POWER STRUGGLES

POWER STRUGGLES:

Hydro Development and First Nations in Manitoba and Quebec

Thibault Martin
and
Steven M. Hoffman
Editors

© 2008, The Authors

University of Manitoba Press
Winnipeg, Manitoba R3T 2N2 Canada
www.umanitoba.ca/uofmpress

Printed in Canada on acid-free paper by Friesens.

Cover design: Doowah Design

Library and Archives Canada Cataloguing in Publication

Power struggles : hydro development and First Nations in Manitoba and Quebec / Thibault Martin, Steven M. Hoffman.

Includes bibliographical references and index.
ISBN 978-0-88755-705-7

1. Water resources development--Law and legislation--Manitoba.
2. Water resources development--Law and legislation--Québec (Province).
3. Indians of North America--Legal status, laws, etc.--Manitoba. 4. Indians of North America--Legal status, laws, etc.--Québec (Province). 5. Indians of North America--Manitoba--Government relations. 6. Indians of North America--Québec (Province)--Government relations. I. Martin, Thibault, 1963- II. Hoffman, Steven M. (Steven Michael), 1952-

E92.P69 2008   343.712709'2408997   C2007-907486-3

The University of Manitoba gratefully acknowledges the financial support for its publication program provided by the Government of Canada through the Book Publishing Industry Development Program (BPIDP), the Canada Council for the Arts, the Manitoba Arts Council, and the Manitoba Department of Culture, Heritage, and Tourism.

To the First Nations of Quebec and Manitoba who must cope with the losses occasioned by hydro development.

—TM and SMH

To my sons, for whom my admiration and respect are without limits, and to Denise, for coming into my life; how fortunate can one person be.

—SMH

Contents

PART III
Toward a Change of Paradigm in Quebec

Tables and Maps

ACKNOWLEDGEMENTS

The editors would like to thank Marie-Claude Perreault and Patrick Morin for all their generous assistance in helping us prepare this book. Thank you as well to the staff at the University of Manitoba Press.

The preparation of this book as well as some of the preliminary research works were made possible through a grant from the Social Sciences and Humanities Research Council of Canada (SSHRC). Additional funding was also provided by the Université du Québec en Outaouais, the University of Winnipeg, and the Association Internationale des Études Québécoises. The editors would like to extend their gratitude to these institutions as well as to all the people who have generously agreed to participate in our research, especially the members of the Community of South Indian Lake.

POWER STRUGGLES

INTRODUCTION

Thibault Martin
Steven M. Hoffman

THE GOAL OF THIS BOOK is to reflect on the evolution of the new agreements signed or in progress between First Nations and hydro corporations in Quebec and Manitoba. These two provinces share much in common, including a decades-long history of hydro development and a significant interest in exporting electricity to the United States. In the mid-1970s, the two provinces and the relevant First Nations also signed so-called "modern treaties," i.e., the *Northern Flood Agreement* (NFA) and the *James Bay and Northern Quebec Agreement* (JBNQA), which allowed several large hydro projects to be developed in Aboriginal territories. Finally, both provinces postponed their hydro projects in the 1990s only to resume them in recent years in order to take advantage of the anticipated soaring demand for electricity in the United States.

However, both provincial utilities, Hydro-Québec and Manitoba Hydro, have diverged in their relationships with Aboriginal communities. Hydro-Québec, at one time heavily criticized by Aboriginal leaders, scholars, and international institutions, has signed agreements with the Grand Council of the Crees and with Innu communities that some have characterized as "groundbreaking" in establishing a new social contract between the state and the First Nations (Saganash 2002). This compares with the approach taken by Manitoba Hydro, which continues to develop what might be called "business-only partnerships." In 2007, for instance, Manitoba Hydro initialled the *Project Development Agreement* (PDA) with the Nisichawayasihk Nation, or Nelson House community, for purposes of building the Wuskwatim hydro project. While many commentators and some First Nation leaders have argued that this type of deal is the best way to involve Aboriginal communities in the inevitable development of their natural resources while simultaneously generating revenues and employment for northern populations, others have criticized Manitoba for continuing a colonial tradition characterized by inherently exploitive relationships.

This book debates the relative merits and limits of these approaches. Notions of "fair deal," "partnership," and "nation-to-nation relationship" are scrutinized and a core set of questions revolving around the different approaches towards hydro development in traditional Aboriginal territories are examined. In sum, the book raises a crucial question: Is Canada, or at least Quebec and Manitoba, on the eve of a new relationship with the First Nations or is the country still dominated by the colonial mindset that has long characterized Canadian-Aboriginal relations, especially in terms of land and resource exploitation?

A second organizing theme for this book concerns the sustainability of the hydro enterprise. Sustainability is a multi-dimensional concept that seeks to call attention, in equal proportion, to environmental, economic, and social impacts associated with development schemes. There is no doubting the enormous environmental impact of large dams and long-distance transmission corridors, particularly in the ecologically sensitive boreal North. While this fact makes the absence of environmental review during the early stages of hydro development all the more remarkable, it is fair to say that in recent years the environmental effects of hydro development have received significant attention. Nonetheless, the growth imperative underlying the behaviour of contemporary utilities companies, including Canadian utilities, makes the primacy of environmental protection problematic despite formal agreements that indicate otherwise. Whether the new agreements provide long-term environmental protection or whether they offer primarily short-term mitigation measures is a central question taken up by a number of authors.

If there is a greater acknowledgement and understanding of the ecological footprint created by large-scale hydro development in the North, the literature regarding the economic and cultural implications of re-engineering landscapes that have been home to human communities for many centuries is still relatively sparse. Given the economically desperate conditions faced by many northern Aboriginal communities, whether and to what extent the various agreements will facilitate viable economic opportunities for these communities are enormously important questions. A number of essays in this book take up this issue, offering conclusions that range from the hopeful to the pessimistic.

Economic viability is only one dimension of social sustainability; equally significant is the viability of culture. Elsewhere, several authors, most notably Richard Salisbury, have suggested that among the important outcomes of the JBNQA was the political empowerment of the Crees, the development of a strong sense of Cree nationhood, and the construction of a modern political leadership (1986). Similarly, Martin (in this volume) stresses the role played by the negotiation of an agreement for the Great Whale project in creating a sense of empowerment for the different Inuit leaderships. At the heart of several essays in this book, therefore, are the questions of whether and to what extent the new agreements facilitate or work against the long-term maintenance and reinvigoration of First Nation culture.

A number of the essays in this book were first developed for a conference held at the University of Winnipeg in 2003. A primary goal of the conference, entitled New Agreements or Old Relationship: Hydro Developments on Aboriginal Lands in Quebec and Manitoba, was to analyze two recent agreements: first, the *Paix des Braves* (2002), which was signed between Hydro-Québec and the Grand Council of the Crees of Quebec; and, secondly, the *Summary of Understanding* signed between Manitoba Hydro and the Nisichawayasihk Cree Nation of Manitoba (2003) regarding the proposed Wuskwatim dam. (The *Summary of Understanding* has been superseded by the 2006 Wuskwatim *Project Development Agreement*.)

Speakers from different backgrounds and perspectives, including scholars, environmental activists, Aboriginal leaders and Elders, as well as spokespersons from the utilities, were invited to speak on these agreements. Hydro-Québec agreed to send a representative to explain the new hydro projects in northern Quebec and the anticipated economic benefits for the Cree communities. The Council of the Crees of Quebec was represented by Romeo Saganash, Jurist and Director of Governmental Relations and International Affairs for the Grand Council of the Crees; his comments are presented in this volume. Unfortunately, Manitoba Hydro turned down a request for a representative to speak at the conference. The province, however, was represented by the minister responsible for Manitoba Hydro, the Honourable Tim Sale, who participated in a debate before a large public gathering.

The second goal of the conference was to bring together Crees from Manitoba and Quebec to provide them with the opportunity to exchange information about hydro development in their respective territories. This was an important element of the conference since, despite the media coverage of hydro developments in Canada, Aboriginal people from various provinces are not well connected and are oftentimes unaware of the nature and economic implications of hydro agreements signed in the other provinces.

The book is divided into three sections, the first of which provides a theoretical perspective to hydro development in general and a number of comparative analyses of developments in Quebec and Manitoba. John Bonner, a resident of South Indian Lake (Manitoba), offers a moving and emotional foreword to this section. Bonner's testimony is rooted in his life experiences before and after the dam development that necessitated his relocation from his long-time family home to a now impoverished community on the shores of Southern Indian Lake.

Thibault Martin then introduces the general theme of the book, which is whether the agreements signed since the 1990 are, in fact, an expression of the new type of social contract between Aboriginal peoples and the state suggested by the Royal Commission on Aboriginal Peoples, i.e., a process of devolution granting at least some broad self-governing powers to Aboriginal peoples. If they are part of a new era, asks Martin, how do they differ from treaties, such as the *James Bay and Northern Quebec Agreement* or the *Inuvialuit Final Agreement*, signed before the work of the Royal Commission?

While many of the papers in this book use colonialism as a starting point for their analysis, Gabrielle Slowey locates hydro developments in the context of globalization. Slowey argues that the opportunities for self-determination "as it emerges under the auspices of globalization, increasingly raises issues of unequal relations, not only between Indigenous people and the state or between Indigenous people and corporations but also between Indigenous groups themselves." The result of this process is the increased stratification of First Nations.

Globalization and colonialism provide useful theoretical reference points for the historical reviews provided by Wera and Martin as well as by Tremblay and Dufour. Wera's and Martin's chapter achieves two goals: first, it outlines the events that contributed to the creation of the respective utilities; and, second, it provides an overview of the treaties and agreements enacted between the Aboriginal communities and the provincial and federal governments. In this respect, the chapter is a useful overview of issues that subsequent chapters discuss in much greater detail.

Whereas Wera and Martin focus on the history of the 'hydro giants' and the agreements that made their development possible, Tremblay and Dufour offer an account of the Aboriginal struggle towards empowerment and self-determination. The authors discuss a number of thematic periods, beginning in the early 1950s, each of which reflects a particular aspect of the so-called 'Long Walk' to gain full rights over ancestral lands and meaningful self-determination. Their survey is intended to answer several questions, including: who were the main promoters of initiatives; under what circumstances and by which mechanisms were Aboriginal leaders' views shared by Aboriginal communities; what positions on various issues have been taken by non-Aboriginal leaders and their communities; have Aboriginal views been accepted piecemeal or as a whole by Canadian governments and the public in general; and what strategies and techniques were used by both governments and Aboriginal communities to make sure that steps were undertaken in the most efficient manner possible?

The second and third sections of the book move from a general framework to the specifics of hydro development in Manitoba and Quebec. By way of introduction to Manitoba, the second section begins with the text of two speeches delivered by members of the Pimicikamak Cree Nation before the Manitoba Clean Environment Commission hearings in the matter of the Wuskwatim generating station project and transmission project. Both these texts reveal the fear Aboriginal people have regarding the potential impacts of hydro projects. These fears are not necessarily proportional to the expected outcomes of a proposed project, but, rather, are the result of prior bad history between the Aboriginal communities and state and hydro authorities (see Hoffman 2002; Chodkiewicz and Brown 1999; Waldram 1988). Thus, Peter Kulchyski argues in this volume that the general attitude of Manitoba Hydro and its unwillingness to fulfill its commitments made through previous agreements such as the *Northern Flood Agreement* contribute to a lack of trust that fuels these fears.

Some insight into the basis of these fears is provided by Steven Hoffman in his brief history of hydro development in Manitoba. Hoffman argues that colonialization is helpful in explaining the historical continuities underlying hydroelectric development in Manitoba. While colonialism provided a basic foundation necessary for the historical expansion of the Canadian state, perhaps its most important contribution for hydro development was a mindset that saw displacement as an opportunity and relocation as a means to move Aboriginal communities out of what one government-sponsored report referred to as a "dead-end way of life." Hoffman explores the implications of this mindset and concludes that recent agreements represent not the "end of colonialism but its zenith."

Hoffman's paper focuses primarily on the historical past; Hoffman and Ken Bradley follow this up with a review of the future that examines Manitoba Hydro's efforts to cement its relations with an expanding range of new, extraprovincial markets. Using Slowey's notion of globalization as a starting point, they discuss the physical necessities of the globalizing impulse, pointing out that "institutionalizing a neo-liberal regime in law and policy is only one part of a sustained process of globalization. In addition to the rules of trade and non-interference in the actions of global corporations physical infrastructure is also required." Recent actions by the company, ranging from the Wuskwatim proposal to working with American and Canadian partners to provide increased transmission capacity to service eastern US and Ontario markets, all speak to a remarkably consistent vision that has been guiding corporate activities for over half a century.

Lydia Dobrovolny concludes this section on a somewhat more optimistic note, taking as her point of departure another element in the provincial/

US relationship addressed by Hoffman and Bradley. There is, argues Dobrovolny, an opportunity to make up some of what has been lost over the last half-century if the parties can agree on a basic framework for aggressively monitoring the effects of dam operations. She is hopeful that the recent order by the Minnesota Public Utilities Commission ordering Xcel Energy to report on the implementation of the *Northern Flood Agreement* will provide such a foundation.

The final section of the book traces hydroelectric development in Quebec. Romeo Saganash introduces the section with optimism based on the *Paix des Braves* agreement, which, according to Saganash, represents a "real partnership." A partnership demands a "genuine equality of status, and equity of outcomes" between the province and the Cree. According to Saganash, the partnership embodies "a common set of goals [and] shared objectives with equitable results, which require the respectful cooperation of the parties."

Saganash's perspective is representative of the positive attention that has been directed towards the *Paix des Braves*. However, as Renée Dupuis, Chief of the Indian Claims Commission, cautions, whatever new perspectives are represented by the agreement, it is important to note that this new deal does not completely supplant the JBNQA. Since whatever social changes might be associated with the *Paix des Braves* will occur within the context of the JBNQA, it is critical to look at a whole series of governance-related questions that have largely been neglected up to this point. Dupuis urges all parties, including Inuit, the Crees, and the provincial and federal governments, to carefully consider whether the results of JBNQA are, in fact, improving Cree and Inuit socio-economic conditions and the role played by the new governance structures in bringing about these results. These same bodies must also be committed to determining whether the structures have improved the operations of local and regional political authorities from the point of view of the responsibility, imputation, and transparency expected today from government administrations.

The impact that dams can have on a given population is well illustrated in Thibault Martin's examination of Hydro-Québec's Great Whale project, which, despite several years of preparatory studies and negotiations, was never realized. Yet, even the preliminary work on the project produced significant social impacts on populations settled within the project area and marked a turning point in the historical relationship between Hydro-Québec and Aboriginal groups in Quebec. Indeed, at a moment when Hydro-Québec had achieved a measure of success in imposing its prescription for development on Aboriginal peoples in the North, a campaign of concerted opposition from Cree and Inuit leaders contributed to the postponement of the project. In addition, the project gave rise to a large-scale mobilization of Inuit and Crees to negotiate an equal partnership with the modern state.

Paul Charest continues the examination of recent agreements between Aboriginal communities and Hydro-Québec, this time extending the analysis to Quebec's Innu communities of the Far North. Again focusing on the meaning of a true partnership, Charest sounds a less optimistic note for the Innu than that taken by Saganash and the Crees. Charest concludes that the recent agreements completed between Hydro-Québec and three Innu communities is an "incomplete partnership, giving a greater advantage to Hydro-Québec. . . . The more time that passes, the more the Innu will be caught between the agenda of Hydro-Québec and its big hydroelectric projects supported by the Province of Quebec in the name of economic development" and its own development and cultural needs.

Brian Craik concludes the book with a brief but centrally important paper that explores the role of the federal government in addressing the economic development needs of the province's Aboriginal communities. It is an obvious fact, says Craik, that both historical and modern treaties, in seeking to extinguish traditional land rights, reduced the areas on which Aboriginal communities are able to pursue economic development strategies harmonious with traditional ways of life. More importantly, however, Craik argues that federal treaties imply federal responsibility. It would be a major error, says Craik, if Manitoba focused only on the government of Manitoba and Manitoba Hydro as the source for Aboriginal development. In that the federal government has constitutional jurisdiction for "Indians and lands reserved for Indians" in Canada and is the Crown signatory to the treaties, both historic and modern, it also has both the obligation and the economic capacity to undertake the developmental effort required to make a difference in Aboriginal development in Manitoba.

This volume is intended to advance our understanding of the complex interplay that defines the relationships among Aboriginal communities, the Canadian federal government, the provinces of Manitoba and Quebec, and the Crown companies of Hydro-Québec and Manitoba Hydro. In some cases, the authors extend the analysis beyond Canadian borders to include in their comments a discussion of the impacts produced by both American governments and non-governmental organizations.

Perhaps because of the specific geographic focus of their analyses, the contributors differ significantly in their final assessments of these relations. To a great extent, those who focus on Manitoba tend to be less optimistic about the directions evident in the province. Thus, Hoffman characterizes the recent 'business-only' approach taken in Manitoba as not a new era in Hydro-Aboriginal relations but as a logical next step in the historical pattern of colonialism that has long dominated the province. And while Dobrovolny is hopeful that the company is more sensitive to the impacts of their actions, the outcry that greeted the recent Minnesota legislation requiring annual progress reports is taken by Kulchyski as evidence that Hydro's basic hostility to fundamental change is little different from the days when the company refused to take seriously the requirements of the ill-fated NFA.

Primarily because of the *Paix des Braves*, those authors who focus on the situation in Quebec tend towards optimism. Yet, even here, the various authors temper their optimism with a significant degree of caution. While Saganash is optimistic that the agreement represents a genuinely hopeful way forward, others tend to leaven their account with caution, urging readers to remember that a single agreement neither displaces prior agreements nor guarantees that the implementation process required of the *Paix des Braves* will proceed unfettered. The 2006 debate over the agreement, which many feared could result in its formal rejection by the Cree, offers ample evidence that the caution urged in these pages is well placed. Thus, despite what many would agree is an imperfect result of a somewhat flawed process, several Aboriginal leaders, including the national Inuit leader Senator Mary Simmons, contend that "Quebec approach is clearly different and welcome" and urge other provinces, as well as the federal government, to follow the lead of Quebec and its Aboriginal leaders (*Globe and Mail*, 25 August 2007, p. A4).

However one views the approaches taken by the respective provinces, what seems certain is that controversy will continue to define the hydro project, a fact demonstrated in the debate over the proposed Bipole III transmission line. The new west-side line, which is crucial to the financial security of the next round of megadams such as Conawapa, was announced in September 2007 after what Premier Doer argues was an exhaustive four years' worth of meetings. The rationale for the additional $650 million required to avoid east-side contruction, as well as what some are predicting to be significant losses associated with the longer span (*CBC News*, 19 October 2007), was the preservation of a "largely intact boreal forest eco-system," whose population is estimated to be 97 percent Aboriginal (Wabanong Nakaygum Okimawin Accord 2007). The decision has sparked enormous controversy, including deep splits among the First Nations living alongside the lake. Thus, the leaders of the Manioba Keewatinook Ininew Okimowin have argued strenuously for a referendum that they claim would show "overwhelming support among members of eleven First Nations living east of Lake Winnipeg for a transmission line and related infrastructure to be built across their territory instead of through western Manitoba" (Paraskevas and Rabson 2007). Premier Doer disagrees, arguing that "people already voted on the issue" in spring 2007 by bringing into power a New Democrat government that had promised to protect the east side of the lake. Controversy and division, it seems, are inherent when re-engineering the landscape.

Whatever the future of the hydro enterprises in Manitoba and Quebec, the editors hope that this volume serves the aim common to all the contributors: a desire to advance the social and economic status of Canada's northern Aboriginal communities and to assist them in their search for a more just and equitable future.

PART I

HISTORICAL AND THEORETICAL PERSPECTIVES
ON HYDRO DEVELOPMENTS, THE STATE, AND THE
FIRST PEOPLES

Foreword

John Bonner
Resident, South Indian Lake
Manitoba, Canada

MY NAME IS JOHN, I grew up in South Indian Lake and I have spent most of my life here. I am thirty-six years old and I have five children.[1]

I am an educated man, I studied at the university and I have a Bachelor's degree. I am very proud of that achievement, but unfortunately I don't have a job and my education cannot help me to get one in my community because there are few positions for qualified workers. Actually, there are almost no jobs in the community. That is why I have to survive on the welfare system, though I try hard to improve my life conditions. I have thought many times to leave my community to find a job fitting with my academic background but I can't resolve myself to do so. I have all my family, all my friends here and our bonds are so strong that I just can't imagine leaving them.

I hunt caribou in winter and I fish in summertime. I go every time I can; sometimes with my friends, or with my family. I do not fish for fun but to perpetuate my way of life. South Indian Lake is a fishing community, or I should say was an affluent fishing community, because today we can hardly make a living from our traditional activity. Still, it is important to work hard to save that way of life and transmit this heritage to the next generations because we have inherited it from our parents who, themselves, were the recipients of long tradition that cannot be lost.

Everything changed when Manitoba Hydro build a dam and forced us to relocate. Before that dam, life was happy and we had enough fish and caribou to feed everyone. We would also have a surplus for sale so we could buy gear and other things to make our life more comfortable. I have lots of memories from my childhood and I remember how life was good at that time and how my parents were happy. All the family was together and there were not many quarrels among us. At that time, South Indian Lake was a wonderful place to be a child. I was a joyful kid and was not worried about the future or anything else; my only concern was to enjoy life. We were definitely a happy community, with few social and economic problems. And we didn't have to rely on welfare assistance, like today. We were independent. We were proud and free.

Sharing has always been at the centre of our way of life and still is. That is why when I go fishing or hunting, I always share with my friends and my family and people who have less than me. However, it is now harder than before to share because the dam has caused so much damage to the river that fish and game are almost all gone. Sharing is the cornerstone of our community and if we can't fish, hunt, or trap, we don't have anything to share and we can't maintain our tradition. Because we share less, our social bonds are broken and our community weakened. Losing our way of life is the first consequence of the dam. But it is not all; it has also had repercussions on our own body because traditional food plays an important part in our diet and if we don't eat enough fish and wild animals our body gets weaker.

Because we can't share as we should, because we can't eat as we should, we are losing our identity. We don't know any longer who we are, and why we are on earth.

The dam and the flooding had also lots of consequences on the land. Before, nature was pristine, intact, our environment was natural, and animals were healthy. Now, everywhere it is a spectacle of desolation. Our living environment has dramatically changed; it was so sudden, so violent that we were not able to adapt and we are still not able to cope with the changes.

Old values have disappeared, Elders are not as respected as they used to be, there is less closeness, respect, mutual aid in families, there is more quarrelling, more squabbling. Even worse, now violence, drug and alcohol abuse are common in our community, while thirty years ago we didn't know anything about these White diseases. It is despairing to see our young people being ruined by all these imported behaviours. The worst is that we cannot do much to stop that social disaster. That's why I am very worried about the youth. I talk to them as much I can of our traditions, our lives, our Elders. I encourage them to have dreams, but they don't dream any more. They have given up on life. It is so sad to see a whole generation sacrificed just in the name of development.

There is no more unity in our community. When I was young, everything was family-oriented; now it is so different and it makes me sad. Before, when someone needed to build a house, everyone in the community would come and help him; now it is a company and paid workers who do the job. People don't depend on each other anymore; the welfare system does what families used to do before. The dam and the relocation made us a dependent people. We need houses, many houses. We all know that overcrowded houses are the cause of many abuses and are very bad for young people who can't study, can't sleep at night, and have no place to hide when adults drink. But instead of working together to build, by ourselves, new houses, we wait for the government to give us money so we can have a White company to build them. Moreover our leaders spend so much time, and waste so much energy, fighting with the government to get that money that they don't have enough time to work for their community.

When I compare our situation with Quebec's Crees, I think it is so unfair. They signed the *James Bay and Northern Quebec Agreement* in the seventies, like we signed the *Northern Flood Agreement*. But contrary to our provincial government, the Quebec government has fulfilled its commitment. Now they have signed a new treaty with the Crees, who will receive $4.5 billion. Here, we will also have a new dam but almost no compensation. If we could only have 10 percent of what Quebec's Crees received, I would be satisfied. I don't ask much, but even that Manitoba Hydro and the province will not consider giving to us.

Sometimes, I am so desperate that I fear I will never see any improvement to our situation. I know I should not give up, I should keep face. We are a strong people; we have survived many hard times and we should be able to force Manitoba Hydro to compensate us for all the social and economic traumas that were caused by the relocation of our community. I am sure we will succeed if we can show the world what Manitoba Hydro did to us. I watched on TV a report on genocide, and I realized that their way of dealing with us was criminal. What they did to us is indeed a cultural and economic genocide and they have to pay for that.

---

1   Oral testimony provided in June 2007 for the research project, Relocation, Social Capital Loss and Rebuilding: A Comprehensive Review of the Nelson-Churchill River Hydro-Projects on the Community and Displaced Residents of South Indian Lake (Northern Manitoba). Martin Thibault, Katia Lienafa, and Steven M. Hoffman, principal investigators. Funded by the Social Sciences and Humanities Research Council of Canada (SSHRC).

1

HYDRO DEVELOPMENT IN QUEBEC AND MANITOBA: OLD RELATIONSHIPS OR NEW SOCIAL CONTRACT?

Thibault Martin

THE PROPOSITION IN THE TITLE of this chapter might seem insulting to those Aboriginal people who have dedicated their lives to preserving their traditional lands. Far from advancing a blanket endorsement of hydro development, however, this article examines how some First Nations have been able to turn hydro development projects imposed on them into instruments of greater economic and political autonomy. Negotiation of such projects is a potentially empowering process, as the Cree people of Quebec demonstrated in their negotiation of the *James Bay and Northern Quebec Agreement* and successful blockage of its subsequent Phase II. The *Paix des Braves* agreement, signed in 2002, provided the Crees of Quebec the political and economic base necessary to envision a brighter future. Today, in 2005, the community is seeking to stop a part of the deal that would see the diversion of the Rupert River. Whether or not they are successful, this effort does illustrate the level of empowerment the community has achieved to date. By contrast, in Manitoba, the provincial government has largely ignored the concerns of the Crees regarding the flooding of their lands. Part of our analysis will discuss the reasons for this difference in treatment experienced by the First Nations of Quebec and Manitoba. To best understand the underlying social and political determinants of contemporary agreements, however, we must first go back to their colonial roots and examine how such agreements have been challenged and questioned by the state.[1]

In order to address the question of Aboriginal peoples' place within Canada, the federal government initiated, in the early 1990s, the Royal Commission on Aboriginal Peoples. The work of the commission lasted several years, was exhaustive, and put countless government practices under the microscope. The report of the commission (Canada 1996) proposed an ensemble of recommendations intended to both counterbalance the harmful consequences of past treatments and to promote Aboriginal self-government (Canada 1996, vol. 2). Above all, the commission recommended that First Nations be treated as equal partners in negotiations with Ottawa on the subject of Aboriginal self-government (Canada 1996, vol. 4). The federal government welcomed the recommendations of the commission, as it had been lacking a firm political mandate since the failure of the Charlottetown Accord to pursue a renewed course of talks with Aboriginal nations on the question of self-government (Russel 2000, 9–11). Despite article 35 of the *Constitution*, which recognizes the inherent right of Aboriginal self-government, relations between the state and First Nations were still dictated by the *Indian Act*, a law routed in the colonial paradigm (Cummins and Steckley 2003, 11). In fact, through repeated amendments, the *Indian Act* stayed true to its original principles (Driedger 2003, 61) forcing Aboriginal peoples to relinquish their ancestral title on the land in exchange for limited privileges (Monture-Angus 1999; Fleras and Elliott 1999).

With the consensus born of the Royal Commission, it seemed natural that Ottawa would begin a process of devolution of powers. Since the report was released, several agreements, some of which afford to Aboriginal peoples broad self-governing powers, were signed. However, are these new agreements an expression of a new social contract between Aboriginal peoples and the state? And if so, how do they differ from treaties, such as the *James Bay and Northern Quebec Agreement* or the *Inuvialuit Final Agreement*, signed before the work of the Royal Commission? To answer this question we will, in the following pages, briefly recall the evolution of relations between Aboriginal peoples and the Canadian state. Later, through the specific analysis of recent agreements negotiated in Quebec and elsewhere in Canada, we will attempt to determine the scope of the change brought on by these agreements. However, this article is not an exhaustive study of all aspects related to the question of First Nations self-government. It is, rather, an attempt to infuse into current debate a sociological perspective on the idea of self-government for First Nations.

In Rousseau's definition, the "social contract" refers to the association of individuals in order to constitute a collective whole (1964). According to Rousseau, the social contract can be translated into several forms of government: aristocratic, monarchist, or democratic. In the democratic regime, the social contract implies that the People delegates to a third party, the state, its sovereignty. This transfer implies that the People and, as a consequence, each member of society, agrees to partially surrender its freedom to continue to exert it through the collective whole. Although Rousseau used the concept of the social contract only to refer to the relations between individuals and the state, we think this concept could also be applied to the relationships that unite groups and the state in multicultural or multinational states. This passage from the micro to the macro social level is feasible because it does not violate the central concept of the social contract: that of the necessary alienation of one's individual liberty for the benefit of the collective (1964). We would contend that this alienation could equally be the act of individuals or groups of individuals.

The nature of each association varies according to the degree to which the individual consents to alienation from his individual liberty. In a democracy, the social contract has the effect of uniting individuals who voluntarily renounce, for the common good, the ability to exert their individual liberty freely and without limit. By contrast, in an undemocratic system of relations, the state imposes, in the name of the common good, limits on individual freedoms. Thus, if we apply this concept to the macro social level, a multicultural state could be defined as a voluntary association of distinct groups, where these groups are cultural communities. Equally, a multinational state would constitute a voluntary union among nations. In all cases, if this association is democratic, it is distinct from a colonial contract that is founded on the limitation of the liberty of colonized groups imposed, and not consented to, by the colonial state for the benefit of the collective whole. In sum, where we make reference here to the social contract, we are employing a metaphor to illustrate a movement to establish systems of relations based on voluntary association and those imposed from the outside, regardless if those affected are individuals or groups of individuals. Indeed, if such a movement were to allow for individuals to free themselves from an absolutist regime in favour of free association, democracy in such a case would prevail; thus, if colonized nations were to emancipate themselves and begin to associate freely and equally, we would see in such a case the emergence of a post-colonial social contract.

THE COLONIAL CONTRACT

Several historians and sociologists contend that there was little or no change in the nature of relations between colonial nations (France and England) and those established between First Nations and the emerging Canadian state (Frideres 1998; Steckley and Cummins 2001). In fact, under the Canadian regime, the position of many Aboriginal people has even deteriorated. The collaborative relations between First Nations and Europeans established by the *Royal Proclamation of 1763* crumbled little by little under the weight of several successive waves of immigration (Hoffman 2002; Buckley 1992). Treaties signed with the British regime and later with the Canadian state throughout the twentieth century established a colonial contract. This contract obligated each party differently. On the one hand, Aboriginal people renounced their entitlement, or what is called today their ancestral rights; on the other, the colonial state committed to protecting and furnishing colonial subjects with specific rights. The development of reserves introduced by the French regime and originally intended to shield Aboriginal people from the influence of immigrants was a consequence of this political outlook. The politics of First Nations' resettlement, displacement, residential schools, and other coercive measures were also components of this outlook, as they were also aimed at protecting Aboriginal peoples while creating better conditions for their development.

This classic interpretation of the nature of the relations between the state and First Peoples has been called into question. Several authors have contended (Churchill 1993, 1997; Davis and Zannis 1973; Nelson 1997) that no real social contract between European and Aboriginal people ever existed because the Europeans' political objective was simply to annihilate

Aboriginal peoples. The two analytical paradigms do, however, share one common perspective. Both contend that European strategies were dictated by the overarching project of land appropriation. Indeed, on the one hand, we see the state offering a contract in the form of protection, conditional to the surrender by Aboriginal people of their title to land; on the other, the Canadian state encouraged the "elimination" (either by assimilation, dispersion, or destruction) of Aboriginal peoples in order to transfer land to new immigrants. In sum, the colonial relation is a product of a conflict that unfolds both on a material plane (the elimination or dispossession of individuals) and on a moral plane through the construction of a discourse that legitimizes this dispossession and appropriation.

QUEBEC'S COLONIAL EXPERIMENT

Today, Quebecers could hardly imagine their province without its northern part. It was, however, only in 1912 that the *Boundaries Extension Act* joined the province of Quebec with the northern territories of James Bay, Hudson Bay, and Ungava Bay. The province took control of that immense territory, which was called New Quebec, with moderate interest, fearing the possibility of having to take responsibility for its Aboriginal population. While First Nations would normally fall under federal jurisdiction, as the *Indian Act* made them wards of the federal government, the Inuit did not have Indian status and therefore fell under provincial jurisdiction. In order to avoid that responsibility, Quebec attempted on four occasions to prove that the Inuit were Indians under the law. Quebec lost the battle but Ottawa recognized nevertheless its responsibility toward the Inuit (Simard 2003, 83). This episode reflects the lack of deep interest that Quebec had, at first, for New Quebec and its population. However, this detachment ended in the 1970s with the launch of the James Bay hydroelectric project, during the Quiet Revolution.

The Quiet Revolution was a social movement by which Quebecers dreamed not only of emancipating themselves but also, in turn, of becoming a modern power. Robert Bourassa, speaking in 1985, summed up Quebec's aspirations: "[T]his inhospitable and desolate land, inhabited only by a handful of Inuit and Crees, is today becoming Quebec's new frontier"

(Bourassa 1985, 14, author's translation). It does not take much sociological imagination to see in this a modern version of the classic *terra nullius* argument historically used to justify colonial expansion. This was the beginning of a shift in the Quebecers' attitude toward the North. Indeed, since their defeat on the Plains of Abraham, French Canadians had lost the ability to exert colonial power. While French Canadians contributed to the opening and "colonization" of lands, this differs from the new approach of "colonialism" popularized by the James Bay Project. Indeed, the James Bay Project can be termed a colonial project, as it sought to expropriate local peoples' property and redirect their resources toward metropolitan areas. As we know, Aboriginal groups resisted and obtained an injunction to stop the construction of the first hydroelectric project, which forced the Quebec government to negotiate with this "handful of Inuit and Crees." At the end of the process the relationship between the Aboriginal nations and Quebec had totally changed. Quebec had become a colonial power, the Native groups of northern Quebec had become its colonial subjects, and the *James Bay and Northern Quebec Agreement* (JBNQA) established the basis of a colonial contract between the parties.

The agreement, signed in 1975, has been termed by some the "first modern-day treaty" (Saku and Bone 2000; Cairns 2000) because it redefined the nature of the protective relationship between Aboriginal peoples and the state. However, as this protection is conditional on the relinquishment of Aboriginal title, the JBNQA is still a colonial treaty. As such, the JBNQA is, in essence, no different from the nineteenth-century treaties. Hence, the JBNQA gave to Aboriginal groups precise rights on several categories of land, and established a certain number of public and semi-public regional institutions. However, the JBNQA did not endow the Aboriginal groups with full autonomy. The role reserved for the Inuit, Crees, and Naskapis under the agreement is to manage a system fixed by the state (Duhaime 1992). With this agreement Quebec simply made a first move toward redefining the nature of "protection" granted by the state to its colonial subjects. Instead of seeking to assimilate or modernize Aboriginal peoples to fulfill its duty as a "colonial father," Quebec acknowledged the necessity of preserving ancestral ways of life.

THE CREATION OF AN AUTONOMOUS NUNAVIK

The signing of the JBNQA did not, however, end the dream of the Inuit for self-government. In 1983, Inuit leaders from Nunavik met with the premier of Quebec, René Lévesque, to air the issue of self-government. This meeting followed Levesque's proposal to officially recognize Quebec's Aboriginal nations.[2] Lévesque agreed to put a body in place charged with developing proposals and procedures aimed at establishing a regional government for Nunavik.[3] In 1989, the residents of Nunavik elected a constituent assembly, the Nunavik Constitutional Committee, in charge of defining a path toward autonomy for Nunavik. On April 10, 1991, the people of Nunavik accepted the committee's plan for a regional government. On November 5, 1999, a tripartite agreement was signed for the creation of the Nunavik Commission. The commission was charged with making recommendations for a form of self-government for Nunavik. In March 2001, the commission published its proposals. The report, entitled *Amiqqaaluta, Let Us Share*, established guidelines for the implementation of the Nunavik government. On June 26, 2003, the governments of Quebec and Canada signed a *Framework Agreement* with the Inuit to implement the commission's recommendations in order to move forward the "creation of a new form of government in Nunavik." The process of establishing self-governing institutions for Nunavik was initiated.

In several respects the Nunavik government will contribute to opening new directions for Aboriginal autonomy. The Inuit will, with the type of governance proposed by the commission, obtain exclusive rights over the protection of culture (language, cultural practices, values, and traditional knowledge). Moreover, the commission proposes to establish institutions that will promulgate traditional ways and will provide a balance to modern institutions. At every level of decision making, one modern institution will be associated with a communal (traditional) one. At the highest level, a council of Elders will interact with the Legislative Assembly (the Assembly of Nunavik elected according to democratic regulations); at the community level, local councils will ensure that modern institutions established in Nunavik, such as health care and schools, do not compromise traditional ways of life. Every community will also have a justice committee in charge of ensuring that the Nunavik Court of Law will not render judgment against community interpretation of Inuit culture. In other areas, where global processes are involved, like environment or resource management, the Inuit of Nunavik will share responsibilities with the federal and provincial governments. This reflects the desire of the Inuit people to operate not on the margins of Canadian society, but rather to remain within a common framework with the federal and provincial governments while adapting that framework to allow their institutions to remain functional (Martin 2003). This will permit the Inuit to incorporate some outside influences, and not simply remain solely within their own traditions, or abandon all their wisdom and ways to adopt external ones.

OTHER CANADIAN AGREEMENTS

Among the numerous agreements either signed or in the process of negotiation with First Nations in Canada, we have chosen to discuss here two recent agreements outside the Quebec context, both signed in 1999: the *Nisga'a Final Agreement* (involving, as in Quebec, a provincial government) and the agreement that created Nunavut. We have chosen to highlight these two examples because they have been considered archetypes of the new Canadian approach in terms of power devolution (Hughes 2003, 97). Although these agreements have similarities, they also exhibit substantial differences. The very existence of these similarities and discrepancies illustrates the ambiguity of the federal stance in terms of its relations with Aboriginal peoples.

The territory of Nunavut enjoys a level of political autonomy equivalent to that of the Canadian provinces. Moreover, according to its founding treaty, the territory of Nunavut stands to receive close to a billion dollars over the next forty years (Dickason 2002). But this money, necessary to exercise political autonomy, does not come without a price. Firstly, the Inuit obtained rights to only 2 percent of the territory's subterranean natural resources (Steckley and Cummins 2001, 243). This conceded to Ottawa control of the majority of natural resources in Nunavut, including gold, silver, oil, and diamonds. In addition, the Inuit relinquished their ancestral rights to all but 17 percent of Nunavut. As a result, some have argued, "the contemporary relationship between the federal government and the Inuit of Nunavut matches fairly closely the central elements of highly problematic internal colonial situation" (Wall 2000, 159).

Also important to consider is the fact that Nunavut allows the Inuit to exert control over their own territory only as long as they constitute the majority of the population (Asch 2002). Indeed, the government of the territory is non-ethnic, meaning that all residents participate in its government. If, at some point in the future, the Inuit cease to be the ethnic majority in Nunavut, the gains they have made in terms of the protection of culture and language could be threatened. To avoid such outside threats to the integrity of Inuit culture, Inuktitut has been adopted as an official language in the territory. However, so was the French language in Manitoba at the time of its creation, but when Anglophones became the majority in the province, bilingualism was repealed. Thus, one can argue that Inuit in Nunavut, to be truly sovereign, should have the ability to control the flow of population and/or define the terms of citizenship.

The agreement signed with the Nisga'a is, with respect to citizenship, different from the agreement signed with the Inuit of Nunavut. The Nisga'a gained through this agreement the right to define who is a "Nisga'a citizen" (Asch 2002, 69). Those who may have feared that such liberty would lead to the discrimination or ostracism of individuals with "not enough Nisga'a blood"—individuals of mixed parentage or spouses of Nisga'a—found their fears misplaced. Indeed, the Nisga'a have established clear rules regarding Nisga'a citizenship; they are actually posted on the *Nisga'a Lisims* (government) Web site under the heading "Nisga'a Enrolment and Citizenship."[4] There are even provisions to define accession of citizenship to non-Nisga'a as well as to non-Aboriginal people. With this ability to control membership, the Nisga'a do not have to fear immigration or inter-ethnic marriages; they could even encourage them, knowing they will remain the ones making decisions.

While progressive in a political sense, the agreement remains somewhat imperfect in that it does not allow the Nisga'a an adequate economic base to exercise their autonomy. Indeed, as a condition of the agreement, the Nisga'a renounced the majority of their ancestral territory and abandoned their Aboriginal title. Thus, as Asch (2002) contends:

> In short, while constitutional recognition of the authority of
> Nisga'a government represents a step in the direction of self-
> sufficiency, problems respecting the inadequate land base and
> insecure financial arrangements indicate that Canadian govern-
> ments still have a long way to go before they can be said to be
> actively promoting a form of self-government. (69)

Neither of the two recent and highly praised agreements is impervious
to sociological critique, although each of them contains several elements
favouring self-determination. Our goal here is not to belittle the genuine
merits of these modern agreements (and if we were to do so, Nunavik would
also need to be questioned, especially in regard to citizenship), but to raise a
more serious issue: why are contemporary agreements so different in terms
of the rights they bestow on their beneficiaries? Why are some groups able
to sign agreements that are praised and deemed to be exemplary, while
other groups have to be satisfied with incomplete autonomy? We could
hypothesize that the differences between the agreements are the result of
the state's pragmatism in addressing Aboriginal groups' most pressing
needs in terms of their ability to self-govern. This pragmatism would lead
the state to identify different needs for different groups, and not impose
a homogeneous plan on all groups (an idea largely supported by Cairns
2000). However, as the next section will suggest, this pragmatism cannot
fully explain the state's actions on the matter of self-government.

THE COLONIAL ROOTS OF MODERN AGREEMENTS

In looking at recent agreements, especially those that transfer important
powers to Aboriginal groups, one must wonder why some groups received
more land and more money than others. Saku and Bone's (2000) research
shows, for example, that the Inuvialuit who signed the *Western Arctic
Claim—The Inuvialuit Final Agreement*, in 1984, received twice the monetary
compensation and thirty times more land per capita than the Quebec nations
signatory to the JBNQA. One cannot ignore the fact that government's moti-
vation in finalizing these two agreements was not only one of benevolence,
as in both cases the goal was to open the land for exploitation of its natural
resources. Is it possible, then, that the amount of compensation allocated

to each Aboriginal group was proportional to the government's desire for natural resources? Knowing that hydroelectricity was at stake in Quebec, while in the western Arctic it was oil, might lead one to assume that the potential value of each resource was proportional to the state's 'generosity'. Perhaps the amount of government monies awarded to Aboriginal groups could be based on the monetary value of natural resources rather than on the real needs of the communities in question. The consequence is that some groups achieve a more solid economic platform for self-government than do others.

Saku and Bone's study (2000) on four Arctic regions (Nunavik, Inuvialuit Settlement Region, Keewatin, and Kitikmeot) shows that the two regions that signed self-government agreements did progress socio-economically, while the others saw their situation worsen. The Inuvialuit Settlement Region, which received the best package, is developing faster than Nunavik. This reveals how important it is for First Nations to achieve some form of self-government. By not signing any understandings with some First Nations or by agreeing to some inadequate deals, the state helps to worsen socio-economic inequalities among Aboriginal groups. For the sake of equity, the state should sign agreements that, while not identical, provide each group with the tools to attain a sustainable form of development. To achieve this, Ottawa should have a uniform policy of treaty implementation. Instead, Ottawa deals case by case with Aboriginal claims and follows not one but two broad and general guidelines, one for land claims negotiations and the other for treaty land entitlement.

One may also wonder why some First Nations cannot achieve any form of self-government. The answer could be that the state seems more inclined to conclude negotiations where there are economic interests involved, but seems less interested in negotiating with groups whose ancestral lands are less valuable for industrial development. As a result, unless provincial or federal governments see an urgent need to conclude an agreement, First Nations have no other option than to seek that agreement through legal channels (Monture-Angus 1999, 65). That puts the quest of Aboriginal nations for self-government in the hands of a system where technicalities govern, and where lawyers' skills in reading evidence are more important than the evidence itself. As a result, a case may not necessarily be judged on its merits. One example of this was the Calder case, brought forth by the Nisga'a and dismissed in the Supreme Court on a technicality, which, despite its failure in the courts, contributed to redefining the political relationship between the state and the Aboriginal peoples as the Supreme Court Justices did acknowledge the validity of pre-existing Aboriginal title.

The preceding poses an obvious problem for the state since its role is to ensure the creation of favourable and equitable conditions for all. The federal government does not hesitate to fulfill this role, particularly with respect to official languages policy. In this latter domain, Ottawa's actions are motivated by the thinking that equality does not signify similar treatment, but, rather, on the contrary, that some minority groups need to receive additional resources in order that they may progress toward parity with the majority. Why, then, does Ottawa not systematically apply this logic to Native groups? The answer may be found in the fact that the state, when it negotiates agreements with First Nations, behaves as though it represents only the non-Aboriginal portion of the population.

> Canada acts as though the national interest of the State largely excludes the national interest of the indigenous peoples for whom the parliament of Canada has direct constitutional responsibility. One need only look at the extensive Canadian jurisprudence to see over and over again the repeated pattern: on one side Canada, a province and a corporation in the courts versus on the other side, the indigenous peoples. This is simply a fact in Canada at the present time. (Saganash 2002, 15)

In sum, rather than negotiating agreements that favour the social and economic blossoming of Aboriginal people as much as non-Aboriginal people, the state enters into negotiations "against" them, trying to limit or to negotiate downward their claim in the name of the interests of the collective (Cairns 2000). Cairns sees here a legacy of the colonial period, when European powers (France and England) negotiated treaties with Aboriginal people who were their enemies.

We could also venture to say that the process of redefining the relation between Aboriginal and non-Aboriginal people is still affected by Ottawa's unwillingness to give up its guardian role. Ottawa's recent attempt to pass a new legislation, Bill C-7, is an illustration of that attitude. Although, according to Ottawa, the proposed bill was intended to modernize the *Indian Act* so that First Nations would be able to participate fully in an increasingly modern society, it also would have allowed the government to intervene in the internal affairs of reserves if and when such affairs were deemed incompatible with Canadian standards of practice. Resistance to this new law was virtually unanimous within the Aboriginal community, and the government chose to reconsider it.

THE *PAIX DES BRAVES*

Recently the Quebec government has engaged in a new direction on the question of Aboriginal rights. This is at least what we can draw from the latest agreements signed or under development in Quebec: the *Paix des Braves*, signed with the Crees in 2002; *Entente Sanarrutik*, or the *Sanarrutik Agreement*, signed with the Inuit in 2002; *Approche commune*, or the *Common Approach*, with the Innus of Mamuitun and Nutashkuan, for which an agreement in principle was signed March 31, 2004. This opinion is shared by several members of the Quebec First Nations, as the following comment illustrates.

> On February 7, 2002, a breakthrough occurred between the Crees and the Government of Quebec. On that day in the Cree community of Waskaganish, Crees from all nine communities assembled to witness the signature by Premier Bernard Landry and Grand Chief Ted Moses, of the "Agreement to establish a new relationship between the Government of Quebec and the Crees". We reached an understanding and a level of mutual respect and recognition that I believe could well be the very beginning of a rights-based approach for indigenous peoples throughout the world. We have fought long and hard for this and I feel that the Cree Nation, has finally been heard and understood, at least by the Government of Quebec. Although the Government of

> Quebec is so far the only government to recognize the mutually
> beneficial nature of this understanding, I believe that others will
> follow. (Saganash 2002, 7)

Hence, the *Paix des Braves* will not change totally the pattern of relations between First Nations and the Quebec government, as this pattern was established and is still governed by the JBNQA. Nevertheless, the *Paix des Braves* is distinguished from the JBNQA in that it recognizes First Nations as partners with whom the state must deal nation-to-nation, as this latter term is understood in Quebec. Indeed, in Quebec the concept of nation refers to a culture, a society (the Quebec nation, the Italian nation), while in English Canada, the concept of First Nations refers often to individual communities (Norway House First Nation, Nisichawayasihk Cree Nation). As a result, when the Quebecers speak of the Innu or Cree Nations, they are referring to a distinct way of life, a distinct form of social association. Defined in this way, the concept of nation is a modern one, and was introduced by Europeans into Aboriginal political thought. In Quebec, where the idea of "nation" or "society" is so important, Aboriginal groups have integrated this nationhood idea due to many interactions with Quebec institutions.

New agreements in Quebec are also based on the parties' desire to create profitable partnerships, the terms of which are not defined by the courts but rather by the parties themselves. Since 1998, the Quebec government has signed with twenty of thirty-one communities not otherwise covered by the JBNQA a pragmatic series of agreements geared toward economic development. In this category the *Paix des Braves* is the most remarkable, as it affects not one but several Cree communities at once. The agreement will grant the Crees $3.5 billion over fifty years, a figure in excess of pre-existing commitments made by the government under the JBNQA. Of course, the Crees also made concessions in the final agreement. They have agreed to abandon the outstanding pursuits they had against the Quebec government and its corporations while also allowing hydroelectric development to continue on their land. But what is of foremost importance is that the *Paix des Braves* addresses not only the main fields of resource development (hydroelectricity, mines, forestry) but also community development; in this way the agreement seeks to create a comprehensive partnership.

The *Paix des Braves* is therefore unlike the treaties of the past, which focused only on a specific field of resource development (such as hydroelectricity or mining) and thus only partially addressed the process of development in a geographic area. The government, through this agreement, has created an environment that compels companies concerned with resource development, notably Hydro-Québec, to limit their appetite for resources and to focus on development strategies that take into account the breadth of First Nations' needs. This approach is in contrast with the strategy formerly employed by Hydro-Québec, which sought to conduct negotiations with individual communities rather than engage on a nation-to-nation basis. Hydro-Québec was thus able to exploit pre-existing divisions among First Nations communities—divisions exacerbated by negotiations with Hydro-Québec—by forcing these communities, often those most in need, to sign agreements they would not otherwise have signed (Charest, chapter 11, this volume). Unfortunately this strategy continues to predominate in Manitoba, Canada's other hydroelectric province.

The nation-to-nation approach has also informed the negotiation between the Quebec government and the Innus of Mamiutun and Nutashkuan. The proposed *Common Approach* will allow the Innu to maintain title to their ancestral lands. This is to say that sovereignty over said lands will be shared. According to the Quebec government's negotiator on the treaty,[5] the project is novel because it recognizes that certain groups can retain distinct rights to the same territory. In fact, Quebec anticipates transferring to participating Innu communities state-like powers that would allow them to establish laws governing a wide range of affairs, notably in matters of marriage, citizenship, fisheries, oil and gas exploration, etc. This marks an important turning point. While treaties like the JBNQA and the *Inuvialuit Final Agreement* made notable strides away from the treaties of the nineteenth century, they were still framed within a colonial paradigm by which the state sought to extinguish at minimal cost Aboriginal peoples' ancestral rights in order to open their lands to modern development (Cairns 2000). More recent treaties (the *Gwich'in Comprehensive Land Claim Agreement* of 1992, the *Sahtu Dene Metis Comprehensive Land Claim Agreement* of 1993, and the *Nisga'a Final Agreement* of 1999) also contain measures by which

First Nations renounce, systematically, forever and always, claims to their ancestral lands. In 1999, the government of Canada was reprimanded by the United Nations Commission on Human Rights, which recommended "that the practice of extinguishing inherent aboriginal rights be abandoned as incompatible with article 1 of the Covenant" (cited by Saganash 2002, 4). Following this critique, the federal government committed on July 9, 2002, before the same committee, that the relinquishment of ancestral rights was no longer a practice encouraged by the Canadian government. It does not, however, seem as though this commitment meant a willingness on the part of the government to grant Aboriginal people complete sovereignty. It is at least what Sheila Fraser, Auditor General of Canada, outlined in her 2004 annual report when she reprimanded the Department of Indian and Northern Affairs for its habit of meeting only minimal legal requirements in the course of implementing agreements signed with First Nations, instead of working to achieve the higher intention of these agreements, that is, greater self-government for First Nations.

Could it be, then, that Quebec, insofar as it promotes a real devolution of powers toward First Nations, is on the forefront of redefining the basis of a post-colonial social contract? This is at least what Saganash (2002) reckons: "Quebec and the Crees have bravely abandoned the old colonial confrontational positions that came with the history of the United Kingdom and grew in our common law" (15). To be sure, it remains for the Quebec government to convince both Aboriginal and non-Aboriginal citizens of the soundness of this new social contract. Indeed, not all Aboriginal people are satisfied with the agreements of this nature either signed or in the process of negotiations; and some non-Aboriginal groups accuse the Quebec government of granting too many rights to First Nations and thus weakening the unity within the province. Despite the uncertainty of the final result of Quebec's attempt to secure a new contract with First Nations, one can hope that the process implemented by the provincial government to reach it will contribute to the progression of Aboriginal rights, not only in Quebec but in Canada at large.

On the occasion of the signing of a new agreement between Ottawa and a First Nation, a ceremony always takes place. At these celebrations, politicians, both Aboriginal and non-Aboriginal, make enthusiastic, even dithyrambic, speeches that sing Canada's democratic and progressive value, and praise and extol the virtues of this latest groundbreaking initiative. All this would seem to suggest that the recommendations of the Royal Commission on Aboriginal Peoples were bearing fruit. The sociologist, however, should not be led astray by these siren songs. Often such public rejoicings celebrate only the end of a long and hard-fought legal battle, and not the result of negotiations in good faith. Putting aside the creation of Nunavut and a few other exceptional cases, overall, Canada has trampled on the question of Aboriginal self-government. Only in Quebec can the state been seen as willing to move ahead on a global agenda for promoting First Nations autonomy. In other provinces Ottawa's procrastination has forced Aboriginal groups to resort to the courts. This slows down, even blocks, any dialogue or process of negotiation that might help to develop a relationship between equals, or nation-to-nation, in terms coined by the *Paix des Braves*.

While only a short time ago the government of Quebec stood accused by Aboriginal leaders of the worst of intentions in its dealings with First Nations, Quebec is today praised by the same leadership for the recent agreements signed. What, then, has happened in *la belle province* to bring about this situation? As neither the provincial government nor Aboriginal leaders seem to have fundamentally changed their negotiating positions, easy explanations for this phenomenon are not in evidence. That said, as Saganash (2004) noted, a dearth of leadership in Ottawa on the question of Aboriginal self-government has compelled Aboriginal groups interested in self-government to advance their agendas in bilateral relations with the provinces. In relatively poor provinces, and where the Indigenous population is present in significant numbers, the government has a diminished interest in championing the cause of Aboriginal people, lest this position result in substantial cost to the public purse. On the other hand, a province with a relatively small Indigenous population, more economic means, and an interest in distinguishing itself from Ottawa in political matters would be motivated to act from quite a different set of conditions.

Accordingly, one could argue that the overarching political objective of sovereignty provides the framework for Quebec's approach to Aboriginal self-government. Quebec's leaders have clearly realized that independence is hardly attainable without first being able to accommodate First Nations' political demands, a lesson they certainly learned in the battle over the James Bay agreement (Martin 2003). As a result, Quebec and several Aboriginal groups have engaged in a process that entails the partial relinquishment of freedom by each party in order that they may live and thrive on the same lands. In other words, the process signifies a drift away from the colonial contract toward the beginnings of a new relationship based on equality. This result was achieved not only through good intentions and good will between the parties, of course, but through conflict and resistance mobilized by the Crees against the provincial government.

The federal government, by contrast, has maintained paternalistic relations through various means, which would include the doling out of selective patronage and research funding, and the mounting of studies, such as that of the Royal Commission on Aboriginal Peoples, whose mandates do not stray beyond assessing Aboriginal peoples' levels of dependency and advancing recommendations that are rarely enforced. In Quebec, equality has been achieved and maintained largely through a process of conflict. One could further argue that First Nations in Quebec have inherited much the same strategy of autonomy as their provincial government applies in their own relations with Ottawa. For better or for worse, the Crees are now well acquainted with this dialectical process.

The last election of the Grand Chief of the Quebec Crees revealed how well this strategy has been ingrained in the community. Matthew Mukash, a vocal opponent whose campaign was mainly structured as a critique of the agreement, defeated Dr. Ted Moses, the main artisan of the *Paix des Braves*. Now elected, Mr. Mukash has declared his commitment to stopping hydro development on the Rupert River. At the same time, however, he is not willing to question the *Paix des Braves* because, he has said, it has provided the Crees with the tools to empower themselves and resist colonial influence. This stance would indicate that the Crees no longer view their relations with government as paternalistic but as equal, even if this equality largely implies recourse to conflict. The fundamental change brought on by the *Paix des Braves* is that both Quebec and the Crees have abandoned the old framework of unequal relations and now favour the settlement of disputes within an equal, nation-to-nation perspective.

---

1   The author wishes to thank Shauna Troniak for assistance in the English translation of this paper.

2   In 1985, the Assembly of Québec was to vote on a motion in this matter.

3   Although Quebec nationalism and its quest for independence have often created conflicts with Quebec's First Nations, it is still important to realize that Quebec's nationalist leaders, especially Lévesque, were and still are genuinely sympathetic to Aboriginal claims for greater powers and the right to self-determination. In the case of Lévesque, it is clear that he was truly moved by the request made by the Inuit for a regional government (see Introduction, Commission du Nunavik 2001).

4   For an exhaustive list of the agreements, treaties, and other related documents, see the Department of Indian and Northern Affairs Web site, <www.ainc-inac.gc.ca/pr/agr/index_f.html>.

5   Remarks made at a conference organized by Recherches Amérindiennes au Québec : Journée de réflexion sur les nouvelles ententes entre le Québec et les Autochtones, Montréal, 20 March 2003.

2

The State, the Marketplace, and First Nations: Theorizing First Nation Self-Determination in an Era of Globalization

Gabrielle A. Slowey

JUST AS COLONIALISM AND CAPITALISM are often treated as uniformly destructive on First Nations systems, globalization is considered to be detrimental to First Nations' self-determination, particularly since these societies are viewed as especially marginalized and ill-placed to resist the tide of globalization. But to what extent is this assumption accurate? In this chapter I argue that self-determination, as it emerges under the auspices of globalization, increasingly raises issues of unequal relations, not only between Indigenous people and the state or between Indigenous people and corporations, but also among Indigenous groups themselves. That is, just as Indigenous nations are not monolithic or unified in organization, neither are their perspectives on, or experiences of, globalization. For some, it may positively affect their quest for self-determination. For others, the experience of globalization may be a negative experience. And for others still, it may be any combination of both. Drawing on the experiences of the northern Manitoba Crees and James Bay Crees, I demonstrate how various First Nations groups experience globalization and neo-liberalism, enabling some to participate and benefit more fully in resource-development projects occurring on their traditional lands while others continue to struggle. The result is that market-driven self-determination leads to the increased stratification of First Nations.[1]

GLOBALIZATION AND NEO-LIBERALISM

It is important to recognize that globalization is not qualitatively new but represents instead the universalization of capitalist social relations. Yet, "globalization" in recent years has become a common term used in both corporate and political circles to describe contemporary economic, political, and even social phenomena. It is a concept that forms part of the climate of ideas that include the information society, late capitalism, postmodernity, the end of state sovereignty, and the end of democracy. It is a phrase that best describes the process in which markets are opened up for unfettered trade and the accompanying internationalizing of production. While most of the rhetoric associated with globalization privileges its economic component, globalization should not be seen exclusively as an adherence to an economic 'logic' or some sort of natural tendency of a market economy. Rather, as Hirsch suggests, "globalization should be understood as a decisive political strategy aimed at the restructuring of postwar capitalism in terms of its economic, social and political dimensions" (Hirsch 1997, 41). This is because globalization is not only an economic force but is also a political force, being closely wedded to neo-liberalism.

For its part, neo-liberalism is a form of classic liberalism that can be defined as a movement toward laissez-faire capitalism in the global system (Klak 1998, 17). To that end, it encompasses a set of political principles that privilege policies designed to attract mobile international capital. It also provides a description of the contemporary economic and social role of government that connotes hostility to government intervention manifested through the downloading of federal authority, the elimination of budget deficits, labour market deregulation, privatization of public services, and the offloading of tax burden from the corporation to the citizen. It entails the "shrinkage of state regulation and protections, privatization, and [an] anti-welfare" bias (Klak 1998, 17). In short, it is a doctrine that, under the rubric of globalization, has changed our "common sense notions" of the government-market-citizen relationship (Brodie 1995, 13).

Neo-liberalism represents a new form of political domination that subverts all previously existing social relations. To elaborate, in the current phase of capitalism, it is in fact neo-liberalism that creates an environment conducive to market systems and the reproduction of capital. In Canada, as in other nation-states around the world, political actors are taking advantage of the restructuring of production and trade and of the inter-state system by pressing for the decentralization, if not the dismantling, of national institutions (Albo and Jenson 1997, 218). For example, different provincial and federal governments have, in the past two decades, "priori-tized deficit reduction over employment and infrastructure development and have continued to attack social welfare programs and system of federal-provincial cost-sharing that was built up piecemeal in the postwar years" (Brodie 1995, 18). What is evident, therefore, is that neo-liberalism leads to profound changes to the welfare state.

With the emergence of world trade organizations, the demise of national social programs, and the pervasive preoccupation with efficiency and competitiveness, it is easy to conclude that the welfare state is a relic of the past (Salter and Salter 1997, 311). The "new political economy," another phrase that captures the many dimensions of globalization, has altered the postwar social order where states gave priority to spending, either through expenditures on services or through cash-transfer expenditures. The logic behind state spending was to offset loss in private incomes during periods of heavy unemployment and to effect a more equitable redistribution of wealth. According to Bakker and Scott, "the Keynesian welfare state was (intended) to be a central instrument of fiscal policy in realizing the goal of continuous stable development" (1997, 287). During this period, the Canadian welfare state functioned as a mechanism to compensate for the discrepancies of capitalism; most obviously it muted distributional conflicts among capital, labour, and regions. It worked to balance out the fluctuations in the market. But if social spending and state intervention characterized the postwar political economy, fiscal restraint and laissez-faire economics characterize the new political economy. Consequently, in the new global order the neo-liberal orthodoxy puts the same demands on all governments, both national and sub-national, that they "eliminate their debts, stop regulating business, sell off all their assets to the private sector and dismantle the welfare state all in order to be more competitive in the international market" (Brodie 1997, 223–224). This is significant because the elements of redistribution, representation, and equity that characterized the welfare state and that dominated the postwar era have been replaced in the new political economy by a regime of privatization and market privilege.

As a consequence of the intensification of capital accumulation on a global scale, Canada, like all western democracies, is currently experiencing a profound shift in state form and governing practices. As Brodie explains, "It is now widely acknowledged that the foundations of the Keynesian welfare state have not survived the combined forces of prolonged recession, jobless growth, the so-called globalization of production, and neoliberal governing practices" (1995, 14). Indeed, the state has played a central role in shaping the new Canadian political economy. Because Canada is a federal state, the very concept of "the state" conflates the two levels of government, national and provincial. That their roles are separate is important to understanding neo-liberalism and public policy. At the same time, that their goals overlap is also important to understand since provinces, like the federal government, have, in recent years, adopted a neo-liberal stance, focused on creating an economic climate conducive to investment by reducing their regulatory regimes. Hence, despite their independent roles, it is useful to draw on the notion of the state to encapsulate the way in which demands in the global economy transform the government-society relationship.

As the postwar social and economic order dominated the past fifty years, there is great interest in the implications of the recent shift in state form, from the large, interventionist, and visible role the state played in the postwar era to the decreasing, minimalist role it is playing at present. It now seems clear that the phenomenon of state intervention has been replaced by the laissez-faire state characterized by the absence of protectionism and state regulation, and the inability of the state to intervene in domestic market production. As Albo and Jenson explain, rather than promoting national markets, "the federal government now pursues the elimination of borders between the Canadian economy and the rest of the world and works to make the country's competitive position in global markets the privileged barometer of well-being" (1997, 215). The shift in government focus is attributed to the demands of external forces that continue to shape Canada's internal development. The result is that the state has moved from assisting capitalism by providing for social needs to ushering in a new set of policies designed to promote unfettered markets.

The explicit transformation of state functions to meet the demands of a global market, dominated by the United States, has led many to speculate that the sovereignty and the practical ability of the state to govern have been significantly diminished, or, at the very least, been transformed. Yet, Canada and Canadians have long been familiar with a type of American imperialism and transformed state sovereignty that is now becoming generalized around the world with globalization, argues Panitch (cited in Bishop and Bigelow 2002). Referencing the Canadian historian Harold Innis, he notes that American imperialism has been made plausible and attractive in Canada and is internalized in the Canadian state and society. Certainly, the process of globalization, far from dwarfing states, has been constituted through and by them. Even in the new political economy, the state is not without power or the ability to lead. According to Brodie, it is important to "stress that the ascendancy of the market over politics does not mean that the state is disappearing. Rather, state power has been re-deployed from social welfare concerns and economic management to the enforcement of the market model in virtually all aspects of everyday life" (1995, 51). Although the state's functions may have changed, the state itself is not disappearing. This distinction is critical since it reinforces the notion that government continues to be active in decision making and public policy in order to facilitate the accumulation of capital. It is also important since it provides a useful analytical framework from which to understand First Nations policy since the legal capacity and power granted to the state are central in the political economy of First Nations people (Warburton 1997, 19).

TRANSFORMING STATE–FIRST NATION RELATIONS

In light of the changes that are occurring, what is it about globalization that leads one to think it affects First Nations' self-determination? Essentially, it is within the global context that state policy becomes of marked importance. As public policy is revised in ways that make states more competitive in the new political economy, globalization provides the rationale for neo-liberal governance. While globalization justifies neo-liberalism, they share similar characteristics. According to Klak, they function as "twin processes, at both ideological and empirical levels. That is, they strongly overlap in terms of intellectual roots and the patterns that emerge in the role of governments and the nature of international economic activity" (1998, 19). It is this overlap that leads to the misconception that state actions reflect global imperatives when the opposite is often true.

The unifying principle dictating current government policy is that anything that increases corporate profit margins and enables them to produce efficiently ultimately serves the interests of Canada and all Canadians. These objectives are largely identical to corporate interests (for example, resource development projects, lower corporate taxes, and so on). Today, as throughout Canadian history, there exists "an ideological hegemony emanating from both the bourgeoisie and the state which is awesome, which is reflected in the sheer pervasiveness of the view that the national interest and business interests are one and which certainly ensures the smooth functioning of the relationship between the state and the capitalist class" (Panitch 1977, 13). The Canadian state has historically served the interests of capitalism in part by dispossessing First Nations people of title to their lands, which stood in the way of development. With the development of neo-liberal society, the state has changed tactics, not goals.[2] This new strategy, embodied in Canada's new approach to First Nations policy, most obviously the shift from paternalism to the promotion of partnerships as evidenced in new First Nation–government agreements, is couched in promises of social cohesion and the prosperity of First Nations people, collectively and as individuals (Abele et al. 1999, 251). Abele cautions, however, that the health and fairness of the relationship between First Nations people and Canada affect all Canadians. It is not simply a matter of getting along or mutual accommodation. It is also a matter of reconciling outstanding conflicts between First Nations people and the state. This reconciliation is critical because, according to Abele et al.,

> in public policy terms, the relationship between First Nations people and the Government of Canada shapes the capacity of the federal government [and the provinces] to regulate land and resource use, to promote economic development, and also to

> address many other important economic issues that are critical to
> the position of Canada in the global marketplace. (1999, 251)

Although government capacity is not currently inhibited by First Nations claims, that could change. In order to avoid any unwanted effects from these changes, the state is now involved in negotiating new treaties and settling outstanding claims. Therefore, the notion that the government is benevolent in its dealings with First Nations cannot be neatly separated from the economic imperatives also driving modern First Nations policy.

Since 1969, when the government first suggested that it release its tight grip on First Nations people by abandoning the *Indian Act*, First Nations–state relations have been undergoing considerable change. Over the past three decades, the state has concentrated on restructuring its relationship with Aboriginal people. This occurs in an era in which First Nations people have asserted their political rights, laid claim to their land, and demanded a renegotiated relationship with the state. An essential part of this renegotiated relationship involves government's meeting its outstanding obligations to First Nations people through the settlement of land claims. According to Mitchell, the decision to negotiate land claim settlements actually originates with the state. She writes that "in the same way the Canadian state had been previously committed to a policy of proceeding with northern treaties only when the land was required for settlement, there was no movement on [First Nations] claims until the state perceived a need for the land for exploration of resources and energy" (Mitchell 1996, 343). Today the settlement of claims, like the negotiation of treaties, are important to the state because they promote stable economic growth and protect the basis for material relations and the basis for Canadian wealth. As issues surrounding First Nations lands and resources have historically constituted an integral part of, and a necessary condition for, the capitalist mode of production, it is imperative that these issues be resolved.

As the gatekeepers to the land and its resources, First Nations people have played and continue to play an important part in Canadian economic development. First Nations people, already present upon the arrival of the first Europeans, quickly became an integral part of the mercantile process as they participated in the production and exchange of resources and commodities. Yet, that which made them valuable allies to the first traders also made them potential barriers to ensuing staple development. As the original occupants, they held underlying title to land and resources, which was perceived as a potential impediment to the development of agriculture and non-renewable resources. As a result, First Nations people were disempowered, colonized, transformed into wards of the state, primarily through federal legislation and related policies. This led to a pattern of dispossession, dependency, and devastation that has characterized more than a century of First Nations policy. As part of its approach to reverse this process, to *decolonize* First Nations, the federal government has embarked upon a new strategy, one that purports to restore First Nations autonomy and authority as well as control over lands and resources.

Many of the changes over the last thirty years in the First Nations policy field have been remarkable as "First Nations people have moved from a position of political irrelevance to a position of considerable importance in the policy process" (Abele et al. 1999, 252). Abele posits that this is because "we have moved from the concept of First Nations people as impoverished because of a paternalistic past … [to recognition of] the need to resolve fundamental issues of land in order to achieve a more constructive future of [First Nations] self-control and improvement" (284). While this may be true, there is also significant pressure on the state to resolve outstanding conflicts to ensure stable access to resources so that development may proceed, fulfilling demands in international (largely American) markets. This is because the settlement of outstanding claims and the resolution of grievances is as important to the continued economic growth of Canada as private property is to capital, especially since the colonial entity of contemporary Canada remains "firmly squatted on First Nations lands and cannot survive without them" (Green 1997, 60).

Nowhere is this more evident than in northern Canada where resources are abundant and pressure to develop them is strong. This is particularly true in northern Quebec and Manitoba where pressure exists to expand hydro-based development, which, Crees claim, has caused a clash between government, hydro development/Crown corporations, and First Nations.

Interestingly, government approaches and Cree responses to resolving these grievances have differed significantly with the consequence being a noticeable unevenness in terms of political equality and economic opportunity. To explain, in 1975 the James Bay Crees (JBC) entered into a land claims agreement with the federal and provincial governments that became known as the *James Bay Northern Quebec Agreement* (JBNQA). This was a modern-day treaty, and at the time the JBC were criticized for allowing the Quebec government to participate in the negotiations. However, Quebec was in charge of resource management and development and social programs, all of which were important issues to the JBC. Thus, it was necessary to include the provincial government in the agreement. In the years following, relations between the JBC and the federal and provincial governments became strained, and the JBC were involved in a series of court cases through which they hoped to have the terms of the 1975 agreement fulfilled. More recently, however, the Quebec government has invited the JBC leader, Ted Moses, to the table in a goodwill gesture to sit down and try to resolve their differences. Together they arrived at a new agreement; known as the *Paix des Braves* (or more formally known as the *Cree New Relationship Agreement* [CNRA]), which was signed in February 2002.

What brought the government of Quebec and the JBC together in 2002 was mutual economic interest. The Quebec government of Bernard Landry was interested in developing more hydroelectric sites; the JBC were interested in participating in the regional economy, essentially premised on resource development projects, and generating employment opportunities. However, what is of significance is the extent to which Cree leaders view this agreement as one between equal partners. They explain that it represents a peace between two parties historically at odds with one another. They argue that it is the result of a new partnership, one between the Quebec nation and the Cree nation over the sharing of benefits accrued from development on their traditional territories.[3] Hence, in their eyes, the *Paix de Braves* is based on the recognition of a nation-to-nation relationship and the affirmation that First Nations governments are, in fact, one of three orders of government. This is most apparent in the terms of the new agreement, which provides the JBC with approximately $70 million per year over fifty years and the responsibility to implement the terms of the agreement as a function of their governance. The combined capital and authority enables the JBC to focus on their goal of developing strong, healthy communities with the overarching aim of becoming important players in the regional economy. Although the JBC acknowledge that colonialism persists, they suggest that it presents them with a challenge, and not an obstacle, that will one day be overcome as they become more self-sufficient (Craik 2004, 25).

In contrast, the Crees of Manitoba entered into the 1875 Treaty 5. As a result they formally relinquished title to their land and were not consulted when hydro development projects were initiated across northern Manitoba in the 1970s. Yet, publicity concerning the negative effects development was having on the Cree way of life eventually led the governments of Canada and Manitoba and Manitoba Hydro to negotiate the *Northern Flood Agreement* (NFA) in 1977. Characterized as generous and imprecise, the agreement proved meaningless because its terms were never fulfilled. In fact, as early as 1985 Manitoba Hydro made the first attempt to extinguish the NFA, offering each of the five bands $30 million to settle. Each of the communities refused to take the settlement, holding out for the implementation of the original terms of the NFA. Subsequently, seven years later, the Government of Canada approached each community with the same proposed Implementation Agreement with the express intent of terminating the original agreement by way of achieving a new settlement. Over the next five years, four of five affected communities accepted an implementation agreement, which effectively relieved the government of its obligations to the communities in exchange for $6 million per year for twenty-four years and a $60 million Hydro bond at the end of the period. The Cross Lake community refused to accept the terms of the settlement because it was concerned about the lack of self-government, especially in terms of providing the Crees with an equitable say in the land management regime, which instead assigned exclusive jurisdiction over the development of land to Manitoba Hydro (Waldram 1988).

What divides the government of Manitoba, Canada, and the Cross Lake Crees is lack of recognition, adequate compensation, and implementation of the terms of the original NFA agreement. Unlike the James Bay Crees, the Manitoba Crees were not treated as equal partners in the negotiation process. Instead, the terms of the settlement were largely dictated to them. No provision for management of resources was included. Instead, they were provided the terms of the agreement and offered the choice to agree or be left empty-handed. Consequently, as Steven Hoffman has argued, the case of the Manitoba Crees does not represent decolonization of state–First Nation relations, or even a step in that direction. Instead, he suggests that it reflects colonialism at its zenith (Hoffman 2004).

What these two cases do share is the commonality of First Nations self-determination being intimately tied to resource development. What they also demonstrate is the extent to which the resolution of First Nations claims is critical since access to resources assumes access to land. Hill and Sloan acknowledge that "land claims have already increased First Nations people' control over significant portions of Canada's land mass" and final land claim settlements have clarified questions of land ownership in many regions (1996, 48). This clarification encourages potential developers and fosters a stable environment necessary for resource development to occur. But that is where the similarities end. As the case of the Crees in Manitoba and Quebec clearly demonstrates, the compulsion of the state to enter into modern-day treaties or to settle outstanding claims on a government-to-government basis is not evenly experienced across the country. In reality, the political will to settle outstanding claims and acknowledge First Nations' rights to benefit from and participate in hydroelectric development projects varies across provinces and jurisdiction. At the same time, the First Nations' response to development, pragmatic partnership versus serious challenger, is also evident. In sum, the discrepancy between these two Cree groups, their approach to development occurring on their traditional lands and their response to it, reflects not only the differing ways in which governments deal with First Nations but also the ways in which First Nations, as a consequence, participate in the global market system.

THEORIZING SELF-DETERMINATION

Challenging the notion that state development strategies and neo-liberal imperatives alone drive First Nations policy, Cassidy writes that the "initiatives of First Nations people and their governments are the real basis of the energy for change and growth in the self-determination policy area and they should be treated as such" (1990, 74). Given the current climate of rapid social change and restructuring that we, as a society, are experiencing, Abele maintains that we must see indigenous nations as dynamic societies that continue to exist among us. She adds that "we need to recognize and understand the aspirations of those who seek change to protect their future and their way of life" (1997, 124). Anderson explains how First Nations today "are struggling to find a place in the new global economy that will allow them to achieve their broader objectives," which include greater control of activities on their traditional lands and an end to dependency through economic self-sufficiency (1997, 1483). What these observations suggest is that First Nations culture is not static and can change as modes of production change. In other words, changing social values reflect changing circumstances. This explains, in part, why the Crees in both Quebec and Manitoba are aggressively pursuing self-determination in the new political economy. What is absent in these and many analyses of First Nations' self-determination, however, are theoretical considerations, structural and social explanations that provide insight into First Nations' self-determination, as it exists under capitalism, as it is driven by ideology, and as it is rooted in material relations. It is, therefore, critical to assess the extent to which the business or bourgeois agenda is central, not only to international and domestic policy or First Nations policy but also to self-determination itself.

Pressure for Canadian resources is a prime force driving land claim settlements and new government-to-government agreements, which are central components in First Nations self-determination policy.[4] In that regard, neo-liberal policies (e.g., devolution, job training, and welfare reform) that promote market solutions to social and economic inequalities (e.g., poverty and employment) are also part of First Nations' self-determination policy. As a capitalist nation with an economy, particularly regional economies, still reliant on staple production, current policies and attitudes of the Canadian state reflect its propensity for the accumulation of capital and its penchant for market logic in the distribution of wealth. Historically, state intervention in the affairs of a society was deemed an effective way to stabilize the dynamics of accumulation. During that time, the Canadian state was seen as directly involved in the class structures and class struggles of society. The role of the state, moreover, is constantly determined by the nature and requirements of the capitalist mode of production, which means that it functions to service the needs of the capitalist class. Today, as resource development corporations seek an environment unencumbered by state regulation and social disruption, they benefit from an economic approach to governance in many regions of the world. As resource development corporations demand low wages, minimal environmental protection standards, and little or no social security benefits, they also require political stability, a highly qualified workforce, and a reserve army of labour. First Nations' self-determination forms part of the neo-liberal strategy to meet these demands. As long as Canadian development is premised on a continuing search for resources to exploit, resource development corporations continue to find a hospitable environment, conducive to harvesting oil and gas and cultivating other natural resources like hydroelectric power as their demands are being met through new governing practices and new labour policies.

RESOURCES, SELF-DETERMINATION, AND FIRST NATIONS

Is resource-driven self-determination the reality for northern First Nations in an age of globalization? And, if so, is it something that necessarily appeals to all First Nations? It is possible that resource-based self-determination may not interest First Nations people who feel pressured into land claims intended only to open up their lands to resource development. It also may not be appropriate if it threatens to destroy those fundamental elements that make First Nations people First Nations. In reality, self-determination is often framed within the choice of progressive development or stagnant traditionalism. Most often, it is in northern Canada where this dilemma unfolds as resource development dominates the economic landscape and the freedoms associated with self-determination are framed in terms of resource development.

With some First Nations choosing to embrace resource development-based self-determination, this choice leads to the polarization of First Nations. Already a new group of First Nations is emerging, one that competes more vigorously in the marketplace than others. In other words, differences no longer occur only between individuals since they also can be found between different First Nations as different models of self-determination lead to different levels of political independence and financial success. In essence, issues of self-determination increasingly raise issues of unequal relations among First Nations. The result is that market-driven self-determination may lead to the separation of First Nations into "have" and "have not" groups.

To elaborate, there is an inherent unevenness in the pattern of neo-liberal restructuring that manifests itself in the development of a divide between those communities that are able to participate in local resource development and those that are not. As some First Nations like the James Bay Crees settle lucrative claims, engage in resource development, receive sizeable amounts of funding, and participate in resource management, others like (at least some of) the Manitoba Crees do not. As a result, there is an increasing incongruity in benefits that First Nations enjoy, creating yet another degree of separation among First Nations. This is further compounded by the fact that an increase of material wealth is not always shared equally or collectively but instead at an individual level, dividing band members even further by accentuating already acute levels of financial disparity.

The contradiction for many First Nations people is that while the status quo of dependency and underdevelopment is no longer acceptable, a future characterized by the further penetration of capitalism into their lives may also be unacceptable (Slowey 2001, 276). In many communities there is internal difference over strategies of economic development as they have their own debates about the issues of meaningful self-determination. Within these debates, voices arguing that land is a resource to be exploited for economic progress have become stronger. For many, including a growing First Nations business elite, self-determination succeeds only if it prepares a community to be self-sufficient to compete in the global economy.[5] The implication is that self-determination must seek not only to meet immediate, regionally specific needs, but also to contribute to a wider vision of growth and well-being. A tenable vision for growth must strengthen the community's position within the global economy. For many First Nations the only way to achieve this goal is through participation in the global capitalist economy. And for some First Nations this begins at the local level since international resource development companies operate in their backyards.

To answer the question asked at the outset, this chapter has argued that shifts occurring in the broader political economy may provide some First Nations groups with the opportunity to ride the wave of globalization. This is in large part attributable to neo-liberalism, which mandates a rethinking of the role of government and a reconceptualization of the place of First Nations governments. There can be no doubt of the power of neo-liberalism and, by extension, globalization, to transform the lives of some First Nations communities, First Nations people, and First Nations institutions. Clearly the challenge remains for those communities whose lives are not transformed but further threatened. At the same time, globalization has provided for political and economic development opportunities that enable some First Nations people to use government agreements and capital business ventures to generate revenue to develop strong, healthy communities. Even though the political and economic agendas of self-determination centre on the enhancement of capitalism, they also make it possible for many First Nations to take advantage of this opportunity to develop a First Nations model for First Nations-oriented governance. Put differently, globalization privileges market solutions to social restructuring, primarily achieved through the dismantling of the Keynesian welfare state. However, it also enables First Nations to construct their own political and economic regimes that meet their own governance needs. Hence, they should not be viewed as passive victims of globalization but instead as active agents participating in their political and economic transformation. This is, in fact, what makes self-determination both unique and appealing as it provides a First Nation with the tools required to meet and/or balance the needs of the community with the demands of the world in which it lives.

As an historic hunger for resources drives First Nations policy in this neo-liberal age, as neo-liberal governments are concerned with political and economic development as a way to access and exploit resources, the settling of outstanding claims, the signing of new agreements, and the overall promotion of First Nations' self-determination may prove to be very effective tools that can be used to meet the needs of the new political economy. They may also prove to be effective tools to meet the needs of a First Nations community. However, just as it is not possible to generalize the First Nations experience under colonialism, it is not possible to characterize the First Nations experience with neo-liberalism as simply good or bad. Instead, to determine if and how effective a tool neo-liberalism may be in opening up space that proves to be beneficial to a First Nation, it is necessary to study different experiences, models, and approaches on a case-by-case basis. In doing so, it is possible to develop an understanding as to how and why different First Nations respond to neo-liberalism differently, thereby revealing strategies that may prove helpful in generating answers (and potentially even more questions) as to why some are successful (in whatever way that may be defined) when others are not.

---

1   The author respectfully acknowledges the Social Science and Humanities Research Council for its financial assistance, and the reviewers for their comments. This chapter is a modified excerpt from my doctoral dissertation, "The Political Economy of Self-Determination: The Case of the Mikisew Cree First Nation," University of Alberta, 2003.

2   Additional causes for the recent shift in state goals pertain to the increased public concern over the social problems faced by First Nations peoples, support of the pressure placed on government by First Nations people themselves, and awareness of the constitutional responsibility of both levels of government for First Nations people.

3   Personal interview with author. Brian Craik, Director of Federal Relations, Grand Council of the Cree, Ottawa, ON, Friday, 14 November 2003.

4   Arguably, there exist other forces driving First Nations policy that include constitutional and legal obligations (s. 91[24] and s. 35), as well as international considerations and pressures.

5   According to Adams, the members of the business elite are not interested in developing or improving Native communities. He insists that "their objectives (are) to suppress the masses, make corrupt deals, and to manipulate government grants." He adds that those who remain in control of the community, either as chiefs or respected businessmen, do not necessarily represent the people. This author does not allege, however, that all chiefs or First Nations business people/ organizations act in this manner. See Howard Adams, *A Tortured People* (Penticton: Theytus Publishing, 1995), 182.

3

THE WAY TO MODERN TREATIES: A REVIEW OF HYDRO PROJECTS AND AGREEMENTS IN MANITOBA AND QUEBEC

Romuald Wera
Thibault Martin

> Une véritable « politique d'État » en matière d'eau sera en mesure de contribuer à la promotion du développement durable, tel qu'il a été défini et voulu par les 130 chefs d'États qui ont signé l'Agenda 21 à Rio de Janeiro en juin 1992, à condition que cette politique soit guidée par une approche solidaire et mutualiste.
>
> —Mario Soares, 1998

> Personne ne se bat pour le plaisir de se battre. Notre lutte a toujours été pour le respect de tous nos droits.... Nous avons le droit à l'auto-détermination, donc de profiter de nos propres ressources sur nos terres.
>
> —Grand Chief Ted Moses, *La Nation,*
> *Eeyou Eenou, La voix du peuple,* December 2001

LEADERS OF CONTEMPORARY ABORIGINAL COMMUNITIES are offering strong resistance to the imposition of external models of development on their society (Martin 2003). They are more and more involved in political, economic, and educational international forums designed to persuade the external world to take into consideration their own perception of development. This movement has contributed to a reversal of the colonial domination and enforced economic modernization imposed on Aboriginal peoples by western governments (Frideres 1998). Canadian northern Aboriginal communities are participating in this process, aiming to achieve strong political leadership by building political autonomy, while simultaneously trying to stop economic exploitation of their territories by western corporations. The internationally renowned Grand Chief Doctor Ted Moses and Grand Chief Mathew Coon Come are among the representatives of this generation of leaders who are using global resources and forums to promote the resistance of their people to industrial development projects.

A major and recurrent issue for the different Aboriginal communities is to assert their rights over the development of ancestral lands and waters. To achieve this end, Aboriginal communities are increasingly seeking judicial remedies. At the same time, they have begun a number of international initiatives meant to create a deeper understanding of the relationship that unites them to the land (Petit 2003). Both these efforts have changed the view that Aboriginal people have of themselves as well as the perception of First Nations held by Western decision makers. One striking result of these changing perceptions is the resistance that Aboriginal communities have demonstrated to further hydro development in their traditional areas.

Throughout the twentieth century, water was a key ingredient in the fabric of the North American society (Lasserre 2001; see also Worster 1985). In Canada, the ability to export large quantities of electricity to the US market induced successive governments to look towards so-called "mega" hydro power projects, which were seen as a renewable and, importantly, storable, source of energy that could be generated through the development of large reservoirs located in remote and less populated regions. Hydro power was also seen as a tool for autonomy, a fact particularly important for Quebec, which has long been in search of a destiny independent of Canadian hegemony (Cans 1997; Martin 2003; Petrella 1998).

More recently, the global demand for ecologically friendly development has generated strong demand for hydro power. The 1987 publication of the Bruntland report alerted the world's environmental conscience to the consequences of industrialization (1987). Promoters of hydro development took advantage of this new discourse to reaffirm the value of hydro power by defining it as an environmentally positive alternative to other sources of energy. According to the industry's supporters, dams do not produce greenhouse emissions, acid rain, or urban smog. Nor do they generate volumes of waste that create a range of harms for future generations and, unlike natural gas, hydro power is deemed to be a sustainable and renewable source of energy. All this, of course, ignores the very real environmental harms that often accompany hydro projects and, perhaps even more importantly, the oftentimes devastating social consequences felt by affected communities. In the case of Canada's northern Aboriginal communities, hydro development might well be the final step in an historic process of dispossession.

This chapter will, first, outline the events that contributed to the creation of the respective utilities, and, second, provide an overview of the major treaties and agreements between the Aboriginal communities and the provincial and federal government.[1]

THE BIRTH OF TWO CANADIAN HYDRO GIANTS

> A l'autre bout du continent, dans la taïga canadienne, les Québécois ont aussi noyé des milliers d'hectares de forêt pour faire des mégawatts. Et ce n'est pas fini. Hydro-Québec, la toute puissante compagnie d'électricité, a l'intention de barrer tous les fleuves qui descendent vers la baie James, au fond de l'immense Baie d'Hudson. « Notre richesse c'est l'eau » répètent les responsables d'Hydro-Québec. C'est vrai : ils n'ont pas de pétrole, comme en Alberta, ni de centrale nucléaire, comme en Ontario. Mais ils ont de l'eau, de la neige et des immensités glacées. C'est pourquoi 95 % de l'électricité qu'elle produit sont d'origine hydraulique. (Cans 1997)[2]

At the 1878 Universal Exhibition of Paris, the world discovered a new reality: electric lighting. The following year, Quebec became the first Canadian city to take advantage of this wondrous new possibility. A new era began in Quebec and Manitoba when several companies, specializing in producing and distributing electricity, appeared. In Quebec it was Montreal Light and the Shawinigan Water and Power Company (Bellavance 1994). In Manitoba, an act of the Manitoba legislature incorporated, on February 14, 1880, the Manitoba Electric and Gas Light Company. One year later, the Winnipeg Gas Company amalgamated with Manitoba Electric and Gas Light Company, giving birth to what later became Manitoba Hydro. In both provinces the abundance of rivers suitable for generating hydroelectricity meant that water was destined to impose itself as a determining factor in the process of industrialization.

Manitoba Hydro

In 1900, the Minnedosa River Plant was the first hydroelectric generating station in Manitoba (Bateman 2005). The plant was located on the Minnedosa River (now known as the Little Saskatchewan River) 2.4 kilometres to the north of its junction with the Assiniboine River. The plant served the City of Brandon, located about fourteen kilometres away, via an 11,000-volt wood pole line and operated only eight months of the year. Development of hydroelectricity continued in Manitoba in 1906, when the Pinawa generating station was opened and became the first hydroelectric generating station on the Winnipeg River. It was also the first hydroelectric generating station. Thanks to the new station, the cost of electricity decreased from 20 cents to 3.3 cents per kWh. The low price set a precedent still followed in the province.

The creation of a hydroelectric system continued with the 1926 completion of the Pointe-du-Bois generating station on the Winnipeg River. This was followed in 1928 by the Great Falls station, about 128 kilometres northeast of Winnipeg, the 1948 Slave Falls station, and the 1952 Seven Sisters generating station. All these stations were located on the Winnipeg River. In 1936, the first export of power to the US from Manitoba occurred when the province issued Manitoba Power Commission a licence to export a limited amount of power to Interstate Power Company, which served North Dakota and Minnesota.

In 1945, the *Manitoba Hydro-Electric Board Development Act* was passed, which stated that the future power requirements of the province would be best served by a coordinated policy on developing and supplying electric energy. In the absence of any immediate reorganization plan for the province's electric industry, the decision was taken in 1949 to establish the Manitoba Hydro-Electric Board (MHEB) and then consolidate the region's production and distribution facilities. In 1952, the provincial government authorized MHEB to acquire Winnipeg Electric Company and in 1961, the Government of Manitoba created Manitoba Hydro to supply the electricity needs of the province.

By the 1960s, the newly created Manitoba Hydro was struggling to stay ahead of surging demand and began to look at options for more dams on the Saskatchewan and Nelson rivers. In 1960, the decision was made to build a four-unit project with a capacity of 479 MW at the Grand Rapids site on the Saskatchewan River where it empties into Lake Winnipeg. While these new units were welcome additions, they were still considered relatively small in size and scale. It was well understood that if the company was to meet its expansionary goals, it would have to look further northward. Thus, early in the decade, Canada, Manitoba, and Manitoba Hydro signed a series of agreements that set in motion the plans for a megaproject. Missing from the set of interested parties were the Crees of northern Manitoba. Indeed, throughout this whole period these communities were unaware of the plans being made for them. At no time were they ever consulted or informed about what would happen to their traditional homeland under the onslaught of the hydro schemes being drawn up by planners living in and operating from the south.

The Nelson and Churchill rivers have long been considered as major sources for hydroelectric power. As far back as the 1920s, and continuing through the late 1940s and 1950s, preliminary surveys on potential power sites both on the upper and lower Nelson were pursued. The capacity of the Churchill River was also examined. These preliminary studies, coupled with the development of long-distance electrical transmission technology, set the scene for the development of hydroelectric generating stations on the lower Nelson River, the diversion of the Churchill River, and the regulation of Lake Winnipeg that, together, constitute what is known as the Northern Manitoba Hydro Project. In the 1970s, the Lake Winnipeg Regulation and Churchill River Diversion projects began to operate (see Table 3.1).

TABLE 3.1

Manitoba Hydro Generating Plants

Generating Plant	Year	Basin	Power Production Capacity (MW)
Jenpeg	1979	Nelson River	132
Kelsey	1957	Nelson River	223
Kettle	1974	Nelson River	1220
Long Spruce	1979	Nelson River	1010
Limestone	1990	Nelson River	1340
Laurie River I/II	1952/58	Churchill River	10
Great Falls	1958	Winnipeg River	131
Pine Falls	1928	Winnipeg River	88
Seven Sisters	1952	Winnipeg River	165
McArthur Falls	1952	Winnipeg River	55
Grand Rapids	1955	Saskatchewan River	479
Pointe du Bois	1958	Winnipeg River	78
Slave Falls	1926	Winnipeg River	67
			Total 4998

Sources: McCullough 2002 and Manitoba Hydro Web Site <www.hydro.mb.ca>

The adverse effects caused by these and other similar projects, such as that on Split Lake, were beyond the worst fears of the Crees and Métis of the region. The local environment was fundamentally and permanently disrupted as the Nelson River pattern of higher flows in the spring and summer with low flows in the fall and winter was changed to accommodate the needs of consumers located far away from the project site. As seen by the Aboriginal peoples of the region, hydro development was the final step in removing forever the opportunity to fully support and sustain their traditional way of life (Waldram 1999, 1988, 1987).

The late 1980s and early 1990s saw a downturn in the demand for Manitoba's energy supplies. This fact, combined with economic recession and pressures on the government to reduce public debt, limited the development of major hydro projects, the result being that the only major project completed during this period was the 1990 Limestone project. By the late 1990s, however, prospects for increased demand were improving such that Manitoba Hydro was beginning to see an opportunity to increase its export sales. As a result, an expansionary vision was planned through major projects such as the Wuskwatim and the Conawapa. But even more problematic is the fact that Manitoba Hydro and the Province of Manitoba have established a business relationship with each Aboriginal community, excluding from the process communities and/or groups of significant land users (see Hoffman and Bradley, chapter 7, this volume).

Hydro-Québec

The creation of Hydro-Québec represented an important social and economic phenomenon in the history of contemporary Quebec. As previously noted, public lighting began in Quebec city in 1879. Some twenty years later, Quebec politicians capitalized on the hydroelectric potential of the province to attract US companies. The early twentieth century was a time of prosperity for the province's electric companies but the rates charged for electricity, and especially the fluctuation in price, created a high degree of public anger. In response, Quebec's Premier Adélard Godbout nationalized Montreal Light, Heat and Power and in April 1944, Hydro-Québec was created and inherited a gas and electric network as well as the Chambly, Des Cèdres, Rivière-des-Prairies, and Beauharnois hydro power stations.

After the Second World War the demand for electricity grew significantly. Hydro-Québec, which had managed to improve the reliability of its transmission and distribution network, continued the development of the Beauharnois central power and in 1953 started its first remote project on the Betsiamites River (north shore of the St. Lawrence River, eastern Quebec). The objective of this project was to transport a huge quantity of energy over 600 kilometres to Montreal, a goal that required Hydro-Québec to become one of the first companies in the world to use a 315kV transport line. Another first was the crossing of the Saguenay fjord, a distance of some 1.6 kilometres, with only one range. In 1959 Hydro-Québec put into service its first megaproject, the Manic-Outardes on the lower shore.

In June 1960, the new liberal government of Jean Lesage entrusted Hydro-Québec with the mandate to develop the resources of all rivers under control by the province. Three years later, on May 1, 1963, the government gave Hydro-Québec the authorization to purchase all the province's private electric distributors. This was the second phase of a nationalization process organized by the government of Quebec designed to satisfy increases in energy demand averaging over 7 percent per annum, a level of demand that necessitated a doubling of production capacity every ten years. To meet the demand, Hydro-Québec chose to increase its hydroelectric production, a decision made at a time when many countries and several North American states and provinces, including Ontario, were choosing nuclear power. The choice of hydro over nuclear was announced by René Lévesque, Minister of Natural Resources, on February 12, 1962, at the opening of the National Electrical Week. Before the owners of the private electric companies, he denounced the rates imposed by the private companies on the Quebec population and the harm being caused by the lack of power supply in remote regions. Lévesque concluded that Hydro-Québec should have the responsibility to organize the development of hydropower resources and to fix rates and standards for the whole of Quebec.

The development of Hydro-Québec was simply one part of a broader social democracy and sovereignty project, one element of which was to substitute indigenous for imported resources. Lévesque's plans were not universally welcomed and Premier Jean Lesage sought to calm the situation by calling early elections, with a pledge to go forward with the provincialization scheme if re-elected. The Liberals were, in fact, re-elected and Hydro-Québec acquired twenty-four companies. In less than three years, all the small companies were unified and tariffs were standardized.

In June of 1966, recently elected Premier Daniel Johnson was confronted with a difficult decision: should he authorize Hydro-Québec to sign a letter of intent to acquire the all the energy produced by the future power station in Labrador, Churchill Falls, a major megaproject that would produce the same energy as the seven power stations of the Manic-Outardes complex? Or should Hydro-Québec try to interest other companies from the US and Canada to acquire a part of the energy of Churchill Falls, despite what appeared to be supplies of supposedly cheaper nuclear power? On October 6, 1966, Hydro-Québec bet on Churchill Falls and on more hydroelectricity. A few years later, the oil crisis convinced the premier of Quebec, Robert Bourassa, to make another big leap and to announce, in 1971, the "project of the century," later known as the James Bay Project. Phase I of the project, which lasted from 1973 to 1985, constituted the most significant building site in Quebec during that period. It included the creation of five reservoirs and the construction of three power stations, La Grande-2, La Grande-3, and La Grande-4, whose working installed capacity is of 10,282 megawatts. The value of the investment reached nearly $14 billion, out of which the Aboriginal communities secured some $18 million in contract funds. Phase II lasted nine years and give birth to five other power stations: La Grande-2A, Laforge-1, La Grande-1, Brisay, and Laforge-2. At the time of its completion, the La Grande system was the largest hydro complex in the world (see Table 3.2).

In 1978, after thirty-four years of existence, the law that gave birth to Hydro-Québec was modified to allow the corporation to create an affiliated firm—Hydro-Québec International—with the mission to promote the expertise and products of Hydro-Québec on the international markets. A contract of mutual assistance that allowed Hydro-Québec to sell electricity to the State of New York in periods of high demand was signed between Hydro-Québec and the Power Authority of the State of New York shortly thereafter.

TABLE 3.2

Hydro-Québec Generating Plants

Generating Plant	Year	Basin	Power Production Capacity (MW)
La Grande-4	1984	La Grande River	2779
La Grande-3	1982	La Grande River	2418
La Grande-1	1994	La Grande River	1436
La Grande-2-A	1991	La Grande River	2106
Robert Bourassa	1979	La Grande River	5616
Laforge-1	1994	La Grande River	878
Beauharnois	1961	Saint-Laurent	1658
Manic-5	1970	Manicouagan River	1528
Outardes-3	1969	Rivière aux Outardes	891
Rapides des îles	1966	Ottawa River	147
Sainte-Marguerite-3	2004	Rivière Sainte-Marguerite	884
			Total 20 341

Sources: McCullough 2002 and Manitoba Hydro Web Site <www.hydro.mb.ca>

In Quebec, as in Manitoba, the end of the 1980s was a period of recess in hydro development. In Quebec, however, the strong opposition of Aboriginal people to the Great Whale project was a significant factor in forcing Hydro-Québec to postpone the further development of James Bay and, indeed, to rethink its entire relationship with Aboriginal peoples. In the late 1990s, however, Hydro-Québec obtained a power marketing licence for the US market, an accomplishment that once again set it on an expansionary path. The Saint Marguerite Project on the north shore of the St. Lawrence River in eastern Quebec was the first dam to be developed. A second major project, the 1250 MW Eastmain project, is also under development.[3] When the Eastmain-1 and Eastmain-1-A/Rupert start-up occurs in 2010–2011, average annual production of energy in the province will increase by approximately 8.5 TWh. These projects represent a $4 billion investment with the potential to create in excess of 10,500 direct and indirect jobs over a nine-year period (Hydro-Québec Production 2004).

FROM USURPATION TO A LEGAL OBLIGATION

As pointed out above, the first hydro megaprojects in Quebec and Manitoba were built without consulting the First Nations living in the territory. In Manitoba, the Churchill–Nelson project led to the relocation of 450 persons and the Grand Rapids project displaced some 1250 residents. The social impacts of both were catastrophic and scarcely addressed by the provincial government (Martin 1998; Royal Commission on Aboriginal Peoples 1996). This disregard is easily understood, given that Canadians have been very slow to recognize the land rights enjoyed by Aboriginal peoples as first inhabitants of the country. In Quebec, the provincial government ignored Inuit and First Nations, since they were considered to be under the responsibility of the federal government. Nevertheless, in 1963, when the Direction Générale du Nouveau-Québec was created, the government decided to renew contact with the Aboriginal communities. In 1971 the report of the Dorion Commission concluded that Aboriginal peoples had rights on parts of Quebec territory, a fact that clearly did not prevent the launch of the James Bay projects.

Neither the Crees nor the Inuit responded quietly to the projects. Instead, they successfully pressed their claims in court, the result being the November 15, 1973, ruling in Quebec Superior Court by Judge Albert Malouf. Even though the decision was overruled seven days later, the legal requirement that Quebec negotiate a treaty covering the territory stood, forcing the Quebec government to provide monetary compensation and the recognition of specific Aboriginal rights in exchange for the development of the vast resources of the territory. Both these points were codified in the 1975 *James Bay and Northern Quebec Agreement* (JBNQA). While generally a positive result for the Aboriginal communities, the agreement also stipulated the extinguishment of Aboriginal title over the territory in lieu of treaty rights accorded to signatory Aboriginal nations. Nevertheless, the obligations imposed on Quebec by a court of law to negotiate and to compensate Aboriginal people before appropriating their land put an end to a long era of colonial behaviours.

Similarly in Manitoba, Manitoba Hydro undertook the Churchill River Diversion and the Lake Winnipeg Regulation projects without consulting the First Nations and the Métis living on the territory. Five Cree nations in the vicinity of the diversion projects were adversely affected by the project. To address the negative impacts associated with the projects, Manitoba Hydro, the five Cree nations, the Government of Canada, and the Province of Manitoba signed the 1977 *Northern Flood Agreement* (NFA). Unlike the JBNQA, the NFA recognized no inherent Aboriginal rights but instead created a claims procedure requiring a long and usually unsuccessful, at least from the Aboriginal point of view, arbitration process.

The NFA and the JBNQA, considered by many to be the first post-colonial agreements signed in Canada, were achieved in a context of tension between Aboriginal communities and the Canadian state over the question of the traditional land rights enjoyed by the First Nations. These disputes had led in the years before 1973 to a major victory for the Aboriginal people in the form of the 1973 *Calder* judgment (*Calder v. AG BC* 1973). The judgment, rendered by the Supreme Court of Canada, affirmed the existence of land rights to Aboriginal peoples, due to their historical occupation and use of the certain territories prior to the arrival of the Europeans. While the *Calder* decision did not clearly define the nature of these rights, it nonetheless marked the beginning of a series of Supreme Court decisions that fostered an attitude of negotiation that moved away from the colonial attitude prevailing to that point.

For hydro corporations and provincial governments the time of negotiation had come. In order to make possible the exploitation of resources from Aboriginal lands, by and for the profit of southern corporations, provincial governments were now compelled to come to terms with the true owners of the land, the First Peoples. Agreement, however, is only the first step; implementation must follow. And in the process of implementation, it is possible for Aboriginal groups to lose ground. A further examination of the JBNQA and the NFA reveals just how this potential is often realized.

The James Bay and Northern Quebec Agreement

The *James Bay and Northern Quebec Agreement* was signed on November 11, 1975. The parties to the agreement included the Crees and Inuit of James Bay and the governments of Quebec and Canada. The agreement regulates the major part of the territory of Quebec, or approximately two thirds of its surface, some 1,066,000 square kilometres. On January 31, 1978, the Naskapis, the third Aboriginal group of the James Bay territory, signed the *Northeastern Quebec Agreement* (NEQA), providing them with the same rights and obligation specified in the JBNQA. At the time of its signing, nearly 12,000 Aboriginal people lived in eighteen villages distributed between the 49th and the 62nd parallels, compared to the almost seven million people who lived south of the 49th parallel.

Both the JBNQA and NEQA divide territory into three categories of land:

- Category I lands are reserved for the exclusive use of Aboriginal people.
- Category II lands belong to the province, but Aboriginal governments share management for hunting, fishing and trapping, tourism development, and forestry. Aboriginal people have exclusive fishing, hunting, and trapping rights over these lands.
- Category III are public lands, where both Aboriginal and non-Aboriginal people may hunt and fish subject to agreed regulations. On these lands, Aboriginal people have exclusive rights to harvest certain species as well as the right to participate in the administration and development of land. Private companies can also develop resources on these lands, but the federal or provincial governments have an obligation to assess the impact of every project.

The JBNQA agreement transferred responsibility for the management of education programs as well as health and social services for residents of Category I lands to Aboriginal agencies. The agreement also created a program to provide income for hunters and trappers, with each Aboriginal group being free to design for themselves the appropriate style of program. The Crees chose to allocate the money to support people whose main economic activity was hunting. Thus, during 1992–1993, 28.1 percent of the 10,645 residents of the nine Cree villages received a monetary allowance if they had spent at least 120 days hunting or trapping outside the community.

The Inuit chose a different strategy to maximize the allocated funds. They used the money to support hunting activity and then provided a community freezer in which individual hunters could store the season's harvest. Almost all Inuit took advantage of the program, either because they received money for their "gift" to the community or because they had free access to the harvest through the community freezer (Martin 2003). Though the money invested in the program was insufficient, according to Aboriginal representatives the programs has nonetheless contributed to the survival of ancestral harvesting activities in northern Quebec communities.

This investment in the protection of traditional activities, institutionalized by the JBNQA, nonetheless came with a substantial price for the Aboriginal communities. The agreement, like the complementary conventions and other agreements that arose from it, not only allowed hydroelectric development to continue but also implied the extinguishment of the Aboriginal title over the land. Hence, while the state was forced to respect the Aboriginal people's demands for compensation, the loss of any land title reveals that Aboriginal people and the state were still, at that time, engaged in an unequal relation.

The Northern Flood Agreement

In order to answer the despair of the Aboriginal people affected by the Nelson-Churchill project, the Northern Flood Committee was formed in April 1974. Initially, the idea was that the committee would consist of both Treaty and non-Treaty communities affected by the hydro project. However, because Canada is responsible for Treaty communities and Manitoba for the non-Treaty communities, the membership of the Northern Flood Committee was narrowed down to the communities of Split Lake (Tataskweyak), York Landing (Kiche Waskihekan), Nelson House (Nisichawayasihk), Cross Lake (Pimicikamak), Norway House (Kinosao sipi), and Fox Lake. The non-Treaty communities, including South Indian Lake, did not form a united committee and as a result were excluded from the negotiation. After much wrangling, the *Northern Flood Agreement* (NFA) was signed in 1977 between Manitoba Hydro, the governments of Manitoba and Canada, and the members of the Northern Flood Committee (Suchan 1999).

The NFA defined lands to be given to Aboriginal people in exchange for the reserve lands required to build the project, provided compensation for adverse effects due to hydroelectric developments, and supported community development activities. However, the Manitoba government was not eager to implement the agreement to the satisfaction of the Cree communities. So deep was the dissatisfaction with the implementation process that by the mid-1980s the provincial government entered into negotiations with each community for an alternative, comprehensive approach. The negotiations were long, complex, and difficult. In 1992, the Tataskweyak Cree Nation accepted the implementation agreement offered by Manitoba and Manitoba Hydro. The three remaining First Nations have since negotiated their own NFA implementation agreements (York Factory 1995, Nelson House 1996, Norway House 1997). Only the Pimicikamak community remains without an implementation agreement.

Though the content of the NFA is similar in its intent to the JBNQA, significant differences exist. Unlike in Quebec, where programs dedicated to support traditional activities were implemented as soon as the agreement was signed and where monetary compensation was given also at the same time, the implementation failures of the NFA left the First Nations of Manitoba without any tools of development until the late 1990s. Moreover, the negotiation of separate implementation agreements with each First Nation exacerbated tensions among and within Aboriginal communities. In Quebec, on the other hand, the JBNQA, by transferring responsibility to the regional Aboriginal administrations, actually strengthened the degree of unity within each nation (see for the Crees, Salisbury 1986; and for the Inuit, Martin 2003). Finally, the decision to exclude the Métis and non-Treaty Aboriginal people in the negotiation only reinforced the traditional colonial strategy of "divide and conquer."

THE WAY TO MODERN TREATIES

Since the 1973 *Calder* judgment, "ancestral rights" or the rights resulting from treaties have been recognized numerous times by courts,[4] the National Assembly,[5] government,[6] statute, and even the Canadian *Constitution*.[7] As a result, a consensus has emerged that Aboriginal peoples have certain rights to the land and should be consulted regarding the management of natural resources over their traditional territory. For example, the Attorney General of Quebec has recently stated that the government should not underestimate the impact of article 35 of the Canadian *Constitution* and should not act as if Aboriginal people were without rights.[8]

Quebec acknowledged this consensus in 1983 when it sought to establish harmonious relations with the Aboriginal nations of the province. Two years later the National Assembly of Quebec officially recognized ten First Nations and one Inuit nation, acknowledging their distinct culture, language, and tradition, as well as the right to hunt, fish, and trap and to participate in the management of wildlife and economic development. Bill 101, which makes French the only official language of Quebec, nonetheless recognizes the right of Aboriginal people to be educated in their own language if they so wish. The second referendum for Quebec independence was a determining factor in the Quebecers' perception of the First Nations. Debates surrounding the event allowed Quebec politicians to realize that Quebecers and First Nations had title on the same land and had to sit together in order to work a compromise that would allow their similar quest for more autonomy to be made compatible. Since that time successive provincial governments, but especially the Parti Québécois, have worked hard to negotiate in good faith with Aboriginal leaders. The best-known result of this work is the *Paix des Braves*.

The *Paix des Braves*, a $3.5 billion, fifty-year agreement, is a comprehensive political and economic agreement establishing a nation-to-nation relationship between Quebec and the Cree nation. The parties agreed to an approach based on four principles:

- respect for Cree values and traditional way of life as well as for their preoccupation for sustainable development;
- greater Cree autonomy and self-determination regarding their economic development;
- establishment of a partnership between Quebec and the Cree nation; and
- mutual cooperation for the systematic follow-up of the agreement and settlement of disputes through dialogue and mediation instead of court mediation.

Quebec committed to pay the equivalent of $70 million per year to Aboriginal people, with a possible increase beginning in 2005, in accordance with revenues generated by the different industries covered by the agreement: forestry, mining, and hydroelectricity. For their part, the Crees have agreed to abandon all legal proceedings against Quebec. Nevertheless, the bottom line of the agreement is that all the Crees in the James Bay territory are entitled to an annual lump sum, whatever the results of the exploitation of their natural resources.

An Example: The Sanarrutik Agreement

Following the February signing of the *Paix des Braves*, the government of Quebec signed on April 9 an agreement with the Inuit, referred to as the *Sanarrutik Agreement*,[9] an Inuit word meaning "development tool." Quebec had no immediate need to sign an agreement since no major projects were in dispute between Quebec and the Inuit. Nevertheless, Quebec wanted to establish the rules regarding future hydro development in Nunavik as well as create the necessary conditions for economic development activities in the Nunavik territory. As with the *Paix des Braves*, the idea was to create the foundation for the renewal of the relationship between the two peoples. The *Sanarrutik Agreement* is similar to the *Paix des Braves* in that it concerns the same sectors of activity and focuses on similar issues. The major difference is the twenty-five-year period of this agreement with any renewal beyond that time frame requiring a renegotiation according to conditions found at that time. The agreement specifies that the government of Quebec and the Inuit will work closely together in order to develop the hydroelectric, mining, and tourism potential of Nunavik on the basis of several key elements, including:

- a mutual desire to cooperate to provide the necessary infrastructure for economic development and job creation in Nunavik;
- the development of Nunavik's potential energy resources while respecting the environment and principle of sustainable development;
- a greater Inuit autonomy and self-determination regarding economic and community development;
- the improvement of public services and infrastructures by funding important projects; and
- the streamlining and increasing efficiency of funding to Nunavik's supra-municipal organization and to the northern villages.

Although one element of the *Sannarutik Agreement* favours development of Inuit territory—the diversion of water from Inuit territory towards hydro reservoirs—it departs from historic precedent by creating rules that benefit the first owners as well as the rest of the province. Negotiation of the agreement was not premised on a 'divide and conquer' strategy and did not interfere into the Inuit's quest for autonomy. Instead, negotiations were done within the framework of traditional institutions (Makivik and Government Regional Kativik) representing all the Inuit of Nunavik. The agreement also provides the Inuit with tools that will contribute to a lesser dependency on federal and provincial transfer payments by helping them to achieve a greater economic autonomy.

Developments taking place in Quebec reveal a great deal about what constitutes an acceptable avenue for Aboriginal peoples regarding hydro agreements. Acceptable agreements reinforce the capacity of the First Peoples to march towards greater political autonomy by recognizing Aboriginal title of the land, not only over the small portion of territory that is granted to them but to all their ancestral land. Acceptable agreements cannot be negotiated with a single community adjacent to a particular dam but must be inclusive of all the Aboriginal peoples within the territory. This view accords with an Aboriginal definition of ownership based on collective responsibility for the protection of the territory.

This review of hydro developments has demonstrated that Quebec and Manitoba succeeded in their development strategy in large part because of their virtually free access to Aboriginal lands, which was made possible, in part, by federal abrogation of the responsibility to protect the interests of the First Peoples. The hydro megaprojects of the 1970s prompted a movement of protestation among Aboriginal groups, one consequence of which was to require the provinces to provide compensation for the adverse effects of the projects. However, the agreements were still the result of an unequal relationship, since the state was offering compensation, mitigation measures, or support to Aboriginal groups on the basis of extinguishment and development according to the imperatives of the industrial south. The *Calder* judgment forced, at least to some extent, a change in this relationship since it established forever the fact that the First Peoples have some inalienable right over traditional lands. Following that judgment, several laws and judgments have confirmed the need for good-faith negotiation, a fact acknowledged by Quebec and its Crown corporation.

Unfortunately, the government of Manitoba is letting Manitoba Hydro move backward by refusing to enforce the new political principles that must guide relations with the First Nations. Thus, in the case of the Wuskwatim project, Manitoba Hydro is offering the Nisichawayasihk Cree Nation the opportunity to invest in a business venture. If the community agrees to that deal, it will receive benefit for the loss of its land only if the market conditions are favourable. Indeed, parts of revenues generated by the sale of electricity have to be used to pay the loan contracted to Manitoba Hydro to invest in the project. Equally problematic is the 'divide and conquer' approach being used by the company in negotiating with each individual community. In this way, Manitoba Hydro, unlike the Quebec authorities, is restricting rather than enabling Crees' political and economic autonomy.

---

1   Preparation of this article was supported by a grant from the Université du Québec in Outaouais, the Arktis graduate school of Rovianiemi, and by a grant from the French Foundation Joel Le Theule. The first epigraph is translated as: "A true 'policy of State' in regard of water will be able to contribute to the promotion of sustainable development, as defined and wished for by the 130 heads of States who signed Agenda 21 in Rio de Janeiro in June 1992, providing this policy is guided by a spirit of solidarity and a cooperative approach" (author translation). The second epigraph is translated: "Nobody fights for the pleasure of fighting. Our fight always was for the respect of all our rights.... We are entitled to self-determination, therefore to benefit from our own resources on our land" (author translation).

2   Translated as: "At the other end of the continent, in the Canadian taiga, Quebekers also drowned thousands of hectares of forest to make megawatts. And it is not finished. Hydro-Québec, the very powerful company of electricity, plan to dam all the rivers that go down towards the James Bay, at the bottom of immense Hudson Bay. 'Our richness is water,' repeat the stakeholders at Hydro-Québec. It is true: they do not have oil, as in Alberta, nor nuclear power, as in Ontario. But they have frozen water, snow and vastnesses. This is why 95% of the electricity produced by Hydro-Québec is of hydro origin" (Cans 1997) (author's translation).

3   The project represents an increase of 15 percent of the production of the James Bay region. Only the fairly small 480 MW Eastmain-1 will be built initially. However, with the conclusion of the *Paix des Braves* and the Boumhounan Convention, the company will be able to build two more power stations, Eastmain-1-A and Sarcelle, if the environmental licences are granted. Water will also be diverted from the Rupert River to the reservoir at Eastmain-1 to be used by both Eastmain-1 and Eastmain-1-A generating stations.

4   Many decisions have been taken on Aboriginal traditional rights from the Supreme Court of Canada and also other Canadian and Quebec courts, for example, *Delgamuukw c. B.C.*, (1997) 3 R.C.S. 1010; *R. c. Marshall*, (1999) 3 R.C.S. 456; *Mitchell c. M.N.R.*, (2001) 1 R.C.S. 911; *R. c. Gladstone*, (1996) 2 R.C.S. 723; *R. c. Van der Peet*, (1996) 2 R.C.S. 507; *R. c. Pamajewan*, (1996) 2 R.C.S. 821; *R. c. Badger*, (1996) 1 R.C.S. 771; *R. c. Adams*, (1996) 3 R.C.S. 101; and *R. c. Gray*, 2004 NBCA 57.

5   Résolution de l'Assemblée Nationale du Québec du 20 Mars 1985 et du 30 Mai 1989.

6   *Partenariat, Développement, Actions.* Secrétariat aux Affaires Autochtones. 1998.

7   Loi constitutionnelle canadienne 1982. Article 35.

8   Mémoire du Procureur général du Québec à la Cour suprême du Canada dans la cause de *Taku River Tlingit First Nation*.

9   Entente Québec—Inuits, Sanarrutik, <www.saa.gouv.qc.ca>.

4

THE LONG WALK OF ABORIGINAL PEOPLES: ACHIEVING RIGHTS, FREEDOM, AND SELF-DETERMINATION (1950–2005)

Marc-Adélard Tremblay
Jules Dufour

THE LONG WALK OF CANADIAN ABORIGINAL PEOPLES did not start at the time of the arrival of the French or the English in Canada, a territory they had occupied since time immemorial, but shortly after the middle of the twentieth century. Initially, the First Nations perceived themselves as generous and welcoming neighbours and as equals who would live harmoniously alongside the newcomers. Disenchantment began soon after the creation of Canadian Confederation (1867) and the failure to recognize them as founding peoples. This failure was compounded by the creation of the tutelage system and the confinement on reserves with the *Indian Act* of 1867. Indeed, it was only after the report of the Hawthorn–Tremblay Commission (1966–1967) and the federal *White Paper* (1969) and its rejection by the Alberta chiefs (1970) that Canadian Aboriginal peoples began to put in place Aboriginal political organizations and a new pattern of cultural identity based on ancestral traditions rather than on the values and behaviours of the dominant social class.

This Aboriginal awakening has been accompanied by a sharp change in attitude at the federal level and among some Canadian provinces. The new stand was made possible by, among other things, the *James Bay and Northern Quebec Agreement* (1975), the insertion into the Canadian *Constitution* of an acknowledgement of Aboriginal peoples' rights (1982), the establishment of the Royal Commission on Aboriginal Peoples (1992), a large number of negotiations dealing with First Nations governance, and the establishment of the Nunavut Territory (1999). This article will discuss some of these achievements.[1]

The paper is divided according to so-called 'thematic periods' meant to reflect the evolution of the relationships between Aboriginal peoples and the governments since 1950, during which time there has existed a continuous effort by Aboriginal peoples to gain full rights over their ancestral lands as well as meaningful self-determination, a process we refer to as the "Long Walk." The thematic periods are defined by the initiatives undertaken individually or jointly by Aboriginal peoples or governments. The elements chosen to cover the thematic periods, or the different stages of the Long Walk, are meant to answer several questions, including who were the main promoters of initiatives; under what circumstances and by which mechanisms were Aboriginal leaders' views shared by Aboriginal communities; what positions on various issues have been taken by non-Aboriginal leaders and their communities; whether Aboriginal views have been accepted piecemeal or as a whole by Canadian governments and the public in general; and what strategies and techniques were used by both governments and Aboriginal peoples to make sure that steps undertaken were done so in the most efficient manner possible.

These questions have wide importance in that we can observe both a power relationship and a communication process where positions are held by three main actors: governments and their main agencies; Aboriginal peoples, including both their organizations and their communities; and non-Aboriginal people and their regional organizations, which defend and promote their views and attitudes.[2] Distinguishing among the three actors is important in that it allows us to identify which of them was at the origin of historical initiatives related to the Long Walk. The theoretical perspective we have adopted also relates to the type of general analysis we wish to build: one that aims at providing an holistic image of Aboriginal initiatives without taking into account some variables that would provide a more refined perspective. However, such a choice will not prevent us from pointing to concrete results obtained in specific instances. Finally, the perspective allows us to identify major initiatives undertaken either by Aboriginal peoples or by governments that produced tangible results related to the needs, socio-economic aspirations, and rights of Aboriginal peoples during discrete, and in some cases overlapping, historical periods.

1950–1967: A PERIOD OF REFLECTION

The post-World War II period in Canada (1945 to 1960) was marked by economic prosperity and major technological and institutional changes. The federal government set in place important social policies aimed at protecting Canadian people against inherent life risks: ill-health, unemployment, and poverty, to name a few. All these social policies and measures were conceived to help individuals to deal with difficult periods of life. During the same period, members of First Nations were still living in reserves under a tutelage regime established by the 1876 *Indian Law*. In principle, "Indians" were eligible to benefit from the various measures of social assistance; in practice, however, some of those measures could not apply to most of them. Their low life expectancy, for instance, did not allow most of them to receive old-age pensions. Moreover, Aboriginal peoples living in the Canadian Arctic region could benefit from Canadian health insurance only if they agreed to be flown to the South and hospitalized away from home and family. As for unemployment insurance, since few of them held a full-time paid job, only a small minority qualified. What money was received did not take into account the high cost of living of families in remote environments and, as a result, could not cover their essential needs.

The Hawthorn–Tremblay Study Commission was established in 1964 with the mandate to examine questions related to the fiduciary function of the federal government. At the time, the financial expenses of the federal government were growing in lockstep with the growth rate of the Aboriginal population, a fact that did not go unnoticed by the non-Aboriginal taxpayers. The then-Liberal government feared that this could have a negative impact on voters, prompting members of Parliament to look for alternatives, including whether some of the constitutional powers of provinces in the fields of health, education, training, and employment could apply to Aboriginal peoples. These financial queries were not, however, explicitly mentioned in the formal mandate of the commission, since it was related to the social, educational, and economic situation of Aboriginal peoples.

The objectives of the study were far-ranging and divided into four topical areas. The first sector to be examined was related to technical training, unemployment, and economic development, and encompassed questions related to the attraction of jobs to remote areas. The second area of interest concerned education and school achievement; the third, Aboriginal leadership on reserves and the conflicts over statutory and traditional leadership elections and roles; and the fourth, the Canadian federal system itself. The goal was to explore some existing possibilities that would permit the transfer of services given to Aboriginal peoples by the federal government to the provinces and the changes required in the Canadian *Constitution* to achieve that end.

In 1966 the commission produced a two-volume report edited by Professor Harry Hawthorn. The first 404-page volume contained ninety-one recommendations. The second, somewhat shorter, volume offered a total of sixty recommendations that dealt with questions of general interest as well as educational and occupational training and employment service issues. Unfortunately, these recommendations did not become an object of serious study on the part of concerned authorities. However, even if those recommendations were not known extensively by Aboriginal peoples, their leaders knew that the results of the research undertaken by the commission were favourable to many of their requests and led to measures that were to improve their position within Canadian society. The reports also made explicit the rights to which Aboriginals were entitled and suggested measures aimed at eliminating poverty. Moreover, some measures suggested important changes in the school system that would allow students to improve their self-image and be better equipped to serve their communities or find work in the non-reserve job market. Aside from the specific recommendations, the reports created an awareness among Aboriginal people that governments were not providing them with the quality services given to non-Aboriginal Canadians, prompting them to ask just how might they go about getting such fundamental rights recognized.

1970–1980: ESTABLISHING NATIONAL ABORIGINAL ORGANIZATIONS

In order to give greater weight to, and better coordinate, their initiatives, Aboriginal peoples established a number of national organizations that later influenced the establishment of regional and band-specific organizations (The Assembly of First Nations 2005). The importance of these organizations can be best understood if put in the context of the historical struggle for identity. The 1927 *Law on Indians* forbade the establishment by Aboriginal people of organizations of a political nature. Any attempt to disobey the rule was readily repressed by state authorities such as the Royal Canadian Mounted Police (RCMP). The band council system was also established at that time. Through this strategy, authorities prevented the legitimate traditional leadership patterns from being reproduced. The *Law on Indians* also prohibited the use of Aboriginal languages and traditional religious practices. These prohibitions were integral parts of ideologies based on ethnocentric perceptions of the superiority of the English and French civilizations compared to Native cultures and were used to justify legal procedures against Aboriginal people.

At the end of the First World War, the League of Indians in Canada was organized. However, given the identity of interests among Aboriginal groups, it received little support and disappeared from the political scene rapidly. In the 1940s, a similar initiative was undertaken to establish what was called the North American Indian Brotherhood (NAIB). Due to limited participation from Aboriginal peoples, internal administrative difficulties, and opposition from Canadian governments, especially in Saskatchewan, the NAIB split into a number of regional organizations, ultimately dissolving at the beginning of 1950.

During the following decade, Aboriginal people sought to coordinate and unite their efforts aimed at common actions. The National Indian Council (NIC) was created in 1961 to represent three of the four major Canadian Aboriginal populations: Treaty and Status Indians, non-Status Indians, and Métis. Only the Inuit were not members of the NIC. The objective of the NIC was to create shared goals and perspectives that could be accepted by all Indians. However, as Aboriginal peoples became better and better organized and their interests and initiatives more and more diversified, the council, through a mutual agreement, split in 1968 into two distinct entities: Treaty and Status Indians formed the National Indian Brotherhood (NIB), while non-Status Indians and Métis organized the Native Council of Canada.

In 1969, the federal government made public its *White Paper* that advocated the closing of reserves and the revocation of the Indian status. The National Indian Brotherhood expressed such strong opposition to these proposals that the government had to withdraw them. All successive leaders of the NIB until 1982 were so successful in building and maintaining a powerful pressure group dedicated to the defence of Aboriginal rights that the federal and provincial governments were forced to redefine their policies and strategies in their relationships with Aboriginal peoples, especially after the rejection of the Meech Accord. In 1972, the NIB submitted to the federal government a memorandum claiming the full Aboriginal administration authority on policies related to Indian schooling. The minister in charge of Indian Affairs, Jean Chrétien, conceded the point and allowed Aboriginal peoples to take on responsibilities related to housing, health care, and economic development.

In 1979, a delegation of 300 Status Indians and band chiefs went to London with the intent to stop the repatriation of the Canadian constitution. Such a fight abroad and at home shook the unity of the NIB and brought into the open long-held misgivings about its representativeness. The end result was the creation of the Assembly of First Nations/L'Assemblée des Premières Nations, which today represents the chiefs of First Nations governments.

The chiefs of all four Aboriginal organizations participated to the Constitutional Conference of Prime Ministers held between 1983 and 1987. Such participation represented for them a major gain since they had been excluded from any formal debate on constitutional matters related to Aboriginal rights and treaty rights. Furthermore, they became conscious of the diversity of their culture patterns and traditions, including their political views and perspectives. Technological developments in the field of transportation and means of communication allowed for frequent internal exchanges as well as giving them the opportunity to tell Canadians and people of the world about persistent prejudices against them. Interactions with governments allowed them to gain a better knowledge of the type of governance

strategies and action patterns developed at both levels of Canadian governments, which, in turn, provided a strong foundation for the negotiations that
would ultimately see their rights written into the Canadian *Constitution*.

The 1983 constitutional conference made obvious the absence of the
required solidarity among Aboriginal peoples in regard to territorial claims,
rights related to natural resources, rights to self-government, educational
rights, and so on. Some provinces denied the existence of inherent rights but
were ready to take into account contingent Aboriginal rights. Such provincial
stands were, on their face, unacceptable to the First Nations Assembly and
the conference ended without reaching an agreement on Aboriginal rights.
However, the conference was helpful in legitimizing the view that territorial
rights ought to get the same kind of constitutional protection given to treaty
rights. In addition, prime ministers agreed to hold three other conferences
to discuss questions relevant for Aboriginal peoples.

The 1984 and 1985 conferences put a single matter on the agenda:
self-government. Discussions led to an impasse among three provinces
(Saskatchewan, British Columbia, and Newfoundland) and Aboriginal
peoples were unable to get a consensus on such a fundamental issue. At
the last conference in 1987, the federal and provincial governments refused
to acknowledge that, due to unique historical circumstances, Aboriginal
people had acquired an inherent right to self-governance. This lack of recognition, however, did not mean that the Assembly of First Nations and its
leader, George Erasmus, had completely failed its mission. Indeed, they
had made explicit the major problems facing Aboriginal nations and got
support for their cause. Furthermore, other Aboriginal organizations agreed
with them on the necessity of enshrining in the *Constitution* Aboriginal and
treaty rights, even if those were not strongly defined. At the same time, they
expressed to government and Canadians alike their strong will to continue
their efforts to obtain due recognition of the whole of their claims.

The Assembly of First Nations was also involved in other issues related
to Aboriginal rights and economic development, such as the Meech Lake
Accord in 1987, the Charlottetown Agreement in 1992, and the *North American Free Trade Agreement*. Furthermore, it steadily worked at getting the
support of powerful international and national lobbies with the aim of

better informing the Canadian public about Aboriginal concerns regarding cultural maintenance, history, and educational needs, as well as a variety of important environmental concerns.

1970–1995: JUDICIAL ACTIVISM

Within the wider scope of the global claims process, Aboriginal peoples in the 1970s began to use the courts as a forum in which to gain recognition of their rights. At the same time, they undertook a process whereby they made international public opinion sensitive to their claims as preparation for a general strategy of judicial appeal. The systematic resort by Aboriginal people to legal systems took place in a risky context where federal, provincial, and territorial Aboriginal policies came in conflict with Aboriginal peoples' desires for more autonomy, for instance, in the case of the Oka crisis in 1990 or the 1995 Quebec sovereignty referendum. According to Quebec Native Alliance, *Sparrow* (1990), *Sioui* (1990), *Van der Peet* (1995), and *Delgamuukw* are among the judgments that had a decisive impact on the recognition and protection of Aboriginal people's rights (Alliance Autochtone 2005).

The 1990 *Sparrow* judgment found that legislation that has an impact on the implementation of Aboriginal rights remains valid even if it interferes with a recognized and confirmed right as spelled out in section 35(1) of the 1982 Canadian *Constitution*. Such legislation, however, will usually require prior consultation with, and some compensation for, the concerned people. The decision recognizes the preponderance of laws that apply to the whole Canadian territory (Lexum, *Judgment Sparrow* 2005). Also in 1990, the Canadian Supreme Court found in favour of the Sioui brothers, allowing them to practise their customs and religious rites on ancestral lands as a result of a 1760 treaty between the Crown and the Huron Nation. Furthermore, the court found that the interpretation of treaties must be flexible and reflect the intent of the parties involved (Lexum, *Judgment Sioui* 2005).

The question of valid ancestral rights and their protection in the Canadian *Constitution* was further explored in the 1995 *Van der Peet* case. Such rights refer to activities that have an element of a custom, practice, or tradition that was an integral part of a distinct culture of the concerned Aboriginal people prior to European contact. The judgment also specified that the tribunal must take into account Aboriginal peoples' viewpoints in the matter but that such a point of view must be consistent with the Canadian judicial and constitutional structure. It is not required to produce—relative to community customs, practices, and traditions—a conclusive proof of a perfect continuity. Thus, a given ancestral practice, which existed before contact with Europeans, could be taken up again after an interruption.

The judgment also specified that ancestral rights were recognized by the common law, and that section 35(1) had not established ancestral rights but simply recognized that these rights cannot be extinguished. They can, however, be regulated. The *Sparrow* case also defined which lands hold an ancestral right, namely those lands to which are attached specific ancestral rights such as hunting rights for subsistence, social, and ritual purposes. Ancestral rights can be attached to reserve lands and to those who hold an Aboriginal title. Aboriginal lands, under the common law, are lands that belong to Aboriginal peoples and that they can occupy and use as they please, under the aegis of reserve title. The Aboriginal title exists when all the ancestral rights are sufficiently important to command the *sui generis* recognition for occupation or use of a landed property or which have been founded on a treaty. The classification of a particular piece of land can be altered.

Finally, the *Delgamuukw* judgment bears on the acceptance of requests claimed by an Aboriginal group, not administered through the *Indian Law*, but representing several dwellings and/or nations. The case also bears on the implication of provincial laws affecting ancestral territory.

In sum, these four judgments recognized and confirmed a set of critically important principles:

- Legislation promulgated and applied by governments that affect the exercise of Aboriginal rights will maintain its validity if it justifies an interference with a recognized and confirmed right as enacted by section 35 of the Canadian *Constitution;*
- Canada recognizes Aboriginal rights to practise customs and religious rites on ancestral lands.

- A fiduciary bond is based on the concept of Aboriginal title and of the inalienability of Indian interests, with the exception of the Crown. The inalienability status is there to facilitate the Crown representation for Aboriginal interests in their negotiations with a third party, that is, to prevent someone from taking unfair advantage of First Nations.

1960–2005: EMERGENCE OF STRUCTURAL FACTORS

This thematic profile is somewhat different from others in that it almost pervades practically the whole era. The profile identifies significant factors or events that had a deep effect on the overall picture of Aboriginal gains by allowing for the consolidation of formerly acquired rights or by confirming the fact that Aboriginal initiatives defended a fair cause whose attainment looks more and more achievable. Since these actions and events occurred over a long period of time, one should not be surprised to find that they also appear under other thematic profiles. For instance, the 1969 *White Paper* so deceived Aboriginal people that it was met with unanimous disapproval and gave rise to the Alberta chiefs' *Red Book*, which, in fact, had been inspired by the Hawthorn–Tremblay Commission's report. The chiefs argued that the content of the *White Paper* negated recognized treaty rights and, as such, should be denounced by all Aboriginal people. The ensuing reaction meant that the federal government had to put the *White Paper* aside.

The 1973 *Malouf* judgment emanating from the Superior Court of Quebec also created an important structural element in Canadian-Aboriginal relations. The decision recognized that the James Bay Crees and the Inuit from Nunavik had rights on the territory where hydro-electric developments were to take place. According to Judge Malouf, such rights ran the risk of not being respected. Therefore, he ordered the suspension of all work being carried out on such a site. This judgment paved the way for negotiations between concerned parties and led in 1975 to the signing of the *James Bay and Northern Quebec Agreement* and, in 1978, to the *Northeastern Quebec Agreement* with the Naskapis.

The Oka crisis, the rejection of the Meech Lake political accord, and the Charlottetown issue also allowed Aboriginal people to argue for the protection of what they considered unalienable or fundamental rights. The partial realization of such long-term goals are evident in recently concluded agreements such as the 2001 *Paix des Braves* signed by Quebec and the Crees and the *Sanarrutik Agreement* signed by Quebec and the Nunavik Inuit. The recent *Common Approach* with the Innus of the north shore of the St. Lawrence River, in collaboration with the federal and Quebec governments, is another case where a long-term perspective was applied by concerned governments.

During this period Aboriginal peoples across Canada, while acting in concert, also began paying particular attention to regional cultural differences. That strategy produced a renewal of Aboriginal cultural identity rooted in traditional patterns, with the objective of avoiding the loss of essential elements required for the survival of each distinct culture. The revitalization of Aboriginal identity is based on a number of socio-political conditions, including the coordinated actions of different national and regional Aboriginal organizations that were in operation at different periods of time, but who nonetheless shared a common priority of defending their rights by promoting the shared concerns of the membership. Here again, the main structuring factor was the publication of the *White Paper* and its answer by Alberta chiefs.

A second factor that reoriented and strengthened Aboriginal cultural identity was the ability to manage their internal affairs and to grow numerically in importance. Of particular importance was the elimination of the tutelage status. A third structural element rests on a strengthened set of positive identification principles. Such principles include a revalorized collective self-image; a way of life that gets its main inspiration from traditional customs while taking advantage of the monetary aspects of the labour market; and a clearer definition of what Aboriginal peoples want to become after contemporary governments have fully recognized their Aboriginal and ancestral rights.

These are not, of course, the only factors necessary for a successful process of collective redefinition. Other factors included:

• the reinterpretation of Aboriginal peoples' history based on traditional knowledge and Aboriginal life-long experiences of their members;

- the careful listening and interpreting of Elders' knowledge with the aim of integrating and assimilating the knowledge and the know-how in the process of being forgotten. In addition, such a task will take advantage of their wisdom related to the collective healing process of individuals and families who have been hurt and traumatized by past abuses of the tutelage system;
- the learning of Aboriginal languages to ensure their maintenance and progress;
- the revalorization of traditional hunting and fishing trades as well as of survival techniques, especially among the youth;
- the strengthening of the sentiment of belonging and of pride in cultural origin;
- the reappropriation of elements of Aboriginal heritage that are in foreign hands as well as the protection of contemporary heritage; and
- the recovery of Aboriginal lands that are in the hands of Canadian governments, industrial corporations, and social institutions.

1995–2005: RECOGNIZING A STATE OF CRISIS

The Royal Commission on Aboriginal Peoples was established to recommend to the federal government solutions that would be acceptable to Aboriginal people and non-Aboriginal people alike. Their report, especially in its summary version, received wide media commentary, and though many comments were critical of the commission's work and conclusions, the inclusive process of consultation and debate legitimated the report's recommendations. Indeed, the report (Royal Commission on Aboriginal Peoples 1996) is undoubtedly the most comprehensive work ever produced on Canadian Aboriginal peoples. It required, on the commission's part, the consultation of many concerned groups and contemporary and historical studies carried out by university researchers. Equally important, however, was work undertaken by Aboriginal researchers that helped commissioners to understand not only traditional life patterns but also contemporary living conditions and life experiences.

The commission advocated a long-term policy of treating Aboriginal people within Canada as distinct nations and recommended setting in place political, economic, and social conditions that would strengthen individual Aboriginal identities. The implementation of this vision will require, on the part of Canadian society, a major social reorganization. The status quo, argued the commission, is unacceptable, in that historical strategies and practices have been dysfunctional and socially devastating to Aboriginal populations. The empirical observations of the report regarding the unfavourable living conditions of Aboriginal people—i.e., low life expectancy, low socio-economic status, high morbidity and mortality rates, poor sanitary conditions, low levels of schooling, an intergenerational gap, high levels of unemployment, high prevalence of social problems (such as high suicide rates, violence against women, alcoholism and drug abuse) and deteriorating environmental conditions—gave urgency to a new approach.

According to the commission, at the core of this new approach is a nation-to-nation relationship. A mutual recognition principle is relevant here since Aboriginal people hold the status of First Occupants, are the main guardians of Aboriginal lands, and hold rights and responsibilities associated with such a major function. The nation-to-nation relationship implies the absence of domination of one group over the other and the respect of status and particular rights being held by Aboriginal peoples, as well as of the culture and the unique heritage of which each Aboriginal person is a depository. Other elements of this approach concern the equitable sharing of received and granted advantages according to criteria stemming from social justice and the responsibility of each party to observe new behavioural rules defining each partner's rights and obligations.

The commission also recognized the importance of dealing with existing ambiguities and that negotiations must remain the only acceptable way to reach necessary compromises on two central concepts: social ethics and transcultural sensitivity (Tremblay 1997). The second concept has not yet received much attention. However, the first one is well documented by the report and is related to the improvement of Aboriginal living conditions, which, as was clearly documented, are deplorable throughout Canada. These conditions, it is argued, can be improved only if concerned authorities engage in concerted and innovative efforts with other partners to share with Aboriginal people the wealth derived from the exploitation of natural resources. Yet, this alone would not be enough. Other actions are also required, including financial aid for economic development, improvement in the quality and the quantity of services, and greater autonomy in the administration of Aboriginal affairs.

1995–2005: MAKING PUBLIC LONG-TERM ABORIGINAL POLICIES

During the last ten years, governments have defined policies and action plans to better serve the concrete needs of Aboriginal peoples and to re-establish harmonious partnerships. They are also working to implement services for Aboriginal peoples that are comparable to those received by non-Aboriginal people. Particularly following the Royal Commission's report, the Canadian and provincial governments undertook a substantial review of Aboriginal policies that reaffirmed their will to provide due responses to fundamental Aboriginal needs. They also designed a general strategy and an action plan meant to harmonize the relationship between non-Aboriginal and Aboriginal governments (Canada 1997). The latter was based on mutual respect and principles of responsibility and sharing, defined in the Royal Commission's Declaration of Reconciliation, that acknowledged past errors and injustices that victimized Aboriginal people. The declaration recommends the renewal of a partnership; the establishment of efficient and responsible Aboriginal governments; the establishment of new financial relationships that will be stable, responsible, and supportive of self-sufficiency; and the improvement of health and public security in Aboriginal communities by investing in human resources that reinforce Aboriginal economic development.

The Declaration of Reconciliation represented an effort on Canada's part to learn from past experiences and to find mechanisms to eliminate the negative influences that historical decisions continue to have on our contemporary society (Canada 1996). The declaration recognized that First Nations have occupied the Canadian territory for millennia, developed close relationships with Mother Earth, organized their societies, and established governments that allowed them to give value to resources in a sustainable manner. The Action Plan elaborates on the declaration by calling for new partnerships with First Nations, Inuit, Métis, and non-Status Indians. The partnerships envisioned include Aboriginal peoples and their organizations, the government of Canada, other levels of governments, and the private sector.

The search for new solutions meant the necessity of determining in a clear way the respective responsibilities of each of the parties concerned. It equally meant the urgent need to acknowledge ancestral customs and the right to celebrate Native heritage and cultures and the fundamental role that Native languages play in their maintenance. The Action Plan also acknowledged the need to assist Native institutions in acquiring the required skills to hold new responsibilities and to establish mechanisms supportive of responsible and sustainable Aboriginal governments and auxiliary institutions. Finally, the Action Plan called on the Canadian government to support social change among Aboriginal peoples by giving priority to health and public safety and by investing in job training and economic development, initiatives that must be planned in partnership with Aboriginal people, their communities, and governments. An important step in the realization of all these aims was achieved with the establishment of the Nunavut Territory in April 1999.

1990–2005: NORMALIZING ABORIGINAL RELATIONSHIPS

The guiding principles established by Canadian governments for Aboriginal peoples were intended to specify negotiation rules, to bring about required actions leading to the full recognition of land and Aboriginal rights, and to better define the parameters at the basis of self-government. Several government initiatives, coupled with reactions from Aboriginal people, bring into the open adjustments necessary for the recognition of fundamental rights and the achievement of greater political autonomy.

As specified by the Royal Commission on Aboriginal Peoples, important decision-making mechanisms regarding the social and economic development of Aboriginal peoples cannot be set in place unilaterally by the Canadian or provincial governments. This is contrary to earlier times when court judgments prevailed to impose on governments the settlement of issues and conflicts with Aboriginal peoples. Today, solutions must result from mutual agreements following bilateral negotiations when a federal territory is involved, as it was the case for Nunavut, and a tripartite one when a provincial territory is concerned, as is the case for Nunavik.

Such a change in attitude on the part of government was not accidental. Instead, the change was the result of a variety of factors, including major court judgments such as the *Malouf* and *Berger* decisions. Governments also promoted their own policies relating to the recognition of Aboriginal rights. The federal government, for instance, enunciated such policies at the time of the repatriation of the Canadian *Constitution* in 1982 and then again during the constitutional conferences of prime ministers with Native chiefs that followed it in 1983, 1984, and 1987.

Quebec acted in a similar fashion when it passed a 1985 National Assembly resolution that provided recognition of ancestral rights endorsed in the *James Bay and Northern Quebec Agreement*. The same resolution urged the government to pursue negotiations with Aboriginal nations with the objective of concluding agreements that ensured the implementation of self-government; rights to their culture, language, and traditions; the right to own and manage lands; hunting, trapping, gathering rights in addition to the right to participate in the management of fauna resources; the right to participate in Quebec development; and access to due benefits. The resolution undoubtedly provided a foundation for the *Paix des Braves* (2001) and *Sanarrutik Agreement* (2002).

As pointed out above, the federal government has established many negotiation processes, the most important of which flow from the global land claims policy, which itself spans a twenty-five-year period, if the *James Bay and the Northern Quebec Agreement* (1975) and the *Northeastern Quebec Agreement* with the Naskapis in 1978 are considered. Other global land claims that have been settled in recent years include the *Final Agreement* of Inuvialuit, the Dene and Métis agreements, the *Gwich'in Agreement*, the *Nunavut Land Claims Agreement*, the Nisga'a *Final Agreement*, and the *Framework Agreement* with the Council of Yukon Indians. Other negotiations in the process of settlement include those with the Dogrib, the Dene of Treaty 8, the Attikamekw and Innus, the Makivik Society in regard to Nunavut and Labrador offshore islands, the Crees concerning Nunavut offshore islands, the Algonkians of eastern Ontario, Labrador Inuit, and the Newfoundland and Labrador Innus.

All these agreements demonstrate that the Canadian Native negotiation policy is a dynamic democratic process, which aims at implementing fundamental rights. It is appropriate, therefore, to provide a few examples of successful negotiation patterns that produced concrete programs and actions, and that derived from the new Canadian government long-term Aboriginal policy.

Sanarrutik (2002): In the footsteps of the *Paix des Braves*, Nunavik Inuit signed the *Sanarrutik Agreement*, a partnership accord aimed at allowing the development of economic projects and the implementation of new social and community services. One part of the agreement bears on the potential hydroelectric and mining development, and the value-oriented use of wide taiga and tundra spaces for conservation and recreation purposes, while another plans to provide social and community services, such as the improvement of the road network and police services.

Common Approach (March 2004): This Agreement in Principle between the Mamuitun and Nutashkuan Innus, the federal and Quebec governments relates to a global land claim negotiation in which the parties agreed to explore new scenarios, concepts, and principles in order to find new solutions at the negotiating table.

Labrador Inuit Land Claims and Final Agreement (January 2005): This agreement between the Labrador Inuit and the Newfoundland and Labrador province is a modern-day treaty and is the first of its kind in Atlantic Canada. According to Minister Andy Scott, the agreement will "provide certainty over land use and title and it will offer a host of opportunities for economic development for Inuit and non-Inuit alike. The Inuit of Labrador now have the tools to build their own government and take greater control of decisions affecting their communities, forging a brighter future for themselves" (*Labrador Inuit Land Claims and Final Agreement* 2005).

Micmacs (2005): Aboriginal peoples and Canadian governments have agreed that, when settlements cannot be reached through the negotiation process or when treaty interpretations are divergent, one party or the other may refer the matter to an appropriate court. The Micmac case is an example of this situation. The Micmac people were attempting to get recognition by governments of the existence of an ancestral right on Nova Scotia and New Brunswick forest resources. According to the court, the 1760–61 treaty does not provide contemporary Micmacs the right to cut trees for commercial purposes without respecting provincial regulations.

Nunavik (2005): In 2001 the Nunavik Commission released its report, entitled *Amiqqaaluta Let Us Share: Mapping a Road Toward a Government for Nunavik*. The report proposed the creation of an autonomous government for Nunavik. After its official launching in Kuujjuarapik, it was distributed to all Nunavik households and in the various federal and Quebec departments providing services in Nunavik. The governmental structure that was proposed by the Nunavik Commission would be the one of a modern government; i.e., one constituted by an Assembly composed of elected representatives holding legislative powers, an Elders' Council playing the role of a consultative body to the Assembly (a sort of Senate), and a traditionally empowered Executive body. It was on this basis that concerned parties decided to negotiate with the aim of creating a new form of government for Nunavik.

Even though the Long Walk of Aboriginal peoples living in Canada has been started and accompanied by steadfast progress, much remains to be achieved by both Aboriginal peoples and Canadian governments. In order for Aboriginal peoples to obtain full and complete respect of ancestral and land rights and to obtain self-government, many steps have to be undertaken, all of which must rest on three fundamental principles: any situation, conflicting or cooperative, that involves governments and Aboriginal people must be examined in the light of well-known government guiding principles agreed upon by Aboriginal peoples; implementation of projects must be in accord with agreed-upon concrete imperatives; and all projects must rest on the assent of a well-informed general population.

The first principle relates to issues of sustainable development and social equity, which, taken together, reconcile the requirements of economic development and the necessity of resource protection in a fragile environment. In other words, the objective is to make sure that the promotion of Aboriginal industries and the creation of industrial trades avoids an increase in environmental risks flowing either from overexploitation of resources or from the establishment of pollution sources. On the other hand, governmental and community programs for Aboriginal people must be comparable in quantity and quality to those available to other Canadians, especially when it relates to health, social services, education, employment, housing, and economic development. At the same time, these programs must respect Aboriginal fundamental values and their worldview.

The second principle flows from the logic of implementation and implies respect for the four following conditions:

- political awareness of both partners who make decisions to be fully at the service of citizens;
- active participation of Aboriginal citizens to make them a significant part of the decision-taking process and transform a top-down pyramidal operation into one solidly anchored at its base;
- full awareness that policies flowing from such a blueprint are part of a systemic perspective and that initiatives taken in one sector are going to engender reactions in other interdependent sectors; and
- concerted strategies to achieve the defined objectives as well as feedback and adjustment mechanisms.

The third principle is tied to the Long Walk itself, which will continue in the right direction only so long as non-Aboriginal Canadians acquire a deeper and more authentic knowledge of Aboriginal living conditions and a willingness to collaborate with them to reverse these conditions. Only when this happens will non-Aboriginal Canadians be able to reconcile the prerequisites of economic development with respect for the fundamental rights of Aboriginal peoples.

---

1   The authors undertook research work for this chapter while they served as commissioners on the Nunavik Commission (1999–2001) and later on as special advisors to the federal negotiator, Nunavik (2002–2005), for the establishment of a public government in Nunavik, which would eventually realize a significant degree of autonomy within the Province of Quebec. The authors' involvements in Aboriginal questions comprise about seventy years of experience.

2   In the past, when conflicts have arisen between governments and Aboriginal peoples, arbitration was relayed to courts. More recently, however, unresolved issues between governments and non-governmental parties have often been resolved through a negotiation process. Such a process, especially in the case of the federal government, makes it hard to discuss a dispute in terms of a nation-to-nation relationship due to the fiduciary role of the federal government as representative of the Crown. Nonetheless, negotiation between concerned parties is viewed in Canada as a superior way to solve conflicts and problems.

PART II

THE MANITOBA EXPERIENCE:
A LEGACY OF DISRESPECT

FOREWORD

Eugenie Mercredi
Women's Traditional Chief and
Leader of the Women's Council
Pimicikamak Cree Nation
Cross Lake, Manitoba

MY ENGLISH NAME IS EUGENIE MERCREDI. My Cree name is Ka-pa-pa-go-wis-qua, which means Butterfly Woman. I am the Women's Traditional Chief and Leader of the Women's Council of Pimicikamak.

I am honoured to speak on behalf of the women of Pimicikamak, sharing one voice, one mind, one spirit. Women are water people because we are life-givers. We are part of the creation, we look after our communities and children. Water is the lifeblood of Mother Earth, flowing through her veins, the rivers and lakes. Without clean water our Mother dies, and we die. Our Mother Earth, which you call the environment, is dying. Those who live in the middle of concrete, glass, and steel in the cities may not see this the way we do. We live in the middle of a poisoned well, where the waters that everyone in this province and beyond depend on are dirty and stinking and killing the fish, animals, birds, and our people.

We as Pimicikamak know first-hand how bad things have become because of the hydro project, for water is the core of our soul and way of life. Pimicikamak means water flowing across the lake. Water was home to all the fish and fishing was our major source of survival, our economy. The rivers and lakes are our highways; we would travel on these in summer and when frozen over in winter, to hunt, trap, gather medicines, and share with each other.

I bring you this water today as evidence of how much the water, and we, have been devastated because of the Manitoba Hydro Project. Our Mother Earth's blood is contaminated, and poisons those who drink it. We, her people, are sick; the fish, birds, and animals are sick. This very water causes rashes on our children when they go swimming. Women will no longer breast-feed their babies because they are afraid the water has infected them.

The water is now filled with mud, silt, rotting plants and trees, and reeds. Instead of nourishing the lands and forests, the rivers now wash them away when Hydro forces the water levels high, flooding and eroding thousands of miles of shorelines. Then when Hydro holds the water back, the lands and forests die of thirst.

The millions of dead trees submerged or floating in the water because of the Hydro Project cause boating and fishing accidents. People die. What used to be the very soul of our people and the source of all life in the boreal is now a feared killer. This water is deadly. We do not want one more inch of deadly water fluctuation to further swallow and poison our lands, forests, shorelines, animals, fish and people.

I implore you on behalf of all women of Pimicikamak to help us carry out our life-giving purpose. We weep because we watch our people and territory suffer, and we try to do what we can to give care and to help heal the wounds. But as long as our Mother Earth's lifeblood is so poisoned our hands have been shackled and we feel raped. As long as all the devastation from Hydro remains left to grow and accumulate, there can never be any justification for adding to it, from Wuskwatim or anything else. We ask you to say this to your Minister of Conservation.

Our children and the unborn depend on you here today to reach into your own hearts through which your own blood flows and do the right thing.

William Osborne
Executive Council Member
Pimicikamak Cree Nation
Cross Lake, Manitoba

MY NAME IS WILLIAM OSBORNE. I am the Executive Council Member Responsible for Intergovernmental Relations for Pimicikamak. I want to speak with you about what you call "Global Climate Change" and what this means to our people. What you call climate change is one of the many labels being used by Hydro and the governments to push for and justify massive new hydro development, starting with Wuskwatim.

I have this agreement between Canada and Manitoba "for cooperation in addressing climate change." It says here: "the Parties recognize the potential for the development of economically competitive sources of hydro electricity and related transmission as a way to reduce greenhouse gas (GHG) emissions." The Agreement then goes on to define hydro as a type of "renewable energy," perhaps trying to justify the push to build more and more hydro developments. This sounds pretty, makes people feel warm and good. But this is really white washing. It is painting over an ugly truth, like that big Hydro billboard at Portage Avenue and St. James Street has done. All the pretty words, pictures, and cloaks in the world cannot turn the devil into a saint.

How gullible we have all been in believing the white wash! This might be funny if it weren't so tragic. Because it is tragic.

It may or may not be true that hydro doesn't cause as much of this GHG climate change as coal. We don't know. But even if it is true, this does not change the fact that industrial hydro like the Manitoba Hydro Project has caused and continues to cause a different type of global climate change crisis.

This is global climate change to Pimicikamak's world—to our way of life, society, economy, and health. This climate change has been and continues to be so devastating that there is no possible way that what has caused it—the Manitoba Hydro Project—can be called "renewable." The *Oxford Dictionary* defines renewable as "not depleted when used." Our lands, waters, birds, animals, fish, trees, medicines, and our people's health and culture, are being depleted over time. This is a fact. This is the truth.

Where my people once lived in a climate of respect for and interdependence with the land, we now live in fear of the land and waters because, since the hydro projects on our territory, our environment has become dangerous. It injures and kills. It cannot support the fish, birds, and animals that we live with and by. The water is polluted, the water fluctuations sweep away at the shorelines, forcing forests and lands to slide into the rivers. The water is filled with dead and rotting trees and plants.

Where my people once lived in a climate of trust for each other and other Aboriginal peoples, there is now sometimes lack of trust. After having been starved out for so long, many were pushed beyond the brink of desperation and were lulled by false promises of wealth and so-called progress. The dollar bill was held out like a carrot. This has caused internal unrest and dysfunction within and between our communities.

Where my people once lived in a climate of self-respect, pride, and joy in pursuing our Creator-granted way of life of fishing, hunting, and trapping, many have now been forced onto welfare and into unspeakable poverty, their souls and pride crushed, caught in a cycle of despair. Many are physically ill from forced diet changes. Many are emotionally ill and try to commit suicide. Some do.

Where the entire climate of our traditional territory had been healthy— with clean water flowing past our homes, teeming with fish, with shorelines alive with birds and medicines, and the forests full of animals and trees— now we live in a climate of disease. Our environment is dying. So are we.

This climate change agreement between Canada and Manitoba says that the Parties recognize that hydro development "should be done in a manner that encourages sustainable development in Aboriginal communities and is respectful of environmental issues." Let me explain to you what "sustainable development" means to Pimicikamak. Developing means healing, so we can sustain ourselves and our Mother Earth as the Creator meant for us to do. It means healing the lands, healing the waters, healing the people to the maximum possible extent so that we can stop this climate of fear and death, and find once again a climate of respect, trust, and health.

I saw some of this healing that my own people started to feel and share when we had a power blackout in our community on May 16, because of a bad snowstorm. Families and neighbours came together to help each other. Grandparents taught the little ones how to build a fire to cook food. Teenagers went out to gather and cut wood. Parents put together the meal, and people helped clean up. Everyone sat around as one, sharing stories of life as it has been before our global climate change. It used to be more like this, more sharing, productivity, self-motivation, caring. We felt our place in the world, and felt good and safe in this place. This foundation has been flooded and ripped out from under us by the hydro project. On May 16 we had a moment of peace in the midst of the pain. We and our Mother Earth need peace and health that lasts.

Unless and until this long-term healing happens, and Hydro and the governments fulfill their legal obligations in this regard, no people should ever be forced to endure further pain and despair from more of the same thing—more unsustainable, unhealthy industrial hydro development.

Hydro tries to back up its claims that further effects from Wuskwatim will be "imperceptible" by relying on its twenty-five years of experience in hydro operations. My people have 10,000 years of experience in living off and with the land in a sustainable and respectful way. We have thirty years of experience in watching all of this stripped away by hydro development. And we have six years of experience in standing up as Pimicikamak and saying "no more."

The above speeches were delivered in March 2004 by members of the Pimicikamak Cree Nation before the Manitoba Clean Environment Commission hearings concerning the Wuskwatim generating station and transmission project.

5

Engineering Poverty: Colonialism and Hydroelectric Development in Northern Manitoba

Steven M. Hoffman

> I am very disappointed in your failure to truly acknowledge and understand what our community has and is going through for Manitoba Hydro and the Government of Manitoba to make hundreds of millions of dollars on the pain and suffering of our people. You mention that Manitoba Hydro has made significant progress in addressing the impacts of previous projects including the "major" $18 million CASIL Agreement. That agreement was signed after South Indian Lake had to fight for almost 17 years after being flooded to be recognized under the Northern Flood Agreement. As I said in my letter to Premier Doer, the negotiations were not fair and just as Manitoba Hydro and the Government of Manitoba tried to pay as little as they could to settle our claims. We were desperate people in desperate circumstances who were tired of fighting and were taken advantage of.
>
> —Excerpt from a letter dated October 24, 2003, written by SIL resident Myrtle Dysart to Manitoba Minister Responsible for Manitoba Hydro, the Honourable Tim Sale, regarding the 1992 *CASIL Agreement.*

SOUTH INDIAN LAKE is a small Aboriginal community located on the shore of northern Manitoba's Southern Indian Lake. The trip from the community dock to the lake's control structure at Missi Falls takes well over two hours in a fast boat. A generation ago, the trip meant an encounter with miles of seemingly endless shoreline dense with primitive boreal forest over waters yielding an abundance of pike and whitefish. Today that same trip reveals a constantly eroding shoreline punctured by large cliffs of exposed sediment and roots; islands losing their struggle to the onslaught of ever-changing water levels; trees suspended at all angles, roots vainly trying to hold onto soil washing steadily into the lake; and waters so degraded that a hand disappears from view before an elbow breaks the surface.

The violation of an apparently undisturbed landscape such as Southern Indian Lake is an affront to many contemporary sensibilities. Particularly for those ensconced in the onrush of modernity, the idea of 'being close to the land,' 'living in harmony with nature,' 'understanding the ways of the wild,' often holds broad appeal. The daily life of those living in intimate association with the land was, however, often far from romantic. Threats posed by forces beyond understanding, much less control, were constant as was the possibility of starvation and domination by competing peoples. Yet, however one evaluates the relative merits of Aboriginal life, there is little doubt that the foundation for even a remotely familiar land-based existence is rapidly slipping from the grasp of not only South Indian Lake residents but all the Aboriginal communities of northern Manitoba. For some, the loss can be traced directly to the massive engineering projects conceived and initiated by Manitoba Hydro. The purpose of this essay is to examine the nature of these projects and the impact they have had on the residents who were caught in the wake of their development.

A COLONIAL FRAMEWORK

The idea of 'colonialism' offers a useful framework for understanding the current status of the northern Manitoba Cree. Unlike imperialism, which may infer a mere physical occupation, colonialism generally implies a much deeper form of control and subordination. Strausz-Hupe and Hazard, for instance, argue that a "colonial relationship is created when one nation establishes and maintains political domination over a geographically external political unit inhabited by people of any race and at any stage of cultural development" (1958, 4). Colonialism also implies, indeed even necessitates, the denigration of Aboriginal systems of social organization and governance since, as Loomba points out, the process of forming a community means "unforming" the existing community (1998, 3). Thus, many authors writing in the midst of the colonial collapse following World War II, while acknowledging the degenerative character of colonial hegemony existing at that time, continued to degrade the cultural, social, and political sophistication of the colonial subjects. Strausz-Hupe and Hazard's 1958 book, for instance, consistently employed terms such as "primitive" to describe the "natives," going so far as to claim that such peoples, or at least the educated among them, were grateful for the advantages of modernity being visited upon them.

Twentieth-century colonialism meant a great deal more than exacting tribute, goods, and wealth from conquered places. Nor was it limited to restructuring the economies of the latter in order to draw them into a complex relationship with their own. Instead, colonization meant interference and perhaps even dismemberment of existing political and cultural structures (Loomba 1998, 6). As such, *de*colonization is not simply a political process entailing "the surrender of external political sovereignty" (Springhall 2001, 2) or putting an end to "commercial and financial hegemony over former possessions," a condition defined by Springhall as "neo-colonialism" (2001, 4). In its deepest sense, decolonization means recapturing a way of life and reinvigorating a prior set of cultural and social relationships that were repressed as a functional part of colonial control.

CREE–CANADIAN RELATIONS

The history of the Cree people is complex and dynamic. Early Cree tribes occupied a land base along James Bay and the western shores of Hudson Bay, north to Churchill, west to Lake Winnipeg, and south to Lake Nipigon. By the early part of the nineteenth century, this base had been expanded to include a large part of the western plains. At least nine major dialects of a common root language were spoken, including Plains, Woods, West and East Swampy, Moose, East, Atttikamek or Tete de Boule, and Naskapi and Montagnais Cree (McMillan 1988, 101–102).

The Cree originated as a woodlands culture, dependent upon a mixture of big- and small-game hunting. Hunting was supplemented with fishing, which, while not as highly valued, nonetheless provided an occasion for the gathering of normally widely dispersed kinship-based hunting groups. A steady march westward began with advent of the fur trade in the last decades of the seventeenth century. Prior to that time, while the Cree were nomadic and dependent upon the seasonal availability of game and fish, they nonetheless occupied a fairly consistent swath of territory. The establishment of the Hudson's Bay Company in 1668 marked a fundamental turning point since prior to that time, the Cree were only indirectly involved in trade relations with the Europeans, though they were routinely acquiring non-native goods such as corn and various merchandise (Mandlebaum 1978, 16). The siting of company posts at the mouth of the Nelson, Moose, and Albany rivers meant that the Cree were now in a position to trade directly with Europeans.

What the Europeans wanted, of course, were beaver pelts. Perhaps more than any other tribe, the Cree took full advantage of their relationship with the Europeans to expand their range of influence. The acquisition and use of the gun, which was gladly provided to them by the English, played a major role in their success. Beyond this, there were several reasons why the Cree became so deeply entangled in the fur trade. First, says Mandlebaum, there was the great demand for fur on the part of fashionable Europeans and a concomitant push to expand the boundaries of the trade. Once the lands near the settlements were stripped of animals, Cree trappers were required to push further and further into their territory to satisfy the seemingly insatiable appetite for beaver-based hats. Second, the Cree were well suited to serve as the dominant hunting group. According to Mandlebaum:

> Being aboriginally a hunting people, dispersed in small groups across a wide territory, they fulfilled the prerequisite of the fur harvest imposed by the scattered nature of the source of supply and the disadvantages of too intensive trapping in any one area. Secondly, they were a canoe-using people and so were readily able to utilize the network of waterways in their terrain to transport the raw materials to the post. [This] gave them a great advantage of over the more distant people who lacked both the early start and

the technique of water transport. For the Cree could reach out into far lands and, armed with guns, repel the previous inhabitants. (1978, 30)

The initial stage of Cree–European relations, therefore, came to be defined by the limits and characteristics of the fur trade, a system that created "a state of economic subservience . . . greatly dependent upon the English and the French not only for arms, clothing, and utensils, but even for provisions" (Mandlebaum 1978, 29). The trade also provided the foundation for westward movement, initially to the fringes of the prairie and ultimately far into present-day Alberta. However, the trade did not fundamentally alter the land-based way of life or the cultural characteristics of the Cree.

The passing of a fashion in Europe and the near-exhaustion of the resource base meant that era of fur trade was over by the early 1800s. Replacing the rapacious demand for fur, however, was a more fundamental appetite, namely, the need for land to satisfy the westward expansion of European populations. While no one event signifies the beginning of this period, Treaty 5 is a suitable historical marker. One of a series of Aboriginal–Canadian treaties, it introduced a period of assimilation and paternalism that, according to McMillan, was based on a goal of protecting "Indians while attempting to 'civilize' them and to prepare them to enter mainstream society. Native populations were declining throughout the late nineteenth and early twentieth centuries, and the government plan was to encourage the gradual disappearance of Indians as Indians" (1988, 291). Underpinning this goal was the belief that

> Indian tribes were racially and culturally inferior to European and, more specifically, Anglo-Saxon cultural groups. Although treaties were ostensibly made between two nations, their effect was simply to get First Nations out of the way of immigrant settlement and onto reserves, where the tribes would either melt away or become 'civilized' enough to become Canadian citizens. (Hoxie 1996, 278)

While the period of assimilation and paternalistic exploitation was long and destructive, neither implied the complete disappearance of traditional life. Indeed, a number of authors have pointed out that even after many years of assimilationist policies, the instrumentalities of modernity ushered in by the post-treaty period facilitated, in at least some cases, the maintenance of traditional practices. In his discussion of regional developments in the James Bay area between 1971 and 1981, for instance, Richard Salisbury argues that

> [residents] point out how new technology, like snowmobiles, has been accepted into traditional activities, like trapping, and has changed the organization of those activities.... The new technology has removed drudgery from a traditional activity, made it more productive and opened the way to other activities, during the time set free. Life is traditional, they may argue, but has become a better life, allowing the hunter more time with his family. (1986, 7; see also Niezen 1993)

While contemporary technology may, in fact, be supportive of traditional activities and the emergence of a post-colonial way of life, at the root of this possibility is a viable land base. The current stage of the Cree–Canadian relationship, defined in large part by a vast system of hydroelectric enterprises, calls into question whether this is, in fact, a continuing possibility.

A NEW ERA: HYDRO DEVELOPMENT IN THE 1970s

The exploitation of northern Manitoba's vast waterways was long a goal of southern policymakers. While initially modest in terms of size and capacity, as the century progressed the imperatives of modernization provided a foundation for projects that became successively larger in scale and geographic scope.

The exploitation of the region's hydrological resources began in 1900 with the construction of the Minnedosa River Plant. This was followed by the Pinawa Generating Station on the Winnipeg River in 1906, the first plant in the region to operate on an annual basis. Following the pattern of power plant construction typical of the era, other stations followed in rapid order, all being larger and operating with relatively higher heads. Ultimately, however, the Winnipeg River was inadequate to meet the region's growing electricity demands and Manitoba Hydro, the province's Crown corporation responsible for energy policy, planning, and development, began to look north to the Nelson and Churchill rivers.

By any measure, the Nelson and Churchill river drainage area is a massive hydrological and ecological system. Together, the basins cover over one million square miles, from the Rockies in the west to the Mississippi and the Lake Superior drainage basins in the south and east, and throughout the bulk of the Canadian provinces of Alberta, Saskatchewan, Manitoba, and Ontario (Manitoba Hydro, *The Hydro Province*, Fact Sheet). A tentative step in placing hydroelectric resources on the Nelson River had been taken in 1960 with the construction of the Kelsey Generating Station, but a systematic inquiry into the full hydroelectric potential of this watershed had to wait until 1963, when the Province of Manitoba entered into a cost-sharing agreement with the Government of Canada to investigate the feasibility of large-scale hydroelectric development on the Nelson. Also in 1963, Hydro commissioned a study to investigate the economic feasibility of developing hydroelectric generating stations on the lower Nelson River, which emptied directly into Hudson Bay (Manitoba Hydro, no date, 31–34).

Though potentially daunting, these plans were understood as a prerequisite for what Alex Netherton refers to as a policy of "provincial continental modernization" (1993). As understood by Netherton, this policy was based on a mix of old and new assumptions, including long-held beliefs that power must be cheap and that the province's hydro policy must be based on the most efficient use of financial resources. Added to these traditional assumptions were at least two new and critically important beliefs: first, that electricity generated in the far north would have to find extraprovincial markets in order for the projects to be economically viable; and second, that Hydro possessed the only legitimate claim to northern land and water resources. Institutional changes were also needed, including the creation of a large, integrated provincial utility not bound by previous interutility agreements and the establishment of mechanisms to remove Aboriginal communities from lands and resources used for hydro (Netherton 1993, 294–295).

The Churchill River Diversion and the Lake Winnipeg Regulation projects (CRD/LWR) were the instruments of this modernizing process. In essence, the CRD project reversed the directional flow of the Churchill River to increase the volume of water moving through the Nelson River, and the LWR project manipulated seasonal discharges from Lake Winnipeg into the river.

The first phase of the project required diverting the Churchill's flow into the Nelson River. According to journalist Larry Krotz, "By 1976, the engineers had achieved their dream. A control dam at Missi Falls, 400 kilometers from the mouth of the Churchill River, cut the flow from an average of 1050 cubic meters per second to an average of 150, and turned all that water back through 180-kilometer long Southern Indian Lake, then through a man-made channel and several smaller rivers into the Nelson" (1991, 38). Simultaneously with the CRD, Hydro began constructing the first of a series of dams located on the Nelson River. In addition to the Kettle generating station, which was brought on-line in 1974, Hydro built three other facilities on the river, representing almost 3600 MW of generating capacity.

The second part of the project involved the regulation of Lake Winnipeg, primarily to coordinate the outflow of the lake with seasonal electric demand. Unfortunately for Hydro, the natural water flows out of the lake are lowest in the winter, when the demands for export power are the highest. In order to optimize hydroelectric production, Hydro needed to control the lake's natural water flows, a feat accomplished with the construction of the Jenpeg control structure and generating station, located sixteen kilometres from the Aboriginal community of Cross Lake. As described by the company,

> [the] station on the upper arm of the Nelson River is one of the key elements in the successful development of the hydroelectric potential of northern Manitoba. In addition to generating [128 MW of] electricity, Jenpeg's powerhouse and spillway structures are used to control and regulate the outflow waters of Lake Winnipeg, which in turn is used as a reservoir to store water to ensure enough water is available to run the northern generating stations. (<www.hydro.mb.ca>)

A number of channels were also constructed, including the 2-Mile channel, the 8-Mile channel, and the Ominawin Channel (Manitoba Hydro, *Information Sheet*, Kettle Generating Station).

These two projects allowed Hydro to develop the Nelson River as a "power corridor" and to turn Lake Winnipeg into a gigantic storage battery. The projects irreversibly altered the hydrological and ecological characteristics of some 30,000,000 acres, or 50,000 square miles, of northern boreal rivers and forest. However, Hydro largely ignored two key considerations: first, the environmental consequences created by the project; and second, the interests of, and impacts on, the Aboriginal communities located on the Nelson River. The company was able to pursue this arbitrary course of action because "any other claims and resource uses were not calculated or recognized in the physical design or economic evaluation of hydro projects" (Netherton 1993, 294). Chief among these potentially rival claims were those maintained by the Cree Aboriginal communities of York Factory, Nelson House, Split Lake, Norway House, and Cross Lake, among others, all of which were located within the geographic areas affected by the CRD and LWR projects.

All these communities were adversely and profoundly affected by the projects. Indeed, according to the 2001 *Report of the Interchurch Inquiry into Northern Hydro Development,* the projects have proven to be "an ecological, social, and moral catastrophe for northern Manitoba and its Aboriginal inhabitants" (Part IX: Conclusion). It is a mistake, however, to presume that the projects resulted in either uniform experiences or responses, a fact illustrated by the case of South Indian Lake.

THE CASE OF SOUTH INDIAN LAKE

The present-day community of South Indian Lake (SIL) is located on the western shore of Southern Indian Lake, an immense body of water 105 miles long and 16 miles wide covering some 1200 square miles of surface area. While human presence in the Southern Indian Lake region might date back some 6000 years, Waldram argues that

> It is not possible to determine the exact date in which a community was formed in the Southern Indian Lake area in post-contact times. . . . However, by the early twentieth century it was likely that a small but relatively stable population of Indians was

living around the region [and] that the economy of the community revolved around the trapping industry and the production
of fish and animal products for food and other domestic uses.
(1988, 117)

For most of the twentieth century, the community was largely traditional in its lifestyle, with family units scattered along a broad swath of land,
including the main body and north end of Southern Indian Lake, Bigami
Bay, South Bay, and Opachuanau Lake (Van Ginkel Associates 1967, 1). As
was the case for much of Cree history, the community gathered together only
sporadically, in this case between Christmas and the end of January (Van
Ginkel Associates 1967, 25). Traditional activities were supplemented by a
viable commercial fishery that was established in 1942 (Waldram 1988, 117).

The community's political and decision-making process was also largely
traditional. According to Van Ginkel Associates, "the population of SIL is
not functionalized—no one is assigned specific roles. Even when an attempt
is made to form an organization to function in a specified area, the members
seldom remain within the area of concern" (1967, 37). In the same manner:

There appeared to be no formal relationship between employer
and employee. This appreciation of the wholeness of the community has kept everyone at more or less the same standard of
living. Though our survey indicated a variance in income, no one
appeared to have much more or much less than anyone else. Two
or three families have fairly large fish and trapping operations,
but their personal standard of living, social status, and political
leadership are neither greater nor significantly different from
anyone else in the community. (37–38)

In 1967, on the eve of the Churchill River Diversion project, some 76.6
percent of SIL's approximately 480 residents were classified as Treaty
Indians, 21.3 percent as non-Treaty Indians or Métis, and only 2.1 percent
white. The main economic pursuits were fishing and trapping, there being
some 80 to 125 licensed fishers and 80 to 150 licensed trappers. These
pursuits were responsible for a remarkably prosperous life. According to
a 1967 report commissioned by Hydro, the average annual income per

employed person was approximately $2500 and the average family income was between $3500 and $4500. Approximately 5 percent had achieved a level of income in excess of $10,000 per year (Van Ginkel Associates 1967, 2). This compared with the "average income of Indians in the North of approximately $500" and, according to the consultants, compared favourably with the national Canadian average. Indeed, "if the current Canadian measure of poverty is applied (an income of less than $3000/year), only 27.9 percent of the total number of families at SIL were poor," a percentage close to the national average at that time (Van Ginkel Associates 1967, 36).[1]

The high level of income enjoyed by the community also meant a high degree of autonomy from the welfare state so commonly associated with contemporary Aboriginal communities. As noted in the Van Ginkel Associates report, "A striking feature of the distribution of income by sources is the relatively small contribution to total income made by welfare and pensions." Thus, a remarkably small 1 percent of the community's income came from welfare payments and 5.5 percent of the community's income was drawn from pensions, and most of the pensioners "are unemployable due to age" (Table 10, 34, 35).

The Van Ginkel Associates report brings home another key aspect of pre-flood SIL: the ability of the land base to support the community and to maintain traditional activities. According to the report, "the most important enterprise is fishing" with the seventy or so licensed fishers in the winter and the 107 in the summer generating $106,000 income, or an average value of $1638 per year (32). Additional cash income was produced by an active fur trade, though the cash value of the trade was only about one-third of that produced by the average fish catch (Table 8, 32). Together, these activities, along with some other minor irregular employment, produced a high standard of living, a fact acknowledged by the consultants: "In summary, by Indian, and even by general Northern Manitoba standards, the people at SIL are very well off economically" (38). In other words, prior to the flooding and subsequent relocation precipitated by the dams, SIL was a community that successfully combined modern pursuits—i.e., a viable commercial fishery—with activities and a pattern of social life strongly associated with the traditional land-based Cree culture.

The relatively stable economic system and the high quality of life enjoyed by the residents of SIL is, of course, strikingly at odds with the characterization of pre-development life generally offered by the company. In testimony before an Interchurch inquiry, for instance, Hydro argued that the communities "were experiencing serious problems of poverty and unemployment long before construction of the Project . . . [and to] . . . assess the specific effects of the Project" or "to quantify the costs and damages of the Project" is extremely problematic (Manitoba Hydro Background Papers 1 and 4, 1999, 1–3 and 4–9). Even in 1967, despite its own findings that SIL was robust both economically and socially, the company's consultants found the community's future problematic. Van Ginkle, for instance, argued that the community's "younger generation . . . was not necessarily prepared to continue to live these harsh circumstance," though evidence to this effect is conspicuously lacking in the report (6). Similarly, the report found that "many parents claim that children who go to residential school—the only secondary schools available—prefer the company of those outside the community" (7).

Underlying an apparent concern for the children, however, was a colonial mindset that understood the integration of a cash economy with a traditional lifestyle as being unsuited to Manitoba's modern, continental society, even if it did produce a high quality of life. Thus, the report argued that "even if one could foresee greater efficiency and productivity and improved marketing of fish and fur for the future, this type of community represents a dead-end way of life" (6). The only choice was to relocate the residents into a permanent settlement and more fully integrate them into modernity. The creation of a new type of cash economy to replace traditional sources of cash income was particularly important since, in the words of the Van Ginkel Associates report, SIL residents "have never lived on welfare" (8). It was therefore of the utmost importance "that a viable economic base be created for every individual that is part of the productive process" (9). Unfortunately, the project, rather than delivering a viable economic base, has helped create a community increasingly dependent upon provincial and company assistance.[2]

SIL's dependency can largely be traced to the 1970s decline of the Southern Indian Lake fishery precipitated by the completion of the CRD project. According to a 1992 assessment by federal authorities, the project resulted in the desiccation of formerly extensive wetland areas; exposure of large river bars and extensive areas of former riverbed; abandonment of former side channel areas; and localized channel down-cutting and bank erosion in formerly apparently stable areas. The result was "locally signifi-cant sediment production [and] considerable shoreline erosion. . . . Sediment output from SIL went from about 120,000 tonnes in 1975, to 400,000 tonnes in 1976, 600,000 tonnes in 1977 and 550,000 tonnes in 1978" (Department of Fisheries and Oceans 1992, 2).[3]

The degradation of the lake had an immediate and overwhelming impact on the Southern Indian Lake fishery. The 1992 Department of Fisheries and Oceans study found that the adult pike population had suffered "a down-ward trend . . . in both catch per unit of effort (from 13.52 per 8 hour period in 1976 to 5.60 in 1988) and in condition factor (from 0.89 in 1976 to 0.84 in 1988)" (1992, 22). The report also noted that

> the commercial fishery at SIL was the largest in northern Mani-toba prior to impoundment and diversion with about 333,500 kg of fish taken yearly. Approximately 85% of the total commercial catch weight was composed of lake whitefish, with the rest being made up of pike and walleye. Immediately following impound-ment there was a substantial drop in catch per unit effort (CPU). In 1982, the whole whitefish catch of the lake was downgraded from export to continental grade, with a concomitant substantial drop in fish price. The lower price and reduced CPU led directly to a collapse of the commercial fishery. (23)

The consequences of this degradation on the community's economic structure was swift and dramatic. In 1972, fishing and trapping were contrib-uting less than half of the community's cash income, as compared to over three-quarters just six years earlier. During the same period, government transfer payments increased almost six-fold to 28 percent of SIL's overall economy (Manitoba Department of Mines, Resources and Environmental Management 1974, 309). The following decades saw further increases in dependency and by 1996 well over one-third of the community's total income was accounted for by government transfers, a rate over three times that for the rest of the province (Statistics Canada, Community Profiles, <www.statcan.ca>, 1996). Since that time, dependency has deepened to such an extent that, according to local leaders, only a small fraction of the community's income is now privately generated.

TABLE 5.1

Average Household Income

	1981	1991	1996	2001
Cross Lake	$5686	$27,213	$32,197	$31,367
Nelson House	$4345	$29,078	$31,742	$34,802
South Indian Lake	–	$24,408	$32,816	$31,185
Thompson	$8812	$53,712	$59,314	$61,759
Winnipeg	–	$42,208	$44,937	$53,176

Sources: 2001: E-STAT, Statistics Canada; 1996: E-STAT, Statistics Canada; 1991: E-STAT, Statistics Canada; 1981: Statistics Canada, 1981 Census

The deterioration of the community's fortunes is also reflected in household and personal incomes. As noted above, prior to the flooding, the people at SIL were "very well off economically" with incomes at or near the northern and Manitoba averages (Van Ginkel Associates 1967, 38). By the start of the new millennium, the average household income has fallen far below that of other northern towns (see Table 5.1) while the median personal income, far from being at or above provincial averages, is now one-quarter of both Thompson and Winnipeg, or $6672, $25,688, and 22,482, respectively (Statistics Canada, Community Profiles). Poverty, rather than prosperity, has followed in the wake of the CRD project.

Surveying the conditions found in SIL in the mid-1980s, Robson found that "commercial fishing was almost completely destroyed, traplines were to a large extent underwater, [and] hunting patterns were thoroughly disrupted by the ecological imbalance caused by the flooding" (1993, 115). In other words, a land base that had supported a viable cash economy *and* at least some version of traditional life had been effectively destroyed. That these results were likely outcomes of the CRD project was well understood at the time. Thus, as early as 1974, the government of Manitoba predicted that

> in the longer run . . . the impacts [of the CRD] will likely be nega-
> tive. There will be disruptions of winter transportation, both
> internal and external, due to lack of suitable ice conditions. Real
> property damage will be extensive. Wildlife habitats, particularly
> in the case of beaver and muskrat, will be temporarily disrupted.
> The fishery could be adversely affected due to possible reductions
> in the lake's productivity over time. A final, and perhaps most
> important effect, will occur in the employment sector. The disap-
> pearance of substantial numbers of temporary jobs could lead to a
> significant drop in community income. Unless new programs are
> forthcoming to ensure employment, there will be a rise in the level
> of transfer payments and, in turn, the social and economic prob-
> lems associated with such a rise. (Manitoba Department of Mines,
> Resources and Environmental Management 1974, 310, 313)

Thirty years later, the adverse circumstances predicted by the province have been realized as the fishery continues its decline and SIL's dependency continues to deepen.

A WORLD OF AGREEMENT: FROM THE NFA TO THE PDA

The state of SIL, while perhaps extreme, nonetheless reflects the general experience of all the Aboriginal communities located within reach of the CRD/LWR projects. To the extent Hydro and the Province have accepted any responsibility for these conditions, they have done so through a series of agreements that have oftentimes deepened rather than alleviated the frustra-tions felt by the affected communities.

The Northern Flood Agreement

The first major agreement reached between the affected communities and the governmental parties was the *Northern Flood Agreement* (NFA). Finalized in 1977, the agreement was entered into by the governments of Canada and Manitoba, Manitoba Hydro, and the Northern Flood Committee, a group represented by the chiefs of Nelson House, Norway House, Cross Lake, Split Lake, and York Landing (Wiebe 1999). The latter did not include South Indian Lake or several other affected communities. The NFA was seen by Hydro as a means for negotiating damage claims brought forward by individual landowners and communities in return for exercising the pre-existing right to flood lands legally owned by the Canadian government. Hydro never assumed that the Cree communities had any right to intervene in a way that would prevent or even delay construction, despite the fact that the projects were being built almost entirely within Aboriginal lands. The best that the Northern Flood Committee could hope for was to negotiate a price for the damages, and suffering Aboriginal people had no choice but to accept.

All parties hoped the NFA would bring some measure of relief, but history proved otherwise. In 1996, for instance, the Royal Commission on Aboriginal Peoples (RCAP) found that the "history of the NFA has been marked by little or no action in implementation of [its] obligations and a long, drawn-out (and continuing) process of arbitration to force governments to implement their obligations" (1996, vol. 2, 517). The report concluded that Canada, Manitoba, and Hydro

> did not intend, and have never intended, to cooperate energetically in measures designed and determined to be effective in confronting the adverse impacts of the project. They have instead used every legal device to limit their individual liabilities under the Agreement. The sixteen-year history of the Northern Flood Agreement is largely a record of the deployment of those devices. . . . To the communities [the history of the *Northern Flood Agreement*] is a manifestation of bad faith by both levels of government. It has done little to address the impacts which continue to confront the communities. (120)

By 1990, frustration over the failure of governmental parties to fully and faithfully implement the NFA prompted the five communities to initiate a negotiation process that ultimately resulted in so-called Master Implementation Agreements (MIA). According to Hydro, the four communities that have accepted the MIAs have done so because the agreements provide an "enhanced land package, firm operational agreements, resource management structures, locally operated claims processes and the flexibility afforded by secure financial arrangements created by means of a trust structure" (Manitoba Hydro Background Paper #2, 2–4). Only the Pimicikamak Cree of Cross Lake have declined to become a party to a Master Implementation Agreement.

While the MIAs might represent an alternative to the failed promises and obligations of the NFA, they also impose a significant cost: the extinguishment of all Aboriginal land claims and their transfer to the government of Canada, which, in turn, can make them available to private parties for development. In other agreements such as the *James Bay Northern Quebec Agreement* (1975), *Gwich'in Agreement* (1992), and the *Sahtu Dene and Metis Agreement* (1993), extinguishment requires "Aboriginal people to 'cede, release and surrender' inherent Aboriginal rights and title to lands for the 'benefits' of land claims agreements" (Grand Council of the Crees 1998, 35–36). In the present case, "rather than fulfill their obligations under the NFA Treaty, the treaty parties . . . embarked upon an initiative of escaping their continuing duties under the Treaty once and for all by inducing the Cree communities to accept a one-time cash buy-out in exchange for full and final extinguishment of their Treaty rights" (Grand Council of the Crees 1998, 33).

Despite the failure of the NFA and the demands imposed by the MIAs, the communities of northern Manitoba continue to seek redress through formal, negotiated agreements, including the 1992 *CASIL Agreement* and the *Wuskwatim Hydro Agreement in Principle* (AIP) and its follow-up agreement, the *Project Development Agreement* (PDA). All these agreements are seen by many as establishing a new partnership model for hydro development in northern Manitoba, one that fosters Aboriginal participation and ownership in hydro development on their traditional lands. In this respect, the agreements present an opportunity to examine the extent to which a new relationship is emerging or whether the old, historic patterns of colonialism continue to dominate Aboriginal-Canadian relations.

The CASIL Agreement

In March 1989, after years of debate and legal manoeuvring, a determination was made that the residents of South Indian Lake were lawful claimants under the *Northern Flood Agreement*. Up to that point, South Indian Lake was not recognized as being entitled to compensation since the residents were variously considered part of the Nelson House community or members of an unincorporated community without reserve status under the authority of the Department of Northern Affairs of the Government of Manitoba. The Community Association of South Indian Lake and the South Indian Lake Housing Association (SILHA) were established to represent and negotiate on behalf of the residents of South Indian Lake and, over the objections of Manitoba Hydro and the Government of Manitoba, were eventually recognized by the NFA arbitrator as having appropriate legal status. Three years later, on February 12, 1992, after an appeal was filed and abandoned, Manitoba Hydro, the Province of Manitoba, and the community agreed to compensation involving both cash and 8500 acres of Crown-owned land for the future establishment of a reserve along with certain infrastructure improvements, most notably the construction of an all-weather road between SIL and Leaf Rapids (Troniak 2004).

The agreement's specific considerations were several. First, it attempted to sort out who can be considered a member of the SIL community, defining a "permanent resident" as

> a person with an historic connection to the Community of South Indian Lake, either by virtue of membership in the Nelson House Band of Indians and full-time residence at South Indian Lake or a present full-time resident who is a direct lineal descendant of a resident of South Indian Lake there residing on or before the Churchill River Diversion Project and does not include any person who has received compensation by virtue of residence on the Nelson House Reserve or Settlement as defined in the Northern Flood Agreement. (article 2.b)

Second, the agreement called for a specific level of monetary compensation, with a total of $18 million being provided to members of the community. An additional $80,000 was provided to the Fisherman's Association "in full settlement of any potential claim" that might be associated with the operations at Sturgeon Narrows. All the funds were to be administered by either CASIL or SILHA, with the explicit understanding that neither Hydro nor the province of Manitoba were to be responsible for the effectiveness "of any of the development purposes" or activities undertaken by CASIL or SILHA or their respective members (article 3.06 [b][c]). Finally, the agreement required that some 8500 acres of Crown land be set aside for the residents of SIL with the stipulation that only land not being "used for another public purpose" was eligible for transfer.

Overcoming Hydro's resistance to their claims was a major step forward for SIL. At the same time, however, the *CASIL Agreement* reflects the strategies and tactics employed by Manitoba Hydro and the Government of Manitoba in negotiating and settling claims emanating from hydro development. First, the agreement is consistent with the company's historic understanding of the NFA and the MIAs, namely, that it is a "once-and-for-all-time" resolution to any damage claims arising from the CRD project. Thus, article 6.04 explicitly states that "neither CASIL nor its members shall be entitled to further compensation except in respect of any damages which were of a nature different than or an extent greater than that which on August 29, 1991 was foreseen or could have reasonably been foreseen." The agreement specifically rules out any further consideration of "alleged socio-economic damages" unless they were caused by "such a physical or biological impact" (article 6.05), the meaning of which was left unspecified. Hydro also gains another layer of protection in that the agreement does not imply any admission of liability under the NFA (article 9.02).

The negotiation process was also typical of previous experiences. Waldram, in discussing the Easterville and South Indian Lake experiences between 1960 and 1977, writes that "in both cases . . . the legal representation of the affected community was either omitted or impaired through poor advice, funding restrictions, legal stalling tactics and the refusal on the part of the Government to disclose the necessary information to allow the communities to properly define their legal positions" (1984, 233). Both projects also involved the failure to provide full and accurate information to the affected communities on the predicted impacts of the flooding of their lakes, and relocation and socio-economic development options (Waldram, 1984). All these tactics were, at least according to many involved in the process, characteristic of the CASIL negotiations (Dysart 2003).

At the same time, rather than leading to a reconciliation of community differences, Aboriginal–Hydro agreements have often deepened rather than narrowed divisions within and among northern communities. In part, this is due to the company's tendency to base compensation on very narrow interpretations of language found in the agreements, and, in turn, on long and often very contentious arbitration and negotiation processes. This has often resulted in extreme frustration, hardship, and divisions in the affected communities.

All these tendencies are again on display in the case of South Indian Lake and the negotiations leading up to the *CASIL Agreement*. The narrow meaning of "permanent resident," for instance, and the subsequent tensions between eligible and ineligible classes of residents, led to the creation of the Association for the Displaced Residents of South Indian Lake (DRSIL). Members of the association, comprised of South Indian Lake residents and their descendants displaced and/or not included under the *CASIL Agreement*, have pursued independent individual compensation under the NFA. Few of the 400 or so claims filed by DRSIL members, including the first eight claims that were filed in June 1994, have reached the point of being heard on their merits (Troniak 2004).

The AIP and the PDA

The *Wuskwatim Hydro Agreement in Principle* (AIP) and the following *Project Development Agreement* (PDA) involving Hydro and the Nisichawayasihk Cree Nation (NCN or Nelson House) also offer important insights into the question of whether a new post-colonial era is at hand. Acknowledging in suitably oblique terms the "difficulties" that "arose in relation to the implementation of the NFA," the AIP pointed out that the 1996 MIA included arrangements for the establishment of a process to "assess future development within the resource management area" (9 and 11). As part of their ongoing discussion and as relevant to their respective interests, the agreement stated that the parties "will endeavour to determine ways in which the [projects] can be developed in a manner that is commercially credible, economically viable, environmentally and socially acceptable, and consistent with the treaty and aboriginal rights of NCN and its Members and with the principles of sustainable development" (article 2.3).

The AIP acknowledged a number of issues that were of significant concern to the community. Citing an opinion survey conducted prior to the onset of negotiations, the agreement recognized that 90 percent of the respondents rated job training and employment and business opportunities as being very important. The protection of Aboriginal life and culture, water quality, big game animals and plants, and the beauty of the site were also rated as being very important. Eighty percent thought it very important to minimize flooding, to protect fur-bearing animals, to address navigation and safety, to provide compensation for historical and on-going damage associated with the CRD project as well as to monitor the effects of such damage, and to find means to effectively involve the community in hydro-related decisions. Substantial majorities also considered it important that NCN own part of the project and that access to NCN resource areas be restricted to members (article 2.4). In recognition of these concerns, the AIP stated that "the parties will review and discuss these issues in an effort to fully understand them, and to the extent reasonable and practicable, and within their jurisdiction and authority, will endeavour to address them in the PDA or otherwise" (article 2.4).

The fact that the AIP even acknowledged these concerns was important and might well have signified a departure from prior agreements. Yet, the agreement specified few explicit or verifiable requirements, instead relying on a language that was conditional and ambiguous. Consider, for instance, the provisions regarding training, employment, and business opportunities (see section 6, generally). Hydro appeared to promise a great deal, and in doing so, might have argued that it addressed in a positive manner the concerns of the community. The required actions were, however, minimal. Far from actually producing jobs, Hydro merely promised to

> a) *consult* to identify potential positions for which Members may be qualified or wish to obtain training in order to qualify for such positions;

b) consult to identify reasonable and practical means for Members to be employed in Hydro operations, including the establishment of annual estimates of permanent, temporary and seasonal employment opportunities; and

c) undertake a study of existing job qualification standards. (article 6.1.2, emphases added)

The same pattern of conditional responsibility was continued in section 6.2.2 where Hydro agreed to work with potential contractors and subcontractors to

analyze the scope and scheduling of all potential work on, and opportunities arising from, the [projects] in a timely fashion; analyze existing and past employment and procurement policies; develop surveys and other planning instruments to assess the readiness of NCN businesses and Members to access opportunities arising from the projects; assess the skills and competencies that will be necessary; and determine at the earliest reasonable time, the academic and other prerequisites necessary for Members to secure project-related employment.

Conditional language continued in section 6.2.3 where the parties agreed to "review any collective agreement … [to] foster and encourage the employment of Members in the projects," and in section 6.2.7 where the "parties acknowledge Members may require special training about labour laws, unions, collective agreements and the obligations of parties to such agreements. The parties will consider appropriate arrangements to ensure that such training is obtained in a timely manner."

Minimal expectations also held with respect to the creation of business opportunities. Thus, Hydro was obligated to provide resources meant "to facilitate the employment of Members," including resources reasonably required for Aboriginal employment support; cross-cultural support workshops for employees; counselling support for Aboriginal and other employees; and programs to facilitate the resolution of problems and conflicts involving Aboriginal employees, other employees, and/or contractors (section 6.4.1). All these activities, of course, might well be considered normal functions within any corporate human relations department.

Despite the fact that no, or at best few, concrete actions were required and no absolute promises of employment were in the agreement, Hydro retained the right to "adopt, amend or terminate its on-the-job employment and business opportunities policies" (article 6.1.3). The company was also insulated from direct responsibility for any job-creating requirements by establishing that "third party contractors and sub-contractors, and where relevant, collective agreements will establish the arrangements under which members will be employed" (article 6.2.1). This point was reiterated in article 6.2.3, which stated that "ultimately the contractors and sub-contractors . . . will be responsible for determining the number of jobs available, the job qualifications, and the scheduling of these jobs." In other words, if community members failed to find project-related work, Hydro could not be considered in breach of the agreement. As in the past, the AIP insulated the company from responsibility for any difficulties that might be experienced by the community or its members.

The same sort of "quasi-commitment" that is established for employment also held true for education and training. Section 6.4.2, for instance, called for the establishment of an accredited curriculum by NCN. But Hydro was required only to "cooperate with NCN in this undertaking and *may* provide funding and other agreed upon resources" [emphasis added]. Again, in section 7.1, Hydro was called upon to "explore arrangements" that may facilitate the objective of "maximizing training, employment and business opportunities" through the establishment of the Atoskiwin Training and Employment Centre (A-TEC). While Hydro agreed to consider a contribution to A-TEC, the contribution would be credited against or repaid by NCN (section 7.5). Future contributions were not called for in the agreement.

One aspect of the agreement did, however, have groundbreaking potential: the opportunity for NCN to become an equity partner in the Wuskwatim/Notigi projects. According to the AIP, "Hydro's Board reviewed its policies, and with the knowledge of its owner, the Province of Manitoba, made a decision to provide NCN with an opportunity to acquire a limited equity interest and to participate as a limited partner in the Project Entity." The AIP was intended to outline the principles that will govern the efforts of the parties, consistent with the Hydro board's decision to explore, and perhaps conclude, arrangements for NCN to participate as a limited equity partner with Hydro in the Project Entity (article 14.b). While again conditional, the agreement nonetheless specified that the NCN would have, "at its option, the right to acquire an ownership interest in the Project Entity, or if a separate Project Entity is used for each project or development, an ownership interest in each Project Entity, which ownership interest will not be less than 25% in each Project Entity" (section 8.6).

The conditions under which an equity partnership might take place were further specified in the October 2003 *Summary of Understandings* (SOU), the bulk of which was taken up with a description of how the proposed financial structure would operate should the partnership proposed in the AIP come into existence. While the SOU moved the idea of an equity stake forward, substantial questions remained, many of which were left unresolved in the culminating agreement, the PDA. Murphy, for instance, when commenting on the AIP, noted that "there is no clear indication as to how NCN will receive its financial revenues or share in the profits. It is evident that Manitoba Hydro owns all the electricity from the Project. However, it is not clear what this means for NCN" (2004). This fact was understood by the NCN leadership who negotiated the PDA. "In the end," admitted Aboriginal leadership behind the deal, "[NCN] can own up to 33% of the estimated $1-billion generation project" (Primrose 2006), a level of ownership requiring some $84 million. Exactly how much of an ownership stake will be realized remains uncertain, as is the source of funds required for equity participation. While NCN leadership claimed that the initial funds would come from the internal community sources, other funds required for securing an equity stake may (or may not) be received from the federal government. Alternatively, the bulk of the money could come from Hydro in the form of a loan to be repaid from the profits derived from the operations of the dam, assuming, of course, that the dam turns a profit. Thus, the actual benefit to be realized in this supposedly new era of equity stakes and partial ownership is, at best, ambiguous. As stated by a long-time community opponent, the PDA *guarantees* "no profits to NCN" and "the estimated future profits to NCN [are] only $15–$20 million a year 25 years in the future and not the 25–56 million" promised at the time the deal was struck (Kobliski 2006).

Thus, the most important and groundbreaking aspect of the PDA turns out to be more of a promise embedded in a set of possibilities than a secured stream of income. Even more importantly, if the returns promised by an equity stake are to be realized, then the on-going "catastrophe" that is the CRD must continue (Manitoba Aboriginal Rights Coalition, 2001). Indeed, the necessity of continuing the ecological and social collapse of the region's Aboriginal communities was implicitly acknowledged by the AIP when it declared that "the typical seasonal and monthly regulation pattern that has been experienced historically since the CRD was fully commissioned in September of 1977 will remain unaltered" (section 4.4.2). In this respect, the AIP and the PDA acknowledge that the land base necessary for even a token participation in an Aboriginal, or pre-colonial, lifestyle is rapidly slipping from the grasp of northern Manitoba's Aboriginal communities.

The relocation of SIL residents, as well as the other 16,000 Aboriginal people living north of the 53rd parallel, was only partly intended to address the grievances occasioned by massive flooding and subsequent environmental collapse. Instead, the relocation is best understood as an on-going, necessary, and functional step in the continuing process of colonialism that had begun more than a century earlier. This point was made in a particularly direct way by the Van Ginkel Associates report in its assertion that "the ultimate solution for every Indian in North America will be to become a member of our technocratic society and whether this society is perfect or not is irrelevant. There is simply no choice but to take part in that society, if the individual is to achieve full status" (8).

From the viewpoint of the dam builders, relocation, the dismantling of a land-based economy, and the subordination of Aboriginal lifestyles were not unfortunate realities occasioned by the necessities of progress. Quite the contrary: everything done to the communities was represented and understood as positive steps that would bring about the necessary transformation of a backward-looking and ultimately unsustainable way of life. Aboriginal people were, to use Loomba's phrasing, seen as "children who need to be brought in line with the rest of the country" (1998, 10). Any suggestion that even a semblance of traditional life could be maintained, except perhaps as a nostalgic display in some sort of ecological theme park, was treated as being, at best, naïve and misguided. At worst, resistance to either relocation or economic transformation was seen as denying Aboriginal communities the opportunity to gain a foothold in modern society.

If by "colonization" is meant interference and perhaps even dismemberment of existing political and cultural structures (Loomba, 1998, 6), then the hydro developments of the last several decades surely represent a profound deepening of that process for the Aboriginal peoples of northern Manitoba. Hydro development, at least in the case of South Indian Lake, engineered poverty, a significant and increasing level of welfare dependence, a fundamental change in traditional social practices, and the virtual sterilization of the land base. In essence, the agreements negotiated between Hydro and the Aboriginal communities acknowledge that in the face of such conditions, a land-based mode of life, even one mediated by the instrumentalities of modern technique, is an historical anachronism.

With the approval and ultimately the implementation of the PDA, the goal enunciated by the Van Ginkel Associates report and embraced by both Hydro and Manitoba—that northern Aboriginal communities should put behind the idylls of the past and fully commit to the advantages of modernity—has finally been achieved. In this respect, the PDA represents not the end of colonialism but its zenith.

---

1   Caution must be exercised in making standard-of-living comparisons based on relative levels of cash income, since communities such as SIL were able to extract consumable items—i.e., fish, fur, and meat—directly from the land, thus avoiding the need to lay out cash payments.

2   A good portion of this assistance is immediately returned to the company coffers in the form of extremely high average monthly energy bills. While energy bills are typically high in the north, it is also true that housing stock in the community is oftentimes of extremely poor quality, particularly for those residents who live in so-called Hydro housing or structures built for residents forced to relocate from traditional structures occupied prior to the flooding (see Robson, 1993, 112–116). Indeed, according to many residents, they are still waiting for the new, modern structures promised at the time the CRD was commissioned.

3   Significant erosion continues to this day and, while the impact of the Wuskwatim and other projects is difficult to estimate, the 1992 study concluded that the net effect will be a further increase in sedimentation and shoreline erosion (2).

6

A Step Back: The Nisichawayasihk Cree Nation and the Wuskwatim Project

Peter Kulchyski

IT HAS BEEN MY GOOD FORTUNE and privilege to have travelled to many Aboriginal communities in the far and mid-north of Canada, especially through the Yukon, NWT, and Nunavut territories, northern Manitoba and northern Ontario.[1] When I do so I have a set of informal issues I use to get a quick sense of where the community sits in terms of its overall well-being. While these snapshot judgments cannot replace what comes with sustained attention and longer term study, I have found more often than not that assessments based on these issues stand the tests of closer scrutiny. Notably, in the piles of statistics developed about northern communities by social scientists and government, three criteria tend to be absent. They are, firstly, are the children playing and laughing in their own Aboriginal languages? That is, not just speaking the language by rote in schools, not speaking it when they 'have to' with family members or in ceremony, but actually using the language in their day-to-day interactions with each other. This will tell me whether Aboriginal culture has much of a future in the community. Secondly, are there Elders in the community who are being treated with respect? In this case, I'm not simply looking for the presence of 'old people,' but rather for the holders of traditional knowledge—the storytellers—who are listened to in community meetings and by community leaders. This will also tell me something about the continuance of Aboriginal cultural values.

Finally, the third test is much simpler: can I drink the water? This will tell me whether the misnamed 'subsistence economy,' the traditional hunting ways, has an ecological basis and is viable in the region. That in turn indicates whether hunting as the sustainable economic basis of the culture has a future.

Hunting cultures continue to suffer from deeply biased misrepresentations. There is an assumption, which appears to cross the political spectrum, to the effect that hunters live with an antiquated set of values and an outdated way of life. Yet, if sustainability were a central standard for judging the success or failure of different social forms, hunting would clearly be seen as the most sustainable form of society invented by human beings: industrial societies have been with us for a few centuries; agricultural societies for about 10,000 years; hunting societies have persisted for over 60,000 years. The notion that continued support for hunting peoples involves a paternalistic or romantic idealization flies in the face of history. In Canada, for over a hundred years, a whole trajectory of social, political, and economic policies has been developed to assimilate hunters. The cumulative effects of these policies have been nothing short of tragic for northern Aboriginal communities. It is the modernizers, those who think they can build, in the subarctic and arctic, 'communities' that will replicate southern suburbs, who are the true paternalists and romantics here: they still have a naïve faith that sporadic wage work on projects that will last one or two decades offers a future for Aboriginal communities. On the contrary, a group of social scientists in Canada—Harvey Feit, Hugh Brody, Michael Asch, Julie Cruikshank, and many others—have taught us that hunters can adapt to modern technologies without losing their values, that hunting offers at least as reasonable a chance to achieve a 'good life' in modern circumstances as other contemporary alternatives, and that without support and against the policy trajectory, hunters have persisted and continued to reinvigorate their cultures and communities.

I take it that offering hunters from South Indian Lake and Nelson House a few words of support in their struggle against Wuskwatim is neither paternalistic nor romantic: ethically it is the least I can do. When I see the maps of the northern St. Lawrence region in Quebec, called *Nitassinan* by its

Innu inhabitants, or maps of the eastern part of Hudson Bay, *Eenu-aschee* in the language of the James Bay Cree, or maps of northern Manitoba, criss-crossed with lines that indicate electric transmission grids, dotted with triangles indicating hydroelectric dams, and showing proposals for more dams and more lines, I do not see something to be celebrated in the name of 'progress'. And I feel sad knowing that some communities have lost, and more are about to lose, the basis of an economy that has proven the most sustainable form of social life invented by human beings.

In the spring of 2002 I was part of a delegation hosted by the Pimicikamak Cree Nation and travelled along the Nelson River. I saw the erosion along the banks created by rapidly rising and falling water levels. I saw burial areas that had been exposed by flooding. I saw uprooted trees posing an insurmountable barrier all along the banks of the river. I saw what had once been clear water according to older people and Elders now opaque with silt. And I drank the bottled water we carried with us, never once daring to drink the water of what had once been a great, life-sustaining river.

While what follows is primarily an impersonal policy analysis of a very important document that is a part of the first of several major hydroelectric projects, I would be remiss not to try to convey some sense of the qualitative dimensions of the issues at stake. The quality of the water that surrounds northern Aboriginal communities is directly tied to the quality of life in those communities. It is a critical factor in determining whether they will be impoverished places hopelessly trying to emulate southern lifestyles, or whether they will be places where a way of life that allows seemingly poor people to enjoy an unmatched wealth measured in time and human rela-tionships persists. The core of this analysis will be a look at *The Summary of Understandings [SOU] between Nisichawayasihk Cree Nation [NCN] and Mani-toba Hydro with Respect to the Wuskwatim Project*, an agreement in principle dated October 2003 that outlines the terms of NCN's equity partnership in the specific hydroelectric development to take place near the community of Nelson House in northern Manitoba. Before I turn to the SOU, a few words are in order about the treaties that preceded it.

TWO TREATIES

Two Supreme Court of Canada decisions made in the last fifteen years have radically altered our understanding of the canons or protocols of treaty interpretation. In the *Sioui* case of 1990 the Supreme Court laid out criteria for understanding what kinds of documents could be interpreted as being treaties and stressed that courts must take a "liberal and generous" interpretation of treaties. Justice Lamer wrote in *Sioui* that a "treaty must be given a just, broad and liberal construction" (see Kulchyski 1994, 187) and that treaties must be read not merely in terms of the literal written language but also in terms of how they were understood by the Aboriginal signatories. Lamer quoted an 1899 decision from the United States, *Jones v Meehan*, writing into Canadian law the words "the treaty must therefore be construed, not according to the technical meaning of its words by learned lawyers, but in the sense in which they would naturally be understood by the Indians," adding in his own words that "these considerations argue all the more strongly for the courts to adopt a generous and liberal approach" (Kulchyski 1994, 188). Nothing less than "the honour of the Crown" was at stake in ensuring that a liberal and generous interpretation of treaties prevailed. The Marshall case of 1999 (*R v. Marshall* 1999) established that the oral histories of the treaties should not be treated as hearsay evidence but rather accorded equal weight with the documentary record of treaties when it came to interpreting treaty ambiguities. While the court was at pains to show this should not mean Aboriginal views of treaty rights are accepted *carte blanche*, the decisions certainly tip the scale towards Aboriginal understandings that treaties be interpreted according to the spirit and intent of the treaties rather than literally. Justice Binnie, writing in the *Marshall* decision and quoting from the earlier *Badger* case, argued that "the bottom line is the Court's obligation is to 'choose from among the various possible interpretations of the *common* intention [at the time the treaty was made] the one which best reconciles the Mi'kmaq interests and those of the British Crown" (emphasis and insertion in original, *R v. Marshall* 1999, paragraph 14). The *Sioui* case was a unanimous decision; *Marshall* involved a healthy majority (five to two). It should also be noted that in 1982 the *Constitution Act* (section 35) specifically "recognized and affirmed . . . treaty rights." Treaties are a major part of the constitutional fabric of Canada.

One key element of Treaty 5, signed on to in a 1908 adhesion by the grandparents of people now living in Nisichawayasihk, is relevant to our discussion here. Although the First Nation signatories agreed to "cede, release, surrender and yield up . . . forever all their rights, titles and privileges whatsoever to the lands included within the following limits" (the document goes on to describe the geographic extent of traditional territories), in addition to reserve lands that were promised, the First Nations also secured promises that

> Her Majesty further agrees with her said Indians that they, the said Indians, shall have right to pursue their avocations of hunting and fishing throughout the tract surrendered as hereinbefore described, subject to such regulations as from time to time be made by her Government of her Dominion of Canada, and saving and excepting such tracts as may from time to time be required or taken up for settlement, mining, lumbering or other purposes by her said Government of the Dominion of Canada, or by any of the subjects thereof duly authorized therefore by the said Government. (Morris 1991, 346)

While a literal reading of these words does not appear to leave doubt that, effectively, 'Government' can have its unimpeded way with the 'surrendered' lands, such a view would certainly not accord with the liberal and generous interpretation proposed by the Supreme Court of Canada. It should be noted that in the speech-making preceding treaty signings, the treaty commissioners often stressed that in signing the treaties, the First Nations would not be expected to give up their hunting way of life, that the Crown would respect their cultural and economic right to live as they had lived 'for as long as the sun shines and the waters flow.' This was as key a promise to the First Nations as the land surrender clause was to the Crown. Hence, the first part of the above clause was no doubt stressed to First Nations signatories; the last part (beginning by "subject to") was something more like the fine print at the bottom of a legal document. Certainly none of the signatories, Crown or First Nations, imagined that the 'tracts' that might be required by the Crown might come to be so large as to destroy the whole basis of the hunting economy.

What would a liberal and generous interpretation of this clause look like? At a minimum, it would mean that the state has a 'bottom line' requirement to ensure that enough land base continues to exist in the Treaty 5 area to support those First Nations citizens in each community who wish to pursue their traditional economic patterns of hunting, trapping, and fishing. At another level, it might mean that treaty signatories should be seen as joint managers of their traditional territories, joint decision makers in determining what takes place: not asked to sign on to plans developed far away, but given a meaningful role in making the plans. Such an arrangement would provide some hope of ensuring that enough land was left in good shape to serve the needs of Aboriginal hunting families. A genuinely generous interpretation might even go further: to recognize that Aboriginal peoples have an inalienable inherent jurisdiction over their traditional territories and begin developing structures to implement and enable that jurisdiction.

The second treaty that needs examination before turning to the current Memorandum of Understandings is the Manitoba *Northern Flood Agreement* (NFA). I agree with the Honourable Eric Robinson, who said to the Manitoba Legislative Assembly that the *Northern Flood Agreement* is a treaty signed by Manitoba Hydro, the governments of Manitoba and Canada, and five of the Cree Nations in the north. Indeed, given the standards of assessment established by the Supreme Court of Canada in the *Sioui* case on this issue, it is difficult to sustain an argument to the contrary. That means the NFA is a constitutionally protected document and cannot be altered without using the constitutional amending formula. So-called implementation agreements signed in the 1990s, which in fact serve to extinguish rights promised in the NFA, are in my view unconstitutional and will not stand the court challenges to which they will ultimately and inevitably give rise. Schedule E of the NFA refers to "the eradication of mass poverty and mass unemployment." It is patently clear that no authority has moved to implement a liberal and generous interpretation of the NFA.

In fact, it is demonstrable and uncontestable that both Treaty 5 and the *Northern Flood Agreement* have been interpreted in a narrow and mean-spirited fashion by both levels of government and by Manitoba Hydro.

The honour of the Crown has been dragged through the mud in northern Manitoba. If we compare the NFA to the situation in northern Quebec, it becomes clear that Cree in northern Manitoba would have been better off had they never signed a treaty. Had that been the case, as with the James Bay Cree, they would have been in a position to negotiate a land surrender modern treaty in the seventies rather than the NFA. Had that been the case, Manitoba Hydro might today be forced to offer these communities deals that compare at least minimally to the *Paix des Braves* agreement recently signed in Quebec. Those who signed treaties with the Crown more than a hundred years ago, experiencing the benevolence and generosity of the Crown, should, one would think, be materially and demonstrably in a better position than those who did not. The reverse is true and will remain true as long as the narrow and mean-spirited interpretation of Treaty 5 prevails.

A NEW PLAN: AN OLD MODEL

The Summary of Understandings between Nisichawayasihk Cree Nation and Manitoba Hydro with Respect to the Wuskwatim Project (SOU), dated October 2003, should be understood in this context: it effectively involves Manitoba Hydro, with the support of governments, and one First Nation, ignoring and giving up on the principle that previous treaties should be respected as the basis of nation-to-nation understandings. It does not contemplate any significant support for the hunting way of life and, in fact, moves in a direction that diminishes the possibility of a future for northern hunters. What follows is a critical analysis of the SOU. While there are provisions that might be seen in a positive light, the overall principles and many of the details do not look favourable, particularly in comparison to similar agreements in other Canadian jurisdictions. Certainly if this is the model that Hydro intends to follow in the next wave of developments it proposes, serious concerns are raised that instead of leading the way as a jurisdiction that respects treaty and Aboriginal rights, Manitoba will be a last bastion of old colonial relations. Among the areas that appear positive are section 7(12), which deals with subcontracts and gives Nisichawayasihk Cree Nation businesses, in some cases, "first option of direct negotiation." Although transmission matters are not a part of the agreement, section 14 provides for interest on

5 percent of "eligible capital costs incurred each year in the construction of the Project Transmission Facilities" to be "distributed annually among eligible aboriginal communities" (SOU 2003, 34–35).

Not until the end of the document does the SOU make it clear that it will not be seen as a treaty. The wording that appears to protect Aboriginal and treaty rights appears at the very end of the SOU. It reads: "nothing in this Summary of Understandings or any other arrangements or agreements contemplated in this Summary of Understandings is intended to alter Aboriginal and Treaty rights recognized and affirmed under Section 35 of the Constitution Act, 1982" (SOU 2003, 36). Had the word "diminish" been used rather than the word "alter," the clause would have been stronger and would have raised the possibility that the SOU itself might be seen as a treaty. The word "alter" ensures that the SOU and agreements that flow from it are intended as mere business contracts. That is, the document is not a nation-to-nation agreement in the manner of the *Paix des Braves* between the Cree of Quebec and the Government of Quebec and contains no such sense of vision. It is rather a business agreement that, if implemented, would tie one Treaty nation to an economic strategy of hydro development. In fact, the SOU itself is actually "non-binding" (SOU 2003, 2) and must be read as a model for the binding agreement that will follow, based upon it.

The core of the SOU is that NCN will be a minority partner with a significant equity position in the Wuskwatim project that can reach a maximum of one-third ownership. The NCN will raise capital for its equity largely through loans from Manitoba Hydro. It should be noted, then, that NCN's benefit comes from two sources: the risk it will jointly assume and the political capital it provides to the project. The project may be successful and, after a lengthy period of time, begin paying dividends to NCN, or it may be less than successful, deferring long into the future when dividends are received, or it may be unsuccessful and leave NCN with a legacy of enormous debt. This is not a resource revenue-sharing model where revenue for the First Nation is generated as a result of its Aboriginal or treaty rights. Compare this with the *Paix des Braves*, an agreement signed between the Grand Council of the Crees of Northern Quebec and the Quebec Government (with Hydro-Québec) in early 2002. Under the *Paix des Braves*, the various Cree nations in northern Quebec will gain significant financial benefit, actually $70 million a year for fifty years to a total of $3.5 billion (much more significant even if the proportions are taken into account), without financial risk. It is not my position to determine whether the financial risk makes good business sense or not; it is my position to suggest that the principles underlying the SOU mean that NCN is making a significant concession to Manitoba Hydro, effectively surrendering the struggle for getting a better deal based on either of the two treaties it signed. Financial compensation for a project, in my view, should derive from NCN treaty and Aboriginal rights to their own traditional territories rather than from taking a significant financial risk. Another core principle underlying the SOU is the structure of the financial partnership. NCN will be a minority partner in the Limited Partnership with Manitoba Hydro; it will have proportional representation—that is, a number of votes determined by the degree of ownership on the dam itself that it achieves, up to 33 percent—on the General Partner responsible for management of the project itself, but no ownership of the General Partner. This kind of shell game will serve to insulate Manitoba Hydro from complaint.[2]

Much has been made of the fact that the overall design of the project has already been influenced by NCN in order to limit its environmental impact. This is referred to in the SOU as the "Fundamental Features" of the project. The fundamental features of the project include some guarantees for NCN respecting water levels and area to be flooded, though the language in the SOU is weak (it uses the term "normally" in dealing with water levels [SOU 2003, 7]), does not include financial penalties, and, at a later part, the document reads: "Hydro will have sole control over water discharge, water levels, water level fluctuations and unit dispatch within the parameters of all relevant licenses . . . and the constraints imposed by virtue of the Fundamental Features" (SOU 2003, 31). Without clear penalties for breach of 'normal' water levels, it is hard to see how the SOU and agreements that will follow based upon it will work as strong environmental impact protections.

The training provisions in the SOU are significant and revealing of old relationships. Of the $5 million allocated to training that are specifically mentioned in the SOU, $3.75 million (75 percent) are allocated to NCN.

However, funds cannot be used for salaries, training is all oriented to manual and lower level employment (there is no contemplation of management training), no specific employment level targets are set, and the overall dollar figure is not impressive. Few jobs will be created and the designers of the SOU assume NCN participation at the most menial levels (SOU 2003, 8–9). Although the minister of energy, the Honourable Tim Sale, has taken exception to comments regarding training, suggesting the dollar figure for training is much higher, these funds must be allocated outside the scope of the agreement and therefore depend upon Government of Manitoba and Manitoba Hydro largesse rather than a contractual obligation. The SOU reads clearly: "Manitoba Hydro has committed *up to* $5 million of Project funds to be used for training for jobs on the Project" (SOU 2003, 8; emphasis added). The remaining part of the section specifies the terms through which these monies will be spent, as discussed above.

It should also be noted that an Adverse Effects Agreement to be signed is not part of the binding *Project Development Agreement* (PDA), which itself would be negotiated as the final version of the SOU. Since NCN will be a limited partner, it starts to become an objective interest of the NCN leaders to limit the liabilities of such agreements; that is, their position as partner starts to create conflicts of interest in relation to responsibility to the First Nation. Since they will need the project to be financially successful, why would they want to create an Adverse Effects Agreement that would place severe penalties on the project for violations of the agreement and for negative impacts? In effect, by becoming financial partners, a conflict of goals and interests will have to be borne by the First Nation. On the one hand, if the project is not financially successful, the First Nation will be left with a legacy of crippling debt; on the other hand, if the project has a greater negative impact on the environment, part of the sustainable future of the First Nation is jeopardized.

One of the critical weaknesses of the SOU regards provisions about community ratification. As noted, the SOU will lead to a *Project Development Agreement* (PDA), which would be legally binding and will "be submitted to NCN Members for ratification when it is finalized. Following meaningful consultation with and ratification by NCN members, the PDA will be formally approved by NCN's chief and council" (SOU 2003, 4). The language here is telling: "following . . . ratification, the PDA *will* be formally approved" presumes acceptance. The PDA submitted for ratification is a "finalized" agreement; that is, community consultation will not contemplate changes. Experience in comprehensive claims indicates ratification usually involves a sales job. Leaders and negotiators hold community 'hearings' in which they extol the benefits of the proposed agreement. The SOU says nothing about percentage of members required (a majority of voters, a majority of the community members, or a significant majority of either are normal alternatives), the time between publication of a 'finalized' agreement and when a vote will take place (the 'finalized' agreement will be more of a legal document than the SOU), and other critical issues. Given the potential long-term impact of the project, one would hope that high standards of approval would be required; that a sufficiently lengthy period of time be specified for debate to allow citizens an opportunity to understand what will undoubtedly be a complex legal document be required; that resources are required to be allocated to proponents and opponents of the agreement within the community; that translation of the document into the Cree language be required; and that a date for a vote be established well in advance as a requirement to ensure leadership does not take advantage of particular moments when it feels it can secure ratification. The SOU does not provide any stringency in the ratification process and appears to take ratification as a *fait accompli*.

The model contemplated by the SOU is a step back from two decades of progress made in the area of Aboriginal and treaty rights. It is not a rights-based document. Its financial value for the First Nation is uncertain and based on the risk assumed by the First Nation. More troubling, it ties the First Nation to continued hydro development and limits the First Nation's ability to act as steward of its own traditional resources. Finally, the SOU contains very loose provisions regarding community consultation (none) and ratification.

SEVEN COMMENTS BY WAY OF A CONCLUSION

It remains up to NCN citizens to determine whether they support or do not support this agreement. I absolutely agree that it is their right and responsibility to decide. One hopes they are adequately informed before ratification and that viable, credible, independently monitored voting procedures are used. Since there will be many resources deployed in selling the deal and many prominent leaders promoting it, in my view it is important that the community have access to critical comments and I have emphasized this approach in my analysis. The agreement contemplated by this SOU does not compare favorably to similar types of agreement in other jurisdictions to my knowledge. See Voisey Bay and the Innu (Lowe 1998); NWT diamond mines and the Tli'Cho (back issues of *News/North*, the Yellowknife-based newspaper, contains the most coverage); in particular compare to the recent *Paix des Braves* with the Crees of Quebec (see Saganash, Martin, and Dupuis in this book). Certainly the SOU does not contain anything innovative or indicative of a desire for a new relationship. The *James Bay and Northern Quebec Agreement* of 1975 contained a section pertaining to hunter income supplements. Recognizing that hydro development would have a negative impact on the ability of hunters to sustain themselves, it accepted the principle that some funds from the profits be allocated to ensuring that hunting families would continue to have a chance at material well-being. This model has existed since 1975. There is nothing in the SOU that would indicate a desire to support hunting families, the very basis of Aboriginal cultural values and communities.

The deal points to the fact that comparisons with other provincial and territorial jurisdictions are becoming increasingly important. Although Aboriginal matters ("Indians and lands reserved for Indians") are a federal responsibility, the role of provinces in resource development has made them key players on the ground in Indian country. Provinces such as Manitoba, which assumed jurisdiction over natural resources through natural resource transfer agreements (such as Manitoba's in 1930), will have to become key players if treaty rights are to be accorded the respect that the Supreme Court of Canada has asserted is due.

The agreement (PDA and other associated agreements) that will follow the SOU involves a critical decision that would link NCN's fortunes to those of Manitoba Hydro generally. The community will begin to have an objective interest in further developments that remove it from the land-based hunting economy that has sustained it for centuries. Effectively, this agreement will work against the current that leaders tried to establish in Treaty 5, and will represent a further surrender of hope to ever implement the broadest promises of the *Northern Flood Agreement*. Experience has also shown that major business developments of this sort very often benefit a class of Aboriginal managers, who will gain very high paying jobs as corporate board members and will be removed from the daily realities of poverty in the community (see for example the experience of Alaska natives after the *Alaska Native Land Claim*; Berger's 1985 study, *Village Journey*, remains an excellent resource on this issue and claim), or problems of corporate misbehaviour among the Inuvialuit leaders who managed resources provided by the *Western Arctic Agreement* (Boldt, 1993, deals with the broad issue in his chapter on leadership in *Surviving as Indians*). Effectively, the project may very well create or consolidate an Aboriginal elite within the community. In that case, the poverty of community members will be exacerbated by the fact that they will have a further eroded land base that once provided an alternative means of subsistence to the welfare system. Also noteworthy is that NCN will not be a partner in ownership of the transmission line, which will have serious and additional impacts on NCN lands and land use rights.

The fundamental rationale for this project remains possible economic gain at the expense of environmental degradation. It has been suggested that continued hydro development in northern Manitoba will be a significant contribution by Manitoba to reducing greenhouse emissions, respecting the Kyoto Accord, and positively contributing to a cleaner world environment; it is also clear that the long-term costs of these developments are borne entirely by northern Aboriginal communities. If the nature of the commitment by Manitoba and Manitoba Hydro were to make such a contribution, why would it not allocate a much more significant proportion of profits to the betterment of northern Aboriginal communities? Then, only after these communities are established at levels of material well-being proximate with their southern neighbours would residual profit be deployed to the benefit of all. Since no such model is contemplated and the only way northern communities are being granted financial benefit is through their assumption of risk, it would appear that financial gain remains the underlying motive of these developments.

The SOU embodies a negative judgment about hunting as a way of life. One of the most difficult concepts to grasp is that although hunting families may look poor from a perspective of those saturated in the comforts of suburban life, if we were to measure wealth in terms of the quality of time we have in our lives as opposed to the things or money we can amass, hunters are among the wealthiest of peoples (see Brody 2000 on this point). While our society at least pretends to pay respect to preserving the family farm as a foundation for rural communities in southern areas, no parallel (even pretence of) respect is paid to hunting families as the foundation of community life in northern regions. There is virtually no program or policy that supports Aboriginal hunting families in northern Manitoba, but a wide variety of structures, programs, and policies that actively discourage the hunting way of life. Hunters are often classed as "unemployed" and are not seen as contributors to the gross domestic product. Their economy and rights are off the map of planners and economic advisors. Yet they have sustained their families, communities, and nations in northern regions for millennia. With this SOU, it appears that some Aboriginal leaders have themselves given up on the hunting economy and the treaty rights that support it.

While what is being proposed by the Summary of Understandings between Nisichawayasihk Cree Nation (NCN) and Manitoba Hydro with Respect to the Wuskwatim Project *is described as a matter of engineering, it is perhaps better seen as a generational legacy.* Three decades ago economists and engineers developed a plan that was supposed to be good for everyone: dam northern rivers, produce hydro power from them, make broad commitments to the Aboriginal communities most affected to compensate them. Within ten years, it became clear that the *Northern Flood Agreement* would be ignored, that the environment was being in many places irretrievably damaged, and that communities were falling into a spiral of misery. Many Aboriginal people in northern Manitoba came to see Manitoba Hydro as an enemy. From Grand Rapids to Pimicikamak to South Indian Lake, the words 'Manitoba Hydro' are dirty words. Small wonder there is so little trust of new promises by economists and new promises by engineers. The record of recent history in northern Manitoba is a record of pain and damage that can be attributed directly to the monumental hubris of engineers and economists supposedly working on behalf of the public. Although anyone with a conscience must agonize over the choices that Aboriginal communities must make when faced with the serious social consequences of a colonial history, and can understand why any jobs and any so-called 'development' has a strong appeal, I have no doubt whatsoever that the model contemplated in the SOU will build an additional legacy of distrust for the generations who will follow.

EPILOGUE

Since writing this, the *Project Development Agreement* was prepared, printed, and eventually voted upon. The PDA is, in some respects, actually worse than the SOU that preceded it. It contains a clause that gave Hydro the authority to redesign any aspects of the project, including the fundamental features, in the event of environmental, engineering, or economic factors changing in a significant way. Furthermore, the language respecting Aboriginal and treaty rights is appallingly, laughably weak: the wording used could have the implication of suggesting that the PDA actually trumps treaties and Aboriginal rights. The agreement was eventually passed in a contested referendum, whose results will likely be legally challenged. Significantly, a few months before the vote, about one quarter of the voters, most of whom opposed the project, were made ineligible as the federal government inexplicably finally stepped in to create a separate band for South Indian Lake (this, after twenty years of struggle, was a bittersweet victory for that sub-band, but the timing was extremely propitious to Manitoba Hydro). While such chicanery may pay for a few more swimming pools among Winnipeg's bureaucratic elite, the legacy that will be handed on to NCN's future generations is not promising.

---

1   This paper was first published by the Canadian Centre of Policy Alternatives, <www.policyalternatives.ca/mbÈ-nakàskàkowaàhk1>. It is dedicated to Thomas Craig Jewiss (8 April 1946 to 2 March 2004), lawyer, professor, and activist, a friend and ally who dedicated much of his life to the struggle for Aboriginal rights.

2   During construction of the Mackenzie Valley Pipeline in the mid-eighties, the owner, Interprovincial Pipelines (IPL), was shielded from complaint because the construction company that had been subcontracted was Pe Ben. During hearings Pe Ben said: "We are tourists in the north." They were not concerned about complaints since they would not remain to continue in business. IPL could defer all complaints to the subcontractor. It should be noted that quorum for the General Partner as defined in the SOU is a simple majority of directors and voting is on a simple majority basis. Hence NCN is not even guaranteed a position at all meetings—meetings can take place without anyone from NCN in attendance—and NCN has no veto powers. NCN will have a majority on a Construction Advisory Committee (sou 2003, 17), but 'advisory' committees have no real powers and, quite rightly, First Nations in the modern era have tended to avoid the word "advisory" for this reason.

7

In Service to Globalization: Manitoba Hydro, Aboriginal Communities, and the Integration of Electrical Markets

Steven M. Hoffman
Ken Bradley

"GLOBALIZATION" HAS BECOME A BYWORD of the early twenty-first century. As Slowey explains, national governments, long concerned with advancing the interests of their citizens, now equate the general welfare with promoting unfettered trade and limiting restrictions on the flow of capital (chapter 2, this volume). In the case of Canada, say Albo and Jensen, "the federal government now pursues the elimination of borders between the Canadian economy and the rest of the world and works to make the country's competitive position in global markets the privileged barometer of well-being" (1997, 215). As a result, argues Slowey, the state has moved from assisting capitalism by providing for social needs to ushering in a new set of neo-liberal policies designed to promote the free flow of capital and commodities across national boundaries. As will be shown below, the impulse towards globalization is clearly manifested in the development of Manitoba's electrical system.

While the exploitation of Manitoba's hydropower resources has always involved debates over timing and sequence, successive Manitoba governments have consistently understood a robust electrical system as a principal means of achieving the elemental goal of provincial modernization (Netherton 1993). In more recent times, the articulation of this goal has meant the continuous expansion of a system capable of serving increasingly distant extraprovincial markets, the implementation of strategies designed to assure a favourable regulatory climate, and the development of mechanisms meant to guarantee the continued subordination of northern Aboriginal communities.

If the specific requirements of the hydro system have changed in recent times, the distribution of benefits and costs has remained remarkably consistent. The winners, of course, are the consumers of some of the cheapest power in North America, namely, the residents of southern Manitoba and the American upper midwest. The losers have been Manitoba's Aboriginal communities. Unless fundamental changes occur in the relationship among these communities, Manitoba Hydro, and the province of Manitoba, this pattern of loss and benefit will continue unabated, albeit clothed in more genial terms.

THE INFRASTRUCTURE OF GLOBALIZATION: DEVELOPING AN INTEGRATED ENERGY SYSTEM

Institutionalizing a neo-liberal regime in law and policy is only one part of a sustained process of globalization.[1] In addition to the rules of trade and non-interference in the actions of global corporations, physical infrastructure is also required. To talk about shipping the products of Brazil to the homes of North America or the iron ore found in northern Minnesota to the foundries of China is empty theorizing absent the ships, the containers, the port facilities, and the highways required to realize these transactions. The same is true for the movement of electrons.

The evolution of the industrialized world's electrical system represents one of the great social and technological achievements of the twentieth century. The articulation of an electrical generation, transmission, and distribution system required groundbreaking accomplishments in electronics, metallurgy, engineering, and myriad other scientific fields, as well as the development of complex organizational and managerial systems. Despite these considerable achievements, however, the system is increasingly unable to meet the demands of a fully continental system of electricity generation and consumption. The blackout of August 14, 2003, that plunged much of

the northeastern United States into darkness, for instance, created a tremen-
dous amount of concern about the brittleness of the continent's electrical
transmission system. Thus, the Brattle Group, in a report prepared for the
Edison Electric Institute, the research arm of the US electric utility industry,
and the Midwest Independent System Operator (MISO), concluded that
"there is widespread concern about the adequacy of the U.S. transmission
grid. . . . [T]he high-voltage grid—at least in some regions—is overstressed.
. . . Moreover, transmission investment clearly has lagged the growth in
demand for a consistent period" (2004, 1).

While much of the post-blackout analysis focused on the immediate
operational problems of the grid, the larger issue confronting the system
is the limitation of a transmission system built primarily to meet local or, at
best, regional, loads but which is increasingly being called upon to handle
intercontinental bulk power transfers. While this trend is at least several
decades old, it was greatly exacerbated by the experiment in deregulation
that occupied much of the last two decades of the twentieth century. The
most egregious excesses of the pre-Enron era have mercifully subsided, but
one important result of the era continues: the creation of ever-larger utility
companies mainly through merger and acquisition. These newly enlarged
entities often have service territories that cover huge swaths of the continent. Xcel Energy Company, for instance, which was formed by the merger
of Northern States Power and Colorado Public Service, encompasses a
twelve-state region that stretches from Minnesota to Arizona. Other firms
are growing by acquiring assets without any sort of physical or geographical
connection. Chicago-based Exelon is now the largest power marketing business in the United States with a variety of coal and nuclear generating and
distribution assets in Illinois and Pennsylvania, including ComEd in Illinois
and PECO in Pennsylvania. Further growth is on the company's agenda, as
evidenced by its efforts to purchase part of PSEG in New Jersey.

Expansion and consolidation is also occurring at the international level.
Scottish Power, PLC, for instance, provides retail service in parts of Scot-
land and sells on the wholesale market in England, Wales, and Ireland. In
1999, through a series of mergers and acquisitions, the company created
what it calls the PacificCorp unit, which served some 1.6 million customers

as Pacific Power in Oregon, Washington state, Wyoming, and California, and Utah Power in Utah and Idaho. PacificCorp, in turn, was acquired by MidAmerican Energy Holdings Company, itself a company whose majority stakeholder is American billionaire Warren Buffett's Berkshire Hathaway Incorporated (Richardson and Smith 2005).

In this respect, the modern electric utility industry serves as an exemplar of the logic and necessities of both globalization and neo-liberalism: it is an industry increasingly dominated by fewer and fewer multinational entities aggressively demanding a minimal state that subordinates, or at least equates, the interests of the public with global corporate interests.[2]

The development of the Manitoba Hydro system has shared in both the opportunities and restraints of this historical process. In the case of Manitoba Hydro, the process began with the construction of the Minnedosa River Plant at the turn of the twentieth century. The company's available generating capacity increased enormously with the completion of the Nelson and Churchill rivers complex in the early 1970s.[3] As will be shown below, the company is now positioning itself to usher in a new era of expansion and growth with the construction of the Wuskwatim station to be followed by, among others, the Conawapa and Keeyask stations.

Though much of the company's early developmental history was domestically oriented, more recent projects have clearly been driven by the opportunities available in non-domestic markets, particularly in the midwestern load centres of the United States. While the official policy has been to frame the developments in terms of satisfying domestic needs, as Netherton (1993) points out, even in the earliest stages of the Churchill River Diversion/Lake Winnipeg Regulation (CRD/LWR) project,

> the problem of excess capacity made the utility dependent upon the export market to gain revenues needed to finance the expensive Nelson River infrastructure. While this conforms to one of the oldest ideas concerning the Nelson River hydro development, it was counter to the position taken by the [government] that the projects were developed for domestic, not export markets. (362)[4]

The first stage in solidifying the export market was achieved with the completion of the CRD/LWR project; the next step was the construction of high-voltage transmission lines between the US and the dams. The initial power transmission line between the two countries was built in 1970 after the US and Canadian governments approved the 230 kV interchange that now stretches from Winnipeg, Manitoba, to Grand Forks, North Dakota. The line was completed and placed in service for a power exchange with the Northern States Power Company of Minneapolis (now Xcel Energy), Otter Tail Power Company of Fergus Falls, and Minnkota Power Cooperative Inc. of Grand Forks. A second 230 kV interconnection was put in place in 1976 to connect Minnesota Power and Light Company of Duluth (now known as Allete) to the international border in southeastern Manitoba. In 1980 a third interconnection, a 500 kV transmission line to connect with United Power Association (now Great River Energy after a merger with Cooperative Power), Northern States Power Company, and Minnesota Power and Light Company in the US, was established. This line more than doubled Manitoba's power exchange capability with the US.

Manitoba Hydro has taken good advantage of this transmission capacity. In 2006, long-term, firm-power contracts resulted in over 12 million MWhs of electricity flowing southward into US energy markets, nearly double that of 2004's 6.6 million MWhs, when the persistent drought experienced in the western portions of the US and Canada depressed generation capacity. In return, Manitoba Hydro realized some $644 million in revenue, again an improvement over 2004's nearly $400 million.[5] While most of this power was transmitted via Minnesota utilities, Hydro also provided over 410,000 MWhs, valued at almost $30 million, to Wisconsin Public Service Company in 2006 (Canadian Energy Board, various years, tables 2A and 3A).[6]

The importance of these sales is obvious. Since 2001 extraprovincial electricity sales have accounted for up to 32 percent of the company's total, a figure that becomes even more significant when measured as a percent of system sales revenues (Manitoba Hydro *Annual Report* 2004). With the exception of 2004, non-domestic sales have accounted for anywhere from 33 to 42 percent of total system sales since 2001 (see Table 7.1). Indeed, 2006 set a record in terms of extraprovincial revenues as a percent of total revenues (37 percent).[7]

TABLE 7.1

Extraprovincial Sales and Revenues

	2006	2005	2004	2003	2002	2001
Total Revenues (millions of $)	2399	2017	1781	1869	1864	1773
Extraprovincial Revenue	881	554	351	463	588	480
% of total	37%	27%	20%	25%	32%	27%
Total System Sales (000,000 kWh)	37,400	29,350	23,712	28,416	29,049	28,763
Extraprovincial Sales	13,800	9569	4389	9463	12,091	12,065
% of Sales	37%	32%	19%	33%	42%	42%

SOURCE: Manitoba Hydro-Electric Board Annual Report; various years

DEFINING THE ABORIGINAL ROLE

While Manitoba Hydro made great strides in expanding its operating system in the latter portion of the twentieth century, it now faces considerable hurdles in taking the next steps required for continued expansion. These hurdles involve all aspects of its operation, the most prominent being increasingly assertive Aboriginal populations and limited transmission capacity. The company is now taking steps to ensure that neither of these will remain obstacles in achieving its historically encompassing goal of continental expansion.

The initial step in moving this agenda forward is the construction of the 200 MW Wuskwatim dam.[8] Small by comparison to the rest of the Nelson River dams, for at least two reasons Wuskwatim is nonetheless a vital first step in securing the construction of much larger dams such as the 1300 MW Conawapa dam, the 640 MW Keeyask facility, and the other ten or so dams being envisaged by the company's planners. The first of these roles is the establishment of a streamlined regulatory process, a necessity acknowledged in the Manitoba Clean Environment Commission's (CEC) report on the project. According to the CEC:

> The Commission recognizes the Wuskwatim projects are relatively small when compared to other potential hydroelectric projects in northern Manitoba. The fact that the effects of future projects may be considerably more significant underscores the need to improve filings and processes. Additional development projects contemplated for the North will have significant implications for the region's infrastructure, housing, social services and other services. (cover letter to report 2004)

A second critical role played by the Wuskwatim project is its ability to move forward the project-by-project and community-by-community negotiating style that has long characterized provincial–Aboriginal relations in Manitoba. While the Wuskwatim *Project Development Agreement* (PDA) between Hydro and the Nisichawayasihk Cree Nation (NCN) does add an important new element to the mix—namely, the opportunity for NCN to obtain an equity stake in the deal—the so-called "business-only" partnership introduced by the agreement nonetheless deeply reinforces an isolationist style of negotiation that has been historically employed by Hydro and provinces.[9]

The implications of this strategy can best be appreciated by comparing negotiations in Manitoba with those in Quebec, and specifically, with the 2004 *Paix des Braves* agreement between the province of Quebec and the Quebec Cree. According to Paul Charest, the latter represents a "true partnership" between provincial governments and First Nation peoples that extends "to all the political, social, and cultural levels of relations between Aboriginal and non-Aboriginal people, who live together on the same territory. Under this type of partnership, there is an absolute equality of all the partners" (chapter 11, this volume). To a great extent, the equality demonstrated in Quebec was the result of the *Paix des Braves* being negotiated between Quebec's Cree *nation* and the Crown utility, the former representing the totality of the Cree communities throughout the province.

In contrast, the absolute inequality prevalent in Manitoba stems from the insistence on the part of Hydro that individual agreements be consummated between the company and various northern Aboriginal communities. Thus, unlike in the case of the *Paix des Braves*, Hydro and the province of Manitoba continue to deal with each and every community as a separate entity and on a project-by-project basis. As a result, separate implementation agreements have been signed with four of the five northern flood communities (i.e., Nelson House, Norway House, York Factory, and Split Lake); the *CASIL Agreement* was negotiated with the South Indian Lake; the PDA and prior agreements were negotiated with NCN; and additional agreements are being negotiated between Fox Lake and other communities that will be affected by future dams.

That an isolationist approach, less generously known as "divide and conquer," continues to describe Cree-Hydro relations was illustrated by the debate surrounding the creation of a new reserve for the South Indian Lake (SIL) community, an initiative spurred on almost entirely by the Wuskwatim development. For many years, indeed almost since the turn of the twentieth century, the federal government and Manitoba resisted granting reserve status to the now-impoverished SIL. However, both Manitoba and Manitoba Hydro publicly stated the Wuskwatim dam would not proceed without the consent of NCN band members, which historically included the SIL members. Since over 80 percent of South Indian Lake NCN members voted against the project in the 2001 referendum on the AIP, it was reasonably feared that if the SIL members were included in the required vote, the proposal would suffer a defeat; hence the urgency in establishing a new SIL reserve, at least from the perspectives of the dam's supporters, which included the NCN tribal leadership at the time. As a result, an accelerated plan for the establishment of the so-called O-Pipon-Na-Piwin (OPCN) reserve was proposed by the governments of Canada and Manitoba (see *Justice Seekers* newsletter, March 2005, volume 3; and *PR Direct Electronic News Service*, March 23, 2005).

The contentious nature of the proposal and the underlying motive was illustrated at the March 23, 2005, meeting of the Interim Supply Committee of the Manitoba Legislative Assembly. Mr. Gerald Hawranik, a representative from Lac du Bonnet, in his questions to a government minister, noted that the 900 or so people who live in SIL have been waiting and asking for band recognition status for decades. The minister appears now to be in a panic to give them status as early as April 1 of [2005]. To give them band recognition status by April 1 would exclude them from a vote on Wuskwatim, which is scheduled for June 1, because they would no longer be members of Nelson House First Nation. . . . The minister knows that most of the Status Aboriginals in South Indian Lake would vote against Wuskwatim. He knows that. Is the minister pushing ahead with reserve status early because he is being forced by [Premier Doer] and the Minister responsible for Hydro to exclude them from the Wuskwatim dam vote? (Committee Transcript, March 23, 2005)

The government's answer was unequivocal. According to Oscar Lathlin, Manitoba Minister of Aboriginal and Northern Affairs:

The situation in South Indian Lake could hardly be characterized as, or at least the creation of a reserve, could hardly be characterized as moving too fast. This issue has been there, I am told, over 70 years. Some people are saying that it goes back even further than that. Some people say it has been there for a hundred years. . . . They have been lobbying the federal government for about seventy years now to get reserve status, for the community to be converted to a reserve by the Minister of Indian Affairs federally. So now it has finally reached that stage where the federal minister has agreed that he will, once certain conditions have been met, in fact, convert South Indian into a reserve. (Committee Transcript, March 23, 2005)

Any delay, according to Lathlin, would only add to the frustrations of the SIL residents in "realizing their . . . long-standing dream" (Committee Transcript, March 23, 2005).

The debate over the SIL reserve status is not the only indication that the traditional mindset continues to dominate relations between the company and Aboriginal communities. As noted above, the Wuskwatim dam will make a relatively minor contribution to the additional generating capacity sought by the company; much more important are the 1300 MW Conawapa and 640 MW Keeyask projects. The latter, although in the early stages of planning, has also excited considerable controversy, including allegations that the company provided contracts worth some $14 million to Hobbs and Associates, a large Canadian consulting firm, to secure community approval for the dam. According to reports filed by the Canadian Broadcasting System (2005), "Hydro needs the band's support for the Keeyask project to go ahead. In 2000, Tataskweyak signed a non-binding agreement-in-principle to build the dam. The original deadline to reach a development agreement has passed, but band members still haven't voted on the project, and there is no development agreement in place." As is the case in Southern Indian Lake and Nelson House, indeed as has been the case since the Easterville project in the 1960s (see Waldram 1988), the payments (as well as a highly publicized visit to the World Bank in March 2005, which, according to critics, presented the partnerships deals as basically done deals) have created considerable internal divisions and have raised the spectre of improper relations between the band's elected leadership, the consultants, and the company (*CBC News,* April 2005).

The Wuskwatim debate, the question of SIL's reserve status, and the controversy surrounding the Conawapa and Keeyask projects illustrate an essential issue surrounding dam development in northern Manitoba: the negotiation process and the implications that derive from that process. As has been the case throughout the dam-building era, the company continues to negotiate with individual communities on individual dams, treating each as though it was unrelated to the system as a whole. The importance of this way of thinking and acting cannot be overestimated. For instance, being safely ensconced in the comforting logic of an isolationist world view allows the company to confidently assert that the Wuskwatim dam will require a mere one-half square kilometre of new flooding (Manitoba Hydro, *Project Overview*). Such a claim allows the company to ignore the reality that the dam could not operate apart from all the constituent elements of the system; i.e., the Jenpeg and Missi Falls control structures, the various diversion channels, the Nelson River dams, and so on.

The isolationist strategy also confronts individual communities with a remarkable reality. First, they are unable to negotiate as anything other than small, isolated, and impoverished communities in a manner that essentially pits them against other equally powerless communities. The Tataskweyak leadership, for instance, *must* ignore whatever effects might be created for other communities, since the negotiations are strictly limited to the Keeyask dam and Split Lake. Collective action, no matter how beneficial, is simply not permitted by those with real power—the company and the province.[10] Second, as individual communities become "business partners," they are, in effect, agreeing to perpetuate ecological damages that are a functional part of the project's operation. In this respect, they become participants in the continued degradation of an ecology that could support a traditional land-based way of life, albeit one expressed in modern forms (see Salisbury 1986). Thus, whatever the outcome of any particular deal, no matter how financially lucrative it might be, each "successful" negotiation reinforces an underlying process that prevents communities from working together. Forced to act individually, each community unwittingly and tragically contributes to the demise of a larger cultural tradition.

TRANSMISSION CONSTRAINTS: THE NEXT PROBLEM

If the new round of dam construction is meant to solve at least two of the company's needs—i.e., additional generation meant primarily for extraprovincial markets and the acquiescence of the province's Aboriginal populations—it simultaneously creates another problem: the problem of transmitting that energy to distant extraprovincial markets.[11]

At the present time, approximately 70 percent of Hydro's total electricity production is sent from northern dams to the Winnipeg area via a pair of transmission lines, known as Bipole I and II, in a single 900-kilometre -long corridor.[12] Such a constrained transmission system makes Manitoba Hydro's system vulnerable to extreme weather events such as ice storms and tornadoes that might also compromise system security and reliability. In addition, the Bipole lines are currently operating near maximum capacity and beyond optimum capacity when considered from an efficiency standpoint (Manitoba Wildlands 2005). Both the Keeyask and the Conawapa dams, which would lie on the upper reaches of the Nelson River, are projected to require new transmission lines.

The number and location of these new lines have been subject to intense scrutiny and debate. According to a 2000 confidential Manitoba Hydro memo obtained by Manitoba Wildlands, a Winnipeg-based environmental organization, the company speculated that it might require up to ten new north-south transmission lines in six different corridors, should it pursue its full expansion aspirations. According to the memo, future corridors—i.e., swathes of land housing one or more transmission lines up to several hundred feet wide—could have included the east side of Lake Winnipeg, two down the centre of the province, and an expansion of a third (through the Interlake region), and one on the west side of the province, west of Cedar Lake and Lake Manitoba.[13] One of the east-side lines, the so-called Bipole III line, would bisect a tract of such pristine wilderness that it is being proposed for designation as a World Heritage site (Manitoba Wildlands 2005).[14] After much pressure from a variety of interests, including Canadian and US environmental organizations, local Aboriginal leaders, and others, the company announced that these routes were no longer to be considered. Instead, the new lines would be sited on the longer and more costly west side routes, thus fulfilling a campaign promise made by then-candidate Doer to launch the province, and its Crown utility, into an aggressively green era (Manitoba Hydro, *News Release,* September 25, 2007, retrieved at <www.hydro.mb.ca>; see also Rabson 2007).

Another piece of the transmission puzzle involves a newer but equally frustrating desire for access to Ontario markets. This market is increasingly attractive because of the imminent retirement of a host of a number of coal plants as well as Ontario's nuclear fleet. At the present time, only three 230 kV lines run east to Ontario, far below the desired capacity. According to Manitoba Wildlands, however, "a push is on to provide Ontario—which is facing energy shortfalls in coming years—with 1500 MW of power from northern Manitoba" (2005). This effort was formalized in a June 2003 Memorandum of Understanding (MOU) between Manitoba and Ontario that committed the respective provinces to strengthening "transmission infrastructure both internally and with other jurisdictions, so as to enhance its overall electrical system reliability and energy security" and to ensure "that its hydro-electric potential and other renewable energy resources are developed for the advantage of domestic and Canadian users, both to the East as well as to the West, in both the short-term and the future." In furtherance of this goal, the MOU specified that the "Governments of Ontario and Manitoba agree to support work . . . associated with evaluating the technical, and financial aspects and agree to cooperate in the study of social and economic aspects of a long term power supply from Manitoba to Ontario" (2003).

The intent to proceed with the initiative was confirmed in a September 2004 press release that summarized the numerous benefits associated with the project. According to the Honourable Tim Sale, Minister of Energy, Science and Technology, benefits included the enhancement of "national energy security and grid reliability and [assistance in] meeting our national climate change targets by helping to displace fossil fuel generation and creating significant economic development opportunities for First Nations and northern communities." Equally important, the project would assist in the long-held goal of continentalization, or in the words of the minister, "nation-building" (*News Release Communique*, issued by the governments of Manitoba and Ontario, 30 September 2004, retrieved at <www.gov.mb.ca/chc/press/top/2004/09/2004-09-30-02.html>).

The first concrete step in realizing the aims of the initiative was taken in November 2005, with a $500 million energy agreement between Manitoba and Ontario. The deal had two significant aims: first, to pave the way for the Conawapa project, and, second, to secure initial upgrades to the transmission system required for the delivery of that power to Ontario. According to the company spokesperson, Glenn Schneider, "[W]hat we have agreed to do is to look at a subsequent phase ... [t]hat would mean that we would need to construct additional facilities. That would mean Conawapa. We are very optimistic that we will reach a second-phase agreement and start working on planning." On the transmission side, the deal involved the transfer of 150 MW of power beginning in 2006, in turn requiring upgrades to the power connections between Winnipeg and Thunder Bay and doubling the existing east-west grid capacity at the Manitoba–Ontario connection point. Power transfers are scheduled to be increased to 400 MW in 2009 (Chilboyko 2005).[15]

The completion of new dams, along with additional north-south transmission lines within Manitoba and an east-west transmission system to meet Ontario's loads, would only partially satisfy the requirements of a more robust version of the modernizing imperative; the more lucrative target has been and remains a larger segment of the US market. The effort to gain enhanced access to this market was initiated in the late 1990s when Minnesota Power (now Allete) and Hydro established an alliance in order to market electric energy in the midwest; i.e., the states of Wisconsin, Michigan, and Illinois, including the lucrative Chicago market. According to Robert Brennan, the CEO of Manitoba Hydro, the alliance, which built on a whole-sale bulk power trading agreement announced in December 1997, allowed "Manitoba Hydro to further strengthen our ties in the U.S. and [affirm] our confidence in working with Minnesota Power" (*PR Newswire* January 15, 1998). It was well understood at the time that the alliance would permit Manitoba Hydro to market its low-cost hydropower throughout the central United States and possibly to markets further east where cheap hydropower would be welcomed, given that average kWh prices are much higher there than in either Manitoba or Wisconsin and Minnesota.

While the marketing agreements are significant, congestion at a key transfer point on the US side of the border was long a major stumbling block in gaining increased access to US markets. According to the 2004 Brattle Group study, the Eau Claire-Arpin 345 kV line, which connects western Wisconsin with points further east and which Hydro is dependent on for eastward-looking plans, "is one of the nineteen most constrained lines or 'flowgates' in the MISO footprint" (Brattle Group 2004, 5). The answer to solving the congestion problem lies in the new Arrowhead–Weston (AW) transmission line, a 345 kV bulk transfer electric/fibre optics line that will cross over some 220 miles of largely rural Wisconsin countryside when completed. The cost of the line was initially projected to cost $165 million; as of April 2005, the estimated cost had risen to some $420 million.

A review of the existing Wisconsin and Minnesota transmission lines illustrates just how the new line will relieve the bottlenecks inhibiting Hydro's efforts to gain access to more eastern US markets. Power generated in Manitoba is currently required to flow down the eastern border of Minnesota and Wisconsin before it can be wheeled to the east. The AW line will bypass this congestion point by linking the Arrowhead station near

Duluth with the Weston station that flows directly into Chicago and then, ultimately, to equally lucrative and profitable markets east of Chicago.

The marketing plan for the AW line followed neatly along the lines established by the CRD/LWR project several decades earlier. Just as Hydro framed the prior undertaking as necessary to solve domestic demand issues, the ostensible rationale for the AW line was to solve local load problems. According to Wisconsin Public Service, the owner of the new line and American Transmission Company, the builder,

> the line is needed to accommodate electric load growth in northern Wisconsin and to improve reliability of the electric transmission system in the region. Building the line will add an important element to Wisconsin's transmission infrastructure—it will bring much-needed reliability to a seriously constrained system. . . . The Arrowhead–Weston transmission project will help ensure that Wisconsin has reliable and affordable energy now and in the future. (<www.arrowhead-weston.com>)

For those charged with something other than placating local landowners and environmental critics, however, larger issues topped the agenda. According to the Edison Electric Institute, for instance, the line is critical in helping to "relieve the highly-constrained interface in western Wisconsin between the northern portion of the Mid-American Power Pool (MAPP) and the Wisconsin–Upper Michigan System (WUMS) . . . [which at the moment] creates reliability problems and inhibits generation competition within WUMS and trade between WUMS and surrounding regions" (Brattle Group 2004, 5). The surrounding region is, of course, Chicago as well as more distant eastern markets. This account pays little attention to local load; instead, it justifies the line by the needs of both regional and national markets. This fact was not been lost on the line's opponents, who argued that "it is clear that the line" would be used primarily to "transfer massive electric sales to points south and east and on through to Chicago." The power to serve these markets would come from two primary sources: "North Dakota coal plants . . . and Manitoba Hydro" (Save Our Unique Lands [SOUL] Web site at <www.angelfire.com/wi/wakeupwisc>).[16]

Manitoba Hydro's leadership also appreciates the vital role played by the AW transmission line, even if this necessity must be cast in a language more easily understood by the public. In discussing the proposed twelve new dams to be added to the CRD/LWR system and the accompanying infrastructure, which by any reasonable accounting would include the AW line, CEO Brennan admits that at this point, they "don't know who the energy will be sold to, Saskatchewan, Ontario, or the States, but there will be a market." Further, the company admits that there is no domestic need "in the sense that the energy for Manitoba isn't going to run out." However, according to Ken Adams, company vice-president in charge of power supply, "Hydro's plan is to maintain its levels of revenue from exports and to build dams because it is still profitable to build them" (quoted in Shoumatoff 2005). Like the rhetoric of localism, a rhetoric of profitability is more easily understood by provincial residents than the historical imperatives of continental modernization and expansion.[17]

Complementing the Wuskwatim project, the dams at Conawapa and elsewhere, the construction of additional transmission capacity in Canada and the United States, and the use of business-only partnerships with northern Aboriginal communities is the role of hydropower in satisfying Canada's commitment to the Kyoto Protocol. According to Pierre Fortin, Executive Director of the Canadian Hydropower Association (CHA), an industry-funded trade group, "hydro generates few GHG and no other air pollutants" (no date). This assertion was based on a 2002 CHA study that found that "results of studies of reservoirs in boreal regions such as Canada show that emissions are much more consistent and always much lower than those produced by fossil fuel electricity generation—approximately 60 times less than coal-fired power plants and 20 times less than the least carbon intensive of the thermal generation options, the natural gas combined cycle. Life cycle emissions of hydropower generation are comparable to those of wind power" (2002).

This argument is strongly supported in Manitoba. Premier Gary Doer, for instance, argues that Conawapa would provide the single largest reduction in greenhouse gas emissions in the country, claiming that if energy from Manitoba Hydro were to replace coal-fired plants in Ontario, it would reduce the country's greenhouse gas emissions by seven mega-tonnes per year (Shoumatoff 2005). Parroting the line of the CHA, the company argues that

> while methane is produced in reservoirs, early research indicates quantities of greenhouse gases from these sources are miniscule compared to thermal generating plants. . . . Manitoba's greatest contribution to national and international efforts could be in the development of additional hydraulic electric generation. . . . [Indeed], the feasibility of future hydro-electric developments may be enhanced as national and international programs are implemented to reduce greenhouse gas production, including encouragement for energy sources which do not produce greenhouse gases. (*The Kyoto Commitment*, retrieved at <www.hydro.mb.ca>)

Manitoba's eastern partner shares the same vision. According to Ontario energy minister Dwight Duncan, projects such as Conawapa and the concomitant phase-out of Ontario's coal plants will make a significant contribution to Canada's Kyoto commitments. Ottawa, says Duncan, should help make Conawapa and its transmission a reality by paying part of the cost since "we're looking at a fairly substantial contribution to help them achieve their Kyoto objectives. Now that Russia has ratified Kyoto, I would think that this opportunity, combined with what Ontario is doing on the coal front, really helps Ontario and Canada get to its Kyoto target" (CBC, 1 October 2004, retrieved at <www.cbc.ca/manitoba>).[18]

The ability to frame hydroelectric projects as environmentally benign, or at least better than the alternatives, is also an important factor south of the Canadian border. In December 2004, in an appearance before the Minnesota Legislative Electric Energy Task Force, the staff of the state's Department of Commerce suggested that "the Department's renewable electricity calculations include all sources deemed renewable under Minnesota law, [including] hydro facilities [and] power from Manitoba Hydro" (2004, 6). According to the department, including Manitoba's production into Minnesota's renewable energy calculation pushes the state into a renewable energy leadership role, with 11 percent of its electricity coming from renewables, a figure that could increase to at least 20 percent by 2015.

AN UPSIDE: NGO GLOBALIZATION

One positive outcome of Manitoba's efforts to secure larger, continental markets has been the creation of some important partnerships among Canadian, Aboriginal, and US organizations. The existence of such transnational alliances is, of course, not unique. Clapp and Dauvergne (2005), for instance, note that a half-century ago, numerous international organizations joined together to work on behalf of the International Convention for the Prevention of Pollution of the Sea by Oil. Since then, international NGOs have played key roles in many policy debates and have provided critical information to policymakers and the public. In many instances, though, the process of creating these alliances has had a 'top-down' character. Thus, even when local organizations have been involved, international NGOs, including the so-called American 'Big 10,' have been accused of consigning local groups to minor roles and attempting to monopolize the policy agenda. The result has often been a gaping disaffection between local, grassroots organizations and national and international NGOs (see Gottlieb 1993). Fortunately, the oppositional efforts directed at hydro projects in Manitoba have not followed this pattern. Instead, opposition has come directly from the communities and has built outward, only recently involving international NGOs.

Inspired by the successful James Bay Cree campaign to halt Hydro-Quebec's Great Whale Project, and working with members of Canada's Mennonite church community, members of the Pimicikamak Nation (Cross Lake) first sought to influence US decision makers in the fall of 1998 with a rally at the headquarters of then-Northern States Power (NSP) in downtown Minneapolis. The rally, which included a meeting between a Cross Lake Elder and NSP's CEO, received significant local press attention (Braun 2005). The visit stimulated further contacts between a number of local Minnesota-based advocacy organizations and representatives from the Cross Lake leadership, including Minnesotans for an Energy-Efficient Economy (now Fresh Energy) and Minnesota Witness for Environmental Justice, an organization affiliated with the Minnesota Friends. These initial contacts led to a number of educational and organizing efforts, including a regional conference on energy policy and environmental justice and the presentation of a resolution at the 2001 Xcel shareholders meeting urging the company to reconsider its relationship with Manitoba Hydro.[19] The Minnesota Public Utilities Commission was also an active venue. While the commission, citing jurisdictional issues, ultimately refused to order an examination of the environmental or social impacts of the CRD / LWR projects, it did order that an Xcel-sponsored monitoring process be established. This was followed up by 2007 legislation requiring Hydro officials to submit an annual report to the state's Electric Energy Task Force on the environmental and social impacts associated with hydro development in the region (see Dobrovolny, chapter 8, this volume).

Throughout the development of the various partnerships, the Minnesota-based groups struggled with the fact that opinions and attitudes within the affected Aboriginal communities were hardly monolithic, particularly as they established relations with communities other than Cross Lake. It was clear that the various communities all had unique problems and held various opinions on what might constitute just, fair, and equitable solutions. Also, there were, and are, significant divisions of opinions within each community and therefore contestation over leadership and who might serve as a legitimate "community voice." Even if all parties agreed with the premise that part of the problem, and therefore some part of the solution, lies on the US side of the border, trying to understand and then effectively negotiate these community differences was extremely challenging for the US-based organizations.

Despite these difficulties, the efforts at outreach by Indigenous people resulted in a set of US/Canadian relationships that now involve national NGOs as well as partnerships with a diverse set of Canadian organizations whose work does not typically involve hydro issues. Thus, the Washington-based National Resources Defense Council (NRDC) became heavily involved in the debate following a visit by the Senior Council for NRDC, Robert Kennedy, Jr. After his visit, Kennedy concluded that it is important to have US NGOs involved in this campaign "because they are the consumers of electricity, mining, and timber. . . . In this geopolitical mix of wealth and resources, it is the North American Indigenous population that bares the brunt of this economic system. They are the canaries in the coal mine."

Oppositional forces within northern communities, including Justice Seekers, a group of community activists in Nelson House, as well other burgeoning movements in Split Lake and South Indian Lake (primarily DRSIL, or the Displaced Residents of South Indian Lake), have also established relationships with organizations that had long worked to protect the boreal forest both in Canada and elsewhere. Thus, the Boreal Forest Network, and its long-time international coalitions such as Taiga Rescue Network (TRN) and the International Pan-Boreal Network, collaborated with residents in many of the affected communities on issues of common concern. Ultimately, the Energy Justice Alliance was formed in the fall of 2003, representing the culmination of a years-long grassroots and bottom-up organizing effort (Sullivan 2005).

The strategy of continental modernization has long animated the perspective and actions of both Manitoba and its Crown utility. While the CRD/LWR project was a vital step in that process, the company understands that it must now move to the next stage of expansion, one that transcends a domestic or even regional basis for its operations. The next round of dam building, the creation of "business-only" partnerships, and the construction of transmission networks capable of moving power to ever-more distant markets, are understood by the company and the province as the inevitable and necessary costs of doing business in a globalized business environment.

One significant cost associated with this way of doing business is the continued undermining of the prospects for the economic and cultural viability of northern Aboriginal communities. A reasonable first step in reversing the downward spiral faced by these communities would be to abandon the divisive "business-only" approach employed by provincial authorities and establish meaningful nation-to-nation dialogue. Such an approach would provide a far more equitable and just basis for a type of development that permits those people most adversely affected by the demands of modernization to flourish. Without this first step, any opportunity for a more hopeful future will be lost and the asymmetries between those who benefit and those who are forced to bear the burdens of globalization will continue.

To a great extent, of course, attempting to ameliorate the consequences of continental modernization ignores a central reality of hydro development: there is no need to continue, and certainly not to expand, the destruction of northern landscapes and communities. As was pointed out above, there is no domestic market for the massive quantities of electrons to be generated by Wuskwatim, Conawapa, and the rest. And, satisfying the demands of extra-provincial markets is most certainly a choice that could easily be spurned.

Ultimately, allowing the necessity of undammed rivers to remain an apostasy within the province must be seen for the folly that it is. Unfortunately, provincial leaders seem willing to sacrifice the natural and cultural heritage of Manitoba to an unfortunate and increasingly anachronistic understanding of progress. Such a view was displayed by NDP Premier Gary Doer in his 2005 State of the Province address, in which he asserted that his party's vision "is to build. The water [from the province's rivers] is going into Hudson's Bay. You can either put a turbine on it and sell it or just let it flow. You can sit on your assets or you can build your assets. We're going to build, build, build" (*Winnipeg Free Press*, December 9, 2005). To accept such a prescription invites an impoverished future for succeeding generations of all Manitoba's citizens and not just the residents of its northern communities.

---

1   Globalization is often characterized as an inevitability. However, an emerging literature calls into question this assumption or at least suggests that the phenomenon will not proceed unfettered. See Stiglitz 2002 and Ferguson 2005.

2   This is not to say that consolidation is not without its challenges. The merger between American Electric Power Company and Central and Southwest Corporation, which would have created the single largest operating utility in the United States, was derailed by a May 2005 ruling from an administrative law judge. The ruling found that the merger violated provisions of the *Public Utility Holding Company Act* dealing with territorial integration. See *Securities and Exchange Commission. Initial Release No. 283. Administrative Proceeding. File No. 3-11616. May 3, 2005.*

3 See Hoffman 2002 and chapter 7, this volume, for more discussion of this developmental history.

4 This enthusiasm has been shared with the rest of Canada's hydroelectric industry as well as the energy sector generally (Watkins 2003). While the gap between electricity exports and imports has been narrowing in recent years, due mainly to the drought condition, Canada remains a net exporter and the demand for Canadian hydropower continues to grow. See National Energy Board, *Electricity Exports and Imports,* retrieved at <http://www.neb.gc.ca.>

5 All dollar amounts in Canadian dollars.

6 This compares with the 400,000 MWhs that flowed into Minnesota from the only other Canadian source, namely, Ontario (retrieved at <http://www.neb.gc.ca>). It appears that these exports sales will continue beyond that covered by existing contracts. In the Xcel Energy Resource Plan filed with the Minnesota Public Utilities Commission (MPUC Docket E002/RP-04-1752, November 23, 2005) regarding the company's base load development process, it was stated that "a more promising option (when compared to natural gas base load) within this category is a possible purchase with Manitoba Hydro. While the development cycle for new hydroelectric development in Manitoba is too long to meet our identified 2015 resource need, there may be potential to restructure our existing contracts to provide additional energy over a longer term" (Xcel Energy 2005, p. 5, C, *Power Purchase Options*). While specific amounts and sources of power were protected as trade secrets, it is reasonable to suppose that the Wuskwatim and possibly the Gull and Conawapa dams featured heavily in the company's thinking.

7 The discrepancy between system sales and system revenues has led to accusations of subsidization of export sales by domestic customers. In 2002, for instance, extraprovincial or export sales accounted for 42 percent of sales. Yet domestic sales, or 58 percent of the total sales, accounted for 68 percent of system revenues. For critics, the difference is evidence of an implicit subsidy for the extraprovincial market. Retrieved at <http://www.hydro.mb.ca/about_us/ar_2004/ar_2004_report_complete.pdf>.

8 See <www.fresh-energy.org>, <www.manitobawildlangs.org>, and <www.hydro.mb.ca> for information and reports on the Wuskwatim debate.

9   The equity partnership is a provision repeatedly trumpeted by both the company and the province as heralding a new era in Hydro/Aboriginal peoples relationships. Yet, as pointed out by many of the dam's opponents, exactly how much return the community will earn on their investment remains highly ambiguous (Kobliski 2006). See also Hoffman, chapter 7, this volume, for further discussion of this issue.

10 The *Northern Flood Agreement* represented a departure from this approach in that the so-called northern flood communities acted collectively. Even here, however, a flawed arbitration process undermined effective collective action and ultimately the agreement. See Manitoba Aboriginal Rights Coalition, *Let Justice Flow: Report of the Interchurch Inquiry into Northern Hydro Development*, 2001.

11 Whether the new generation is destined for domestic or extra-provincial markets has been controversial. Under oath in March 2005 before the CEC hearings, a senior company official stated that the rationale for moving up Wuskwatim from 2020 to 2010 was to export the power to the US. Two days later the same official stated before the Minnesota Senate Committee that Wuskwatim Power was not to be exported and would be needed domestically in Manitoba starting from its proposed in-service date of 2010. Manitoba Liberal leader Jon Gerard raised this in the Manitoba Legislature during Question Period in March 2004.

12 The term "Bipole" refers to High Voltage Direct Current (HVDC) transmission infrastructure used and, to some extent, pioneered by Manitoba Hydro (see Manitoba Wildlands 2005).

13 Manitoba Hydro Interoffice Memorandum from W.N. Zurba to C.V. Thio, June 27, 2000. Obtained from Parks Canada under the *Access to Information Act*.

14 Just as the Wuskwatim and Keeyask dams seem to deny the onset of a new reality between Aboriginal communities and the company, the willingness to violate such a pristine region is problematic for an organization that claims to have entered a new era of environmental sensitivity. Among the environmental damages associated with Bipole III would be the extensive use of chemical herbicides associated with tree removal. Caribou herds, already severely stressed throughout Canada, would also be affected mainly due to their need to avoid open space and subsequent predation (Granger, "Hydro Lines Threat to Caribou Herds." See Sierra Club 2005 for discussion of caribou herds generally).

15 Such projects naturally proceed in fits and starts. In July of 2006 Manitoba Premier Gary Doer stated that the Conawapa Project and proposed east-west power transmission grid to transport power to Ontario was "in a state of suspended animation" due to the January 2006 election of a national Conservative government under Prime Minister Stephen Harper. It was hoped that much of the $1 billion cost of the east-west transmission line, facilitating construction of the $10 billion-plus Conawapa hydro dam, would be underwritten by the federal government. With the change of national government in Canada, these funds may be in jeopardy.

16 A permit was issued by the Wisconsin Department of Natural Resources, 22 December 2004, to undertake pre-construction work along the transmission corridor. While some local county boards went on record opposing the line, the project turned first turned dirt on 19 June 2006; the last of the segments is scheduled to be completed in May 2008.

17 This rhetoric continues to be used despite serious questions about the eventual profitability of the fairly inexpensive Wuskwatim project and the much more costly Conawapa-type projects. In the 2004 hearings before the Clean Environment Commission of Canada, Hydro estimated the cost of the 200 MW Wuskwatim project to be $756 million. By early 2005, an additional $130 million had been added to the project. The Conawapa project has been estimated to cost $10 billion (*Winnipeg Free Press*, 30 September 2004).

18 The assertion that hydro power has positive greenhouse effects is the subject of increasing scientific scrutiny. Recent research has shown, for instance, that greenhouse gases are emitted from all the dozens of reservoirs where measurements have been made, with variations caused by the area and type of ecosystems flooded, reservoir depth and shape, the local climate, and the way in which the dam is operated. Reservoirs emit greenhouse gases due to the rotting of organic matter, including submerged vegetation and soils and the detritus that flows into the reservoir from upstream. The diffusion of carbon dioxide into the atmosphere from reservoir surfaces accounts for most of the global warming impact of dams in boreal and temperate regions, as well as deep tropical reservoirs. See <www.irn.org/programs/greenhouse/index.php?id=resemissions.html.> for relevant literature.

19 Some 9.4 percent of those in attendance voted in favor of the resolution, a figure that exceeded the threshold for reintroduction the following year.

8

Monitoring for Success: Designing and Implementing a Monitoring Regime for Northern Manitoba

Lydia Dobrovolny

FORTY YEARS AFTER HYDRO development was initiated along the Churchill–Nelson rivers system in northern Manitoba, the extent of associated impacts and fulfillment of responsibilities by involved parties remains unresolved. Debate regarding the nature and magnitude of environmental and socio-economic damage is ongoing. Plans for future development have provoked further controversy over outstanding issues and potential consequences of additional development.

The issue is seemingly intractable. Each side posits a very different reality, and the complexity of the situation has made it difficult to conclusively delineate the causal relationships between development and impacts. When the Minnesota Public Utilities Commission approved a contract for Minnesota's largest utility, Xcel Energy, to continue importing electricity generated from hydro development in northern Manitoba on the condition that Xcel Energy "monitor and report" on implementation of the 1977 *Northern Flood Agreement* (NFA), it simultaneously presented an opportunity and issued a challenge. In providing a mechanism to assure Minnesota consumers that the price Manitoba Hydro charges reflects the true costs incurred, as mandated by Minnesota state law, the Minnesota Public Utilities Commission faced the heart of this intractable issue head on and called for an assessment of a system for which no yardstick exists.

Nobel Prize winner Amartya Sen, who has worked to develop yardsticks for human well-being, achievement, improvement, potential, and other seemingly unmeasurable issues, dedicated *On Economic Inequality* to his daughters, "with the hope that when they grow up they will find less of it no matter how they decide to measure it" (Sen 1973). Sen and others have demonstrated that too often issues deemed unquantifiable are simply unquantified. Since that which is not measured is not valued, new metrics are being devised to track issues previously unmeasured and existing metrics are being expanded to provide a more holistic accounting. For example, the United Nations now ranks countries on a quality of life index, and China has announced plans to establish a green GDP in three to five years, which will extend this traditional metric of economic strength to consider natural resource inputs and outputs.

Conversely, that which is not valued is not measured. Partly in response to this problem, clearer and wider reaching statements asserting the fundamental value of environmental and human rights have emerged in the past few decades. The Rio Declaration on Environment and Development, the World Charter for Nature, Agenda 21, and the Declaration on the Right to Development all include provisions for environmental protections and directives for balancing development concerns. The first five principles from the 1972 Stockholm Declaration from the United Nations Conference on Human Environment include statements on the fundamental rights of humans to freedom and equality "in an environment that permits a life of dignity and well-being" and argues that natural resources need to be maintained and safeguarded for present and future generations (United Nations Environment Programme 1972).

All these statements underscore the necessity of fully assessing past and future hydro development in northern Manitoba. A central task in undertaking this assessment is the development and implementation of a practical and transparent indicator system. The benefits of such a system were emphasized in a 2004 report authored by the US Government Accountability Office, which determined that indicator systems enhance collaboration to address public issues; help inform decision making and improve research; increase public knowledge about key economic, environmental, social, and cultural issues; and provide an effective tool for monitoring and encouraging progress toward a shared vision. This chapter assesses the history and issues associated with hydro development in northern Manitoba and proposes an indicator system based on the blueprint outlined in the NFA. This preliminary summation is neither exhaustive nor conclusive. Steps that would be necessary to fully develop an indicator system for monitoring implementation of the NFA include selecting and revising indicators, acquiring data to compute indicators, engaging data providers, assessing the quality and reliability of the indicators or data, and seeking and maintaining funding.

HISTORICAL PERSPECTIVES ON HYDRO DEVELOPMENT IN NORTHERN MANITOBA

Since the early twentieth century, the Canadian federal government and the provincial government have been interested in development of hydropower in northern Manitoba. A geological survey conducted by the Canadian Department of Mines in 1913 concluded that of Manitoba's rivers, "the Nelson, by reason of its great volume and numerous falls, is the most important from the point of view of power development" (McInnes 1913). In 1938, the Economic Survey Board of the Province of Manitoba championed the potential to develop water resources in the north:

> [S]ituated almost in the center of a district rich in forest and mineral resources this river with its abundance of cheap power is the key to the utilization of these resources and, with the advent of further improvements in the transmission of power and increased markets in the southern part of the province, will prove a valuable source of additional power to those markets when present sources have been fully utilized. (Atwood 1938)

On February 15, 1966, the federal government and the Province of Manitoba signed an agreement to cooperate in the development of the hydroelectric potential of the Nelson River. Manitoba Hydro, a Crown corporation, was appointed to carry out the obligations and agreements for Manitoba. This 1966 agreement specified, among other things, a methodology for land transfers and a distribution of profits arising from export sales between the three parties in proportion to investment.[1]

The resulting Churchill–Nelson Hydroelectric Project consisted of the Churchill River Diversion, the Lake Winnipeg Regulation, and a series of generating stations on the Nelson River. By some estimates, up to 85 percent of the Churchill's waters were diverted into the Nelson River so that generating stations could be built along one waterway instead of two. The Churchill River was dammed at the eastern outlet of South Indian Lake and the level of the lake raised three metres by the Notigi Control Structure at Missi Falls, which was completed in September 1976 (Manitoba Hydro, History and Timeline). The lake overflowed southwards through a constructed channel into the Rat–Burntwood rivers system, which empties into the Nelson River.

The Nelson River drains Lake Winnipeg, the eleventh largest freshwater lake in the world. The Jenpeg Control Structure, completed in 1975 at the north end of the lake, effectively causes Lake Winnipeg to function as a large reservoir. Water is held back during spring and summer high flows, and released during the winter when electricity demand is greatest. The flow potential from Lake Winnipeg was doubled with construction of the Ominawin, Eight Mile, and Two Mile channels, which bypassed shallow and narrow passageways (Aitchison et al. 2001). Since the 1960s, five major dams have been constructed on the Nelson River.

Early in the development process, concerns were raised about the environmental damage predicted to result from the flooding and altered flow regime. The Manitoba Environment Council, which operates under the Manitoba Minister of the Environment and is responsible for providing advice to the Manitoba government on environmental matters, held a meeting on January 19, 1973, to assess potential impacts from the hydroelectric development. New Democratic Party (NDP) Minister Sidney Green declined to participate and, instead, responded in a letter to the Manitoba Environment Commission that the government had already been advised of potential environmental damage in previous reports, including The Crippen Report (January 1970), The Underwood McLellen Report (February 1970), The Hydro Task Force Report (October 1970), and the McTaggert–Cowan Report (August 1972). According to Manitoba Environment Council co-chair Ken Arenson, Minister Green wanted it "clearly understood that he did not wish the [Manitoba Environment] Council to advise him on this matter. He does not believe that the Council's advice will help him because the government is already aware of the potential environmental damage" (Axworthy and Arenson 1984).

The reports cited by Minister Green called for attention to the issue and contained recommendations like this one from the Underwood McClellen report: "The socioeconomic structure of a community is as sensitive to changes as the ecological balance existing in nature. . . . It is essential to realize that abrupt and major changes among these people are about to occur, particularly in the communities of Nelson House and South Indian Lake. A relatively short period of time remains to institute programs which will alleviate the possible detrimental effects of change" (Underwood et al. 1970).

A joint federal-provincial Study Board composed of representatives from Manitoba Hydro, the federal government, and the government of Manitoba was appointed in 1971 and given a mandate to examine potential impacts. The Study Board activities were conducted while development was underway (construction began on the Kettle Generating Station in 1966); its summary report, which enumerated numerous anticipated impacts, was not released until 1975.

Despite the consensus among reports that major changes were about to occur among affected northern Aboriginal communities, community members were not officially informed by the government about the Churchill–Nelson River Diversion project until after development had begun. In 1975, affected communities received letters from Premier Ed Schreyer along with an information bulletin "intended to provide residents of your community with some additional information about the Lake Winnipeg Regulation Project and its possible effects on your community" (Schreyer 1975). In spite of the findings of the Study Board that had been recently released, the premier downplayed the potential impacts of development and wrote that "it would be generally fair to say that the conditions which will actually occur will be at least favourable, or more favourable, than those predicted because the predictions are based on the worst possible consequences being foreseen in order to prepare for, or guard against, them." The report outlined effects to wildlife and fishing, concluding that "in general, the future of fishing possibilities in Cross Lake is good" and that the benefits of development included "direct color TV broadcasts of improved quality" and direct telephone service (Schreyer 1975).

In 1977, with hydro development underway, five of the affected Cree communities created the Northern Flood Committee and signed the NFA with Canada, Manitoba, and Manitoba Hydro. The NFA addresses the land exchange required for hydro development as well as the environmental and socio-economic problems created by the Churchill–Nelson rivers development. The NFA asserts that the hydroelectric development modified the water regime and caused adverse effects, and that "all persons as defined herein, who may be, or have been, directly or indirectly, adversely affected by the Project shall be dealt with fairly and equitably." Specific promises in the NFA include replacement of every flooded acre with four acres of undamaged land, monetary compensation for lost hunting, fishing, and trapping profits, and the eradication of poverty and unemployment.

The NFA communities were already covered by the 1875 Treaty 5, which was used by the federal government to acquire Aboriginal land title for expansion and consolidation of Canada. In return to the surrender of all title to treaty lands, the Aboriginal people received reserve lands and other benefits, including cash payments and provisions. They also reserved the right "to pursue their avocations of hunting and fishing throughout the tract surrendered as hereinbefore described."

The NFA was recognized as a modern treaty by Eric Robinson, Minister of Aboriginal and Northern Affairs, in a statement before the House on December 15, 2000: "For the first time in the history of this house, the Government of Manitoba recognizes that the Northern Flood Agreement is a modern day treaty and expresses its commitment to honor and properly implement the terms of the Northern Flood Agreement" (Robinson 2000).

THE ENVIRONMENTAL AND SOCIO-ECONOMIC ISSUES OF HYDRO DEVELOPMENT

Hydro construction, impoundment, and operations throughout Manitoba resulted in the flooding of approximately 600,000 acres, resulting in lost forest land and serious harm to the aquatic environment (Brennan 2004).

The land most affected by the hydroelectric development in northern Manitoba was the traditional domain of Cree, who still represent the majority of Manitoba's northern population.[2] The area is characterized by northern prairie and boreal forest interspersed with wetlands, rivers, and lakes. Manitoba's boreal forest is a mixture of conifers like black spruce and tamarack, and deciduous trees like quaking aspen and balsam poplar. The diversity of animal species includes grizzly and black bears, caribou, and wolverine (Gunn et al. 2001).

Some of the environmental impacts from hydroelectric development, —rotting vegetation and the impacts from construction activities—are ephemeral. Other environmental impacts that are ongoing or permanent may be static, like inundated land; variable, like water levels and erosion; or cumulative, like nutrient loading and the accumulation of methyl-mercury. Modifications to the aquatic habitat that have an impact on aquatic species at various life-cycle stages include alterations in flow regimes and water temperature, introduction and accumulation of contaminants, displacement of species, and disruption of food sources (McAllister et al. 2001; Culp 2000; Hartman 1996; FEMP 1992).

Upstream and reservoir impacts have included flooding, land inundation, and alteration of shorelines, which resulted in loss of habitat and biodiversity, increased sedimentation, changes to the river flow regime, and changes to the water chemistry. Impacts in the downstream areas included altered hydrology, such as lowered flow levels and diminished seasonal variation, erosion from bank-cutting, sedimentation, and changes in water chemistry and temperature. Diminished water quality resulted from the large amount of biomass left in the flooded area, and permanent increases in sedimentation resulted from changes in water level and flow (Goldemberg 2000).

The environmental impacts of large-scale hydropower development have social and human health implications, and, in the case of northern Manitoba, cultural dimensions. In a statement to the Minnesota Public Utilities Commission in 1999, Pimicikamak Cree member Kenny Miswaggon described these linkages.

> The mega-hydroproject, and the continuing use of the power
> it generates, has virtually destroyed our economy and culture,
> which is based on the environment. It has destroyed vast areas
> of forests, polluted the waters, generated large amounts of green-
> house gases of carbon dioxide and methane, and it has reversed
> the seasonal state of nature. It has killed or poisoned the fish with
> methyl-mercury, killed animals, birds and their habitats. Over
> the years, some of our people have lost their lives from drowning
> in hazardous water and ice conditions, and through a suicide
> epidemic, brought on by hopelessness, mass poverty and depri-
> vation of fundamental human rights. (MN PUC 1999)

Water contamination from the flooding of old mines, nutrient loading, and the build-up of methyl-mercury from altered flushing regimes continues to affect the health of local communities, through consumption of contaminated water and food sources like fish. Without intervention, mental and physical health impacts on humans residing in the region are likely to continue from poor water quality, injuries or fatalities resulting from unpredictable thin ice caused by fluctuating water flows, and suicide.

"MONITOR AND REPORT"

The legacy of these effects were in play on March 18, 2003, when the Minnesota Public Utilities Commission approved a contract for Xcel Energy to purchase 500 MW of power from Manitoba Hydro (MN PUC 2003). This purchase power agreement effectively renewed a twelve-year export agreement that has allowed Manitoba Hydro to export a maximum of 500 MW of firm power in Minnesota annually from May 1, 1993, to April 30, 2005 (Manitoba Hydro, History and Timeline).

Xcel Energy is Minnesota's largest single utility and provides half of the electricity consumed in the state (Nobles 2005). Electricity provided by Manitoba Hydro represents a relatively minor 4 percent of Xcel Energy's total energy portfolio (Brunetti 2004). However, 40 percent of the energy generated by Manitoba Hydro's fourteen hydro plants, two gas-fired thermal plants, and one coal-fired facility flows southward into the United States, and Xcel Energy is the single largest importer of this energy.

During the review process that preceded approval of the power purchase agreement, testimony before the Minnesota Public Utilities Commission from interested stakeholders highlighted the complexities of the agreement. Yet, there was a notable point of consensus: "none of the parties involved in the case, including Xcel Energy and the [Public Utilities] Commission, disputed the proposition that power generation in Manitoba had caused environmental and socioeconomic harm to relator" (MN Court of Appeals 2004). Whether this harm had been adequately addressed, however, was the key issue.

Attention focused on remediation of the environmental and socio-economic impacts of the hydro development in Manitoba, and specifically on the question of adherence to Minnesota Statute 216B.2422. Subdivision 3 of this statute requires the Minnesota Public Utilities Commission to quantify and establish a range of environmental costs associated with each method of electricity generation. A utility must then use these values to factor in externalities, including socio-economic costs, when evaluating and selecting resource options.[3]

In considering the responsibility of Xcel Energy to account for the external costs associated with power purchased from Manitoba Hydro, the Minnesota Public Utilities Commission concluded that the *Northern Flood Agreement*, a treaty signed by five Aboriginal communities, Manitoba Hydro, the Manitoba government, and the Canadian government on December 16, 1977, provided a mechanism for internalization of the socio-economic and environmental costs associated with large-scale hydroelectric development. "Based on its review, the [Public Utilities] Commission finds that the treaty provides comprehensive relief for 'all the adverse results of the Project', i.e. the negative socioeconomic effects of the hydro projects at issue in this matter" (MN PUC 2001). The Minnesota Public Utilities Commission also found that the NFA "contains specific provisions providing for compensation lands, wildlife and fishing rights, programs to compensate for adverse effects on trapping and fishing, the construction of remedial works, the provision of a continuous supply of potable drinking water, removal of obstructions to navigation, comprehensive community planning and other matters" (MN PUC 2001). Based on these findings, the Minnesota Public Utilities Commission concluded that by signing the NFA, Manitoba Hydro had effectively signed a promissory note to internalize the socio-economic and environmental costs, and, therefore, the bid price presented to Xcel Energy by Manitoba Hydro would account for these costs.

Stakeholders opposed to the power purchase agreement on the basis of compliance with Minnesota law were denied their request for a contested case hearing by the Minnesota Public Utilities Commission. This ruling was subsequently upheld by the State of Minnesota Court of Appeals on March 30, 2004: "The environmental and socioeconomic impacts caused by the Manitoba Project are capable of being addressed under the NFA" (MN Court of Appeals 2004). The Court of Appeals determined that the Public Utilities Commission had met its obligations under the Minnesota statute and referred further responsibility for meeting Minnesota law to Xcel Energy: "Under the statute, any further examination of the effects regarding the extent of uncompensated and unremediated environmental and socioeconomic costs of the Manitoba Hydro Project were to be carried out by the utility, Xcel Energy" (MN Court of Appeals 2004).

Having determined that the NFA was the appropriate mechanism by which external costs associated with power generation by Manitoba Hydro could be internalized, focus shifted to assessing NFA implementation. Xcel Energy reported that since its 1998 Resource Plan, it has been monitoring implementation of the NFA (Clark 2002). In testimony before the Minnesota Public Utilities Commission (PUC), legal counsel for Xcel Energy expressed a willingness to supplement future resource plans with information from this monitoring (Clark 2002). Subsequently, when the power purchase agreement between Xcel Energy and Manitoba Hydro was agreed upon on March 18, 2003, the PUC directed Xcel Energy to "monitor and report" on the implementation of the NFA (MN PUC 2003).[4]

Concerns were raised throughout the power purchase review process regarding whether action in Minnesota constituted interference with tribal and Canadian sovereignty. The Nisichawayasihk Cree Nation (NCN), one of the five NFA communities, for instance, questioned whether the Minnesota Public Utilities Commission should take the NFA into account, arguing that "the [Public Utilities] Commission lacks jurisdiction to consider claims about the NFA and whether it has been fulfilled" (MN PUC 2002). Throughout the contract review process, however, fulfillment of NFA obligations had been cited as the specific avenue by which Minnesota state law could be met for the energy imported from Manitoba, notwithstanding the fact that as a Canadian treaty, the NFA is subject to international and Canadian terms of enforcement. Thus, once imported into Minnesota, the energy from Manitoba Hydro was found to be subject to the conditions of Minnesota state law and the NFA was determined to be an appropriate safeguard for Minnesota interests. In requiring that Xcel Energy monitor and report on implementation of the NFA, the PUC affirmed the responsibility of Xcel Energy to account for externalities and assure Minnesota consumers that the NFA is in fact conferring the environmental and socio-economic protections required by state law.

IMPLEMENTATION OF THE NFA

To "monitor and report" on implementation of the NFA, Xcel Energy must consider the record of preceding NFA activities. Implementation proved problematic after the NFA was signed. By 1986, full compensation within the timeline proposed by the NFA had not been provided and comprehensive negotiations were undertaken to pursue implementation. Each of the NFA parties appointed a negotiator to work towards a "Proposed Basis of Settlement of Outstanding Claims and Obligations." By summer of 1990, the negotiations were complete and recommendations were forwarded to the five NFA communities. By August 1990, Split Lake Cree Nation opted to proceed and, in June 1992, signed an Implementation Agreement. Three of the four remaining communities also eventually signed implementation agreements: Nelson House in 1995, York Landing in 1996, and Norway House in 1997. The agreements vary between the four communities, but in general include financial compensation, usually in the form of Hydro bonds placed in a trust to be used by the First Nation to address adverse effects on members and to provide capital for the long-term benefit of the community; compensation lands; provisions relating to water levels and flows; establishment of a resource management board for the resource management areas for each of the First Nations; and provisions for ongoing environmental monitoring.

Both between and within affected communities, including those who have signed implementation agreements and those who have not, controversy remains over whether the NFA has been implemented, and whether these agreements have provided satisfactory reparations for damages. Each implementation agreement includes a clause that calls for termination of that community's claims under the NFA,[5] although Eric Robinson, as Minister of Aboriginal and Northern Affairs, has stated: "[T]he Government acknowledges the comprehensive implementation agreements negotiated in good faith and signed with four NFA First Nations as one method of addressing and implementing the terms of the NFA" (Robinson 2000).

The Pimicikamak Cree Nation (PCN), which has not signed an implementation agreement, is pursuing implementation of the NFA through various action plans. On December 16, 2002, a plan was announced among Manitoba, Manitoba Hydro, and the Pimicikamak Cree Nation with initiatives to implement the NFA over a period of fifteen months. The plan included provisions to clear the Jenpeg forebay of debris, address outstanding land exchange issues, and develop recreational resources (Manitoba Hydro 2003). Results at the conclusion of the fifteen-month action plan were mixed. According to the PCN NFA implementation officer, the Jenpeg forebay was cleaned, but Sipiwisk Lake was not, and the promised playgrounds and skating rinks were not built (personal communication, Cross Lake, 2004). PCN entered into a new action plan for 2004–2005 and will receive $5 million from Manitoba Hydro and the province to continue implementation activities.

Additionally, the original NFA did not include all affected groups. Settlements have since been sought by South Indian Lake, displaced residents of South Indian Lake, Métis groups, and other organizations, and negotiations are ongoing to secure redress for all who were or continue to be affected by the hydro development.

Manitoba Hydro has expressed a desire to advance beyond the controversy. Victor Schroeder, chair of the board of Manitoba Hydro, for instance, has said, "Certainly, if we were to do it over again, it would not be done the way that it was done. The basics can't be undone. How do we now go forward?" (Knoy 2000). One potentially important mechanism for "moving forward" is the development and implementation of a practical and transparent monitoring system. The Environmental Impact Statement (EIS) by Manitoba Hydro for the proposed development at Wuskwatim, for instance, demonstrates that Manitoba Hydro appreciates the need for monitoring, and lays out a plan in the Wuskwatim proposal to monitor environmental impacts (Wuskwatim EIS 2003).

While it is an acknowledgement of the importance of monitoring, the Wuskwatim monitoring plan falls short. The proposal from Manitoba Hydro assumes as a baseline for future developments the current regulated system instead of the historical natural system. There have been no suggestions from the company that it will explore a comprehensive monitoring approach to address the outstanding controversies over past development and NFA implementation, even though the World Commission on Dams (WCD) determined that "opportunities exist to optimize benefits from many existing dams, address outstanding social issues, and strengthen environmental mitigation and restoration measures" (WCD 2000). Capitalizing on these opportunities requires:

1) introduction of a comprehensive post-project monitoring and evaluation process, and a system of longer term periodic reviews of the performance, benefits, and impacts for all existing large dams;

2) identification and implementation of programs to restore, improve, and optimize benefits from existing large dams;

3) identification and assessment of outstanding social issues associated with existing large dams, and processes and mechanisms developed with affected communities to remedy them; and

4) assessment of the effectiveness of existing environmental mitigation measures and identification of opportunities for mitigation, restoration, and enhancement (WCD 2000).

In addition to advocating that existing dams be addressed and outstanding issues be tackled before additional development proceeds, the WCD calls for annual and freely accessible publications of monitoring results to all stakeholders. Although there are partial records of intended activities in northern Manitoba, such as the action plans that have been negotiated by PCN, there is no comprehensive report summarizing current implementation activities of the NFA. The last comprehensive report by one of the parties to the NFA that summarized activities related to implementation was published in 1987 by Indian and Northern Affairs Canada. No such reports have been identified from Manitoba or Manitoba Hydro and there is no evidence of a more recent report from any of the Crown parties on implementation activities.

In addressing the PUC order, therefore, Xcel Energy faces the lack of an organized and ongoing monitoring regime and the lack of a comprehensive, up-to-date summary of NFA implementation activities. However, as Jason Miller, a youth council representative from Cross Lake Cree Nation, observed, "the real measure of whether the NFA is being implemented or not is the objective conditions in the communities" (Miller 1999).

EFFECTS AND COMPLIANCE MONITORING

Collecting data and organizing it systematically—i.e, developing an effective monitoring regime—will make it possible for consumers in both Manitoba and Minnesota, Aboriginal communities, and other interested stakeholders to evaluate conditions in the communities to determine whether the NFA is being implemented and the socio-economic and environmental costs of hydroelectric development are being internalized. In developing a monitoring regime, Xcel Energy can pursue either effects and/or compliance monitoring. Effects monitoring measures the accuracy of predicted impacts and requires suitable baseline data for comparison. In situations where baseline data are unavailable, the focus of the monitoring shifts from effects monitoring to compliance monitoring of regulations and standards, or, in the case of Manitoba, the NFA.

It would be useful to establish a baseline of the impacts of hydro development in order to assess the actual impacts and effects of preventative and corrective measures, but a lack of pre-development studies makes this difficult. For instance, a 1996 report designed to evaluate the adequacy of baseline studies for examining impacts to the Split Lake Cree Nation, one of the five NFA communities, found a lack of sufficient pre-project and post-project data for wildlife populations, plant communities, fisheries harvest, subsistence wildlife, transportation and navigation, and recreational uses. Information on water quality, sedimentation, waterfowl, fish habitat, historic resources, and health and safety was determined to be geographically or temporally incomplete, or methodologically flawed (Lawrence 1996, vol. 4). "Limited scientific information exists on the biological impacts, and, with respect to impacts on the socio-economic environment, such information is scarce, except with respect to commercial resource harvesting" (Lawrence 1996, vol. 5).

The lack of baseline information makes effects monitoring difficult; it does not, however, preclude compliance monitoring. Furthermore, the NFA provides explicit structure for a monitoring system. Where information gaps exist, the NFA can be monitored by identifying proxy indicators for which there are records, assembling incomplete records with complete disclosure of their deficiencies, incorporating traditional knowledge, and identifying comparable systems from which a comparative assessment could be done. As the reviewers at Split Lake determined, "generic and project-specific predictions of impacts do exist that provide an indication of the type of adverse and beneficial effects to expect" (Lawrence 1996, vol. 5).

INDICATORS AS A METHOD OF MONITORING

An indicator is a quantitative measure that describes an economic, environmental, social, or cultural condition over time; an indicator system is an organized effort to assemble and disseminate a group of indicators that together tell a story about position and progress (US GAO 2004). Carefully chosen indicators that are relevant, reliable, outcome-based, easy to understand, and based on accessible data are a useful method for translating monitoring regimes into tangible, measurable outcomes. A set of indicators linked to specific NFA provisions would be a useful tool to assure Minnesotans and Manitobans alike that externalities are accounted for. By emphasizing outward results along a chosen set of acceptable goals, indicators could provide a measure to quantify whether the NFA is being successfully implemented and the extent to which implementation is advancing over time. This systematic approach would be more productive than monitoring the ever-changing negotiations and action plans being developed, as the focus would be on tangible outcomes rather than process. Additionally, much of the data to complete these indicators exists;

completing the indicators is a matter of identifying suitable information sources and aggregating them appropriately to address the issue at hand.

To monitor implementation of the NFA for northern Manitoba, indicators should be developed to verify predictions, clarify uncertainties, and track historical and ongoing changes to the physical environment as a result of the hydro development. Indicator design should be intentional and transparent. Useful monitoring systems currently in place could be identified and evaluated, and the responsible agencies, their operating mandates, and options for restructuring or expanding reporting identified, or, when necessary, independent and objective mechanisms proposed. In addition to community councils, local NFA offices, and Manitoba Hydro, there are numerous agencies in Manitoba and Canada collecting information that Minnesota can adapt to inform indicators, such as Statistics Canada; Aboriginal and Northern Affairs in Manitoba; Indian and Northern Affairs, Canada; Manitoba Office of Health Canada; and Environment Canada. However, it is important to avoid biasing indicators towards areas with existing measures; the focus of an indicator system must be on addressing the provisions contained within the NFA, not simply on the areas currently being measured.

In order to address concerns of transparency and accountability for Minnesota consumers as required under the PUC's ruling, Xcel Energy should develop a reporting structure about NFA implementation that is open and accessible. Minnesota consumers should be granted access to the information being used to evaluate their energy purchases. Additionally, the protocol should be both practical and amenable to revisions as necessary to incorporate learning. Whatever monitoring protocol is developed and reported on, it should contain adequate feedback loops that allow it to evolve and adapt as needed.

The structure and scope of the indicators must match the goals of monitoring. In the present case, Xcel Energy is charged with monitoring implementation of the NFA in order to ensure that externalities associated with energy generation have been incorporated in accordance with state law. Because hydroelectric generation in northern Manitoba is achieved through the operation of the system in its entirety, with no differentiation with regard to exported energy, the indicators should account for the Churchill River Diversion Project as a whole.

THE NFA AS A FRAMEWORK FOR AN INDICATOR SYSTEM

The NFA addresses environmental and socio-economic issues, and clearly identifies items that can be assessed, including human health, physical and cultural heritage, land and resource use, and the physical and biological environment, including terrestrial and aquatic ecosystems. Socio-economic, cultural, and environmental indicators can be identified from NFA provisions, and used to structure an indicator system to monitor implementation.

What follows are a few specific examples of how indicators might be used to assess the NFA themes of employment and income, shorelines and debris, water fluctuations, and arbitration. Additional provisions of the NFA are then presented, along with preliminary suggestions for possible indicators. This assessment is not complete or definitive, but is meant to examine the provisions of the NFA with the goal of suggesting a potential system for impartial and quantifiable measurement.

Employment and income. In addition to Schedule E, which calls for the eradication of "mass unemployment," the NFA contains provisions specifically addressing employment and training opportunities. Article 18.5 states that "it is in the public interest to employ, to the maximum possible extent, residents of the subject Reserves in all works and operations related to the Project and to implement forthwith practical measures necessary to achieve that objective, including opportunities for education, training, and particularly on-the-job training of any able and willing resident," and to report on the results obtained in meeting this objective every three months. Article 12.3 calls for Canada and Manitoba to offer the opportunity and any assistance or training necessary to carry out the measures and works required for protection and restoration of community infrastructure, shorelines, and property of residents. Article 15.7 calls for Manitoba to provide training opportunities for residents to become qualified for employment as conservation officers.

A number of indicators could be monitored to assess fulfillment of these NFA articles and there are numerous agencies in Manitoba and Canada collecting employment and income information that is useful to inform these indicators. A range of options exists for structuring and evaluating the different data available to address these issues, including community income levels, government transfers as a percentage of total income, community employment,[6] and work opportunities available to community members.

Shorelines and debris. For the purpose of maintaining the rights of community residents to free and normal navigation, articles 5.3.2 and 5.3.3 state that Manitoba Hydro will clear standing trees that become a navigation problem "now or in the future" and will "remove debris of any nature which results from the actual construction or from the flooding of land or by diversion of waters in the total area encompassed by the overall Project." Articles 12.5.5 and 13.1 call for shorelines to be cleared to retain the traditional and intended use of shorelines by residents. Additionally, articles 12.3 and 12.5.1 and 12.5.2 call for protection and restoration of shorelines.

Shorelines can be catalogued by their degree of, or susceptibility to, slumping and erosion. A report by the University of Manitoba civil engineering department that classified the shorelines in the Churchill–Nelson system was released in January of 1973. Examinations along previously regulated waterways led the researchers to conclude that while shorelines, riverbanks, and valleys not affected by artificial controls naturally adjusted to normal process rates of erosion and deposition, "shorelines, riverbanks and valleys subject to flooding or increased flows generally exhibited an unstable form in which erosion and deposition processes were greatly accelerated. In all cases of controls that changed the regime of lake levels or flows by a significant amount (+/- five feet in level or 50 percent in flow), the water-land interfaces were in a transient state in spite of ages of projects that ranged up to 34 years" (University of Manitoba 1973).[7]

The current state of shorelines in the project area could be assessed by comparing the amount of shorelines with debris to those that have been cleared. After an initial assessment of the total amount of affected shorelines, an annual report on shoreline clean-up could be reduced to the quantity of areas needing attention relative to the quantity of those that have been cleared. The system total of remaining shorelines with debris could be calculated to determine how much clearing remains over time.

Water fluctuations. The NFA places limits on water level maximums. Article 3.9.1 gives static inundation levels for waterways adjacent to each community that Manitoba Hydro, by controlling the flow of water on the regulated waterways to the extent that is possible and within its control, is not to exceed. Article 3.9.2 states that Manitoba Hydro will use all practical means to prevent any inundation of reserve land between the static inundation level and the severance line (the upland boundary of the easement land). Article 9.3 requires Manitoba Hydro to provide two-week written notice before making any operating changes that will affect the water levels or flows. Article 9.4 requires radio notice in both English and Cree for at least three successive days, as well as any other reasonable forms of notice the communities may periodically request.

Historic flow and water level records exist or have been estimated, and illustrate the reversal of water highs and lows brought about by regulation of the system. In Cross Lake, for instance, water level highs traditionally occurred in late summer (August) and lows occurred in spring (April). With regulation, water level highs now occur in January and lows in June (Federal Ecological Monitoring Program 1992). Such fluctuations have multiple impacts, which could each be assessed individually: the impact of low summer water levels on fish; the effect on the use of the lake for recreational and resource harvesting purposes from low water levels in summer and poor ice conditions in winter; and the aggravation and acceleration of shoreline erosion, to name a few.

An indicator could be developed that monitors fulfillment of reporting provisions for water fluctuation events. Community members have requested greater communication of imminent changes, and that reasonable warning be given so that people who are affected by the lake fluctuations have enough time to remove their fishing nets. There is already significant monitoring of daily and real-time water levels throughout the system. Environment Canada operates a Web site that reports real-time monitoring of daily water levels and contains data on historic flows and levels for several of the regulated waterways.[8] Sudden changes in water levels and flows are obvious when graphed over time. Establishing an accepted threshold level and tabulating the instances of extreme water fluctuations in a year through a review of this data would indicate the number of times community members should have been warned of impending changes. Manitoba Hydro can provide Xcel Energy with the same warning reports that it issues to communities, and Xcel Energy can compare the reports from Manitoba Hydro with the hydrometric data.

Arbitration. Article 24 of the NFA, or the arbitration clause, contains a lengthy and detailed account of arbitration matters. Historical use of arbitration suggests that rather than providing a mechanism for implementation, it became a method of non-implementation, as claims for compensation originally promised under the NFA were often instead referred to the arbitrator, which increased the time and effort required to receive the promised compensation. Arbitration has been cited in PUC hearings as a key mechanism for implementing the NFA. If the NFA is being implemented and arbitration is working, the number of claims and lawsuits being filed should be decreasing.

Details of all arbitration claims from the NFA Arbitration Claims and Settlements Office could be monitored and reported. The most recent report available on the status of arbitration claims, from 1977–1987, indicates that of 147 claims that had been filed, 75 had been settled (Indian and Northern Affairs, *Arbitration Claims* 1987). This report should be updated with the number and description of claims, the outcome, and the time required from the filing of the claim to resolution of the claim; the time elapsed from the date of the claim to the date of final settlement would allow for more comprehensive assessment of the effectiveness of arbitration as a mechanism for implementing the NFA.

Continuation of traditional activities. Provisions in the NFA support the continuation of traditional activities for sustenance and income. Article 15.3

states that "Manitoba has encouraged and will continue to encourage the residents of Reserves to achieve the maximum degree of self sustenance in food supplies and to maximize the opportunity to earn income and income-in-kind from the wildlife resources," and article 15.8 states that "the parties agree to facilitate and encourage the functions served by the community traplines, by reason of their contribution to the community." Article 19.4 states that compensation will be provided for adverse effects on fishing "to encourage the fishermen in each community to continue to fish."

Measurements of resource harvesting could be obtained through proxy indicators like fur transactions, or directly, such as surveying the number of days spent living on the land. Program 56 of Pimicikamak's proposed 04/05–05/06 Action Plan encourages active participation in life on the land by providing individual support payments for these activities; registration through this plan will generate a record of participants, which would provide appropriate and useful data for MN to consider.

Energy. Article 18.4 states that Manitoba Hydro, Manitoba, and Canada should use their "best efforts to ensure that potential benefits of the Project are made available as a practical manner to the residents of each reserve." As a direct benefit of the hydroelectric development, it is important to measure patterns of household energy use in the communities. There was a policy of charging higher rates to northern households in effect until 2000 (Robinson 2000). The pricing policy has since been changed and households in northern and rural communities are supposed to pay the same basic rate for hydro services as households in urban centres (Robinson 2000). However, rates relative to northern household incomes are reportedly still high. It is not an uncommon occurrence for households to have their electricity disconnected for non-payment of bills, even in the winter, and many Elders in the community pay as much as two-thirds of their retirement benefits to Manitoba Hydro (Waldram 1988; personal communication, Elders 2004).

In addition to equitable distribution of hydro development benefits, energy consumption can serve as a proxy indicator of poverty and housing quality. The average size of energy bills in northern Aboriginal communities relative to other areas in Manitoba may serve to demonstrate the quality of

housing. The number of people who have had their energy service disconnected for non-payment may indicate poverty (although the correlation
may not be complete, particularly in Cross Lake, where non-payment of
energy bills has become a form of protest). Data to inform an indicator
reflecting energy consumption should be available from Manitoba Hydro.

Education and training. The duration of the NFA is the lifetime of the hydro
development project. Therefore, it is important to monitor education and
training opportunities at all levels to meet the employment and training
provisions contained in articles 12.3, 15.7, and 18.5, and to work towards
the "eradication of mass poverty and mass unemployment" promised in
Schedule E.

Indicators could consist of standardized test scores, and funding for
training and educational programs. Monitoring standardized test scores
along with graduation rates provides an indication of the health of the
schools. Anecdotally, the current situation in Nelson House is disquieting:
last year, all the eighth graders in NCN failed their provincially administered standardized test (personal communication, Nelson House 2004).
But while western measurements of education performance can illuminate
the prevailing inadequacy of education that exists in many Indigenous
communities, the solution to monitoring this situation is not to rely solely
on western education standards and systems (personal communication,
PCN counsel 2004). Rather, funding and support provided to indigenous
communities that allow them to develop and implement their own culturally appropriate education system should be monitored as well. Manitoba
Department of Education, Citizens and Youth, and Indian and Northern
Affairs Canada could be a source for data on standardized test results, graduation rates, and program funding. The extent to which training programs
exist and the levels of enrolment indicate the availability of opportunities for adults, and it is important to monitor and report on these as well.
Funding for the development and operation of training programs as well
as enrolment data could be obtained from the government of Manitoba and
Manitoba Hydro.

Navigation and transportation. Articles 5.1 and 5.3 of the NFA state that "residents of the reserves have a right to free and normal navigation of the waterways" and that "Manitoba and/or Hydro undertake to maximize the free and normal use of the navigable waters." Article 8.2 states that "Hydro shall provide a large scale map or maps to each Band Council indicating areas which may from time to time be rendered unsafe for travel in summer or winter as a result of the Project," and article 12.5 provides for alternate transportation facilities to compensate for adverse affects on transportation.

Indicators could track the occurrence and frequency of safe-ice route marking. Members of PCN report that safe-ice routes are marked infrequently over the winter period, and are concerned that this does not adequately account for the fact that the ice is constantly changing with the changes in flow. Indicators could also record local data on accidents and loss of equipment (boats, motors, snowmobiles, dog sleds) and lives during summer and winter months on the water and ice. Local police and fire departments often are involved in search-and-rescue operations and would have relevant data. The Pimicikamak Cree NFA Claims Office and other communities should have information available that will reflect the efficacy of mapping, warning, and clearing programs for providing "free and normal" transportation and navigation.

Land exchange. Article 3 states that communities would receive four acres of land for every acre of affected land, and articles 3.12.2 and 8.1 provide for maps to show the land transfers. NFA article 8.1 directed Manitoba Hydro to provide, as soon as possible, maps of each community showing the affected lands in order to provide a quantitative record of the affected land and a basis to evaluate any subsequent transfers.

Housing and infrastructure. Article 12.1 states that "measures and works which are required for the protection, restoration or adjustment, in relation to the new water regime, of community infrastructure, shorelines, and/or property of residents shall be undertaken at Hydro's expense." Articles 12.5.4 and 12.5.6 call for the replacement of docks and the protection and/or relocation of roads, houses, and other structures. Schedule E of the NFA committed to setting forth "the improvement of the physical, social and economic conditions and transportation."

Resident concerns, particularly in South Indian Lake, regard outstanding claims for adequate replacement of housing destroyed by flooding. Infrastructure indicators could include maintenance reports and funding appropriations for housing. Housing conditions could be tracked, with proof of NFA implementation of this provision being a shrinking number of houses needing attention. Maintenance and funding records could also be tracked for the wastewater plants and sanitation systems provided by Hydro when the communities were relocated.

Canada Housing and Mortgage Corporation and Indian and Northern Affairs Canada generate monthly and yearly operating reports. The Manitoba Bureau of Statistics may also be able to provide housing data. Infrastructure information could be obtained from permitting and regulating agencies, such as registrations with Manitoba Environment for operating sewage and waste management facilities.

Drinking water quality. Article 6.1 states that "Canada accepts responsibility to ensure the continuous availability of a potable water supply on each of the Reserves. The quality of the water shall meet the health and safety standards set by Canada to protect the public health." Article 6.2 charges Manitoba Hydro for half the expenses for providing water if need for that water is attributable to the effects of the project.

Manitoba Hydro built and operates the Nelson House water treatment plant, but there are concerns voiced by residents, who report tasting chlorine in the water and incidents of intestinal health problems, that the plant is not maintained appropriately. As of August 2004 in Nelson House, home water storage tanks that were supposed to be cleaned every month had not been cleaned since summer of 2003 (personal communication, Nelson House 2004), and residents report a broken sewage line that leaks refuse into the bay of the same lake from which drinking water is drawn. Independent testing of water samples from resident tanks and the community water supply in September 2004 revealed high levels of e-coli bacteria, coliform, and heterotrophic plate counts. A doctor in Cross Lake voiced similar concerns about maintenance of the PCN water treatment plant (personal communication, Cross Lake 2004).

Indicators to monitor drinking water quality could include water test results, maintenance records of treatment plants, and maintenance and operational expenditures. Manitoba's Office of Health Canada is required to monitor and report local water quality to ensure safe drinking water, which is evaluated according to Canadian drinking water quality standards. Currently, these data are unavailable to the general public. If the data cannot be supplied to Xcel Energy by either Manitoba's Office of Health Canada or Manitoba Hydro, a third party should be charged with acquiring quarterly water testing results.

Recreation. Articles 12.5.3 and 12.5.7 of the NFA promised the construction of new beaches or locations suitable for swimming and the provision of alternate recreational opportunities or facilities. The NFA provides for recreation facilities because hydro development severely damaged and rendered unsafe natural recreation opportunities provided by ice in the winter and beaches and lakes in the summer.

An indicator tracking recreation opportunities available in the community might include a record of available and usable facilities, the annual number of users, the number of programs, and a record of funds used to facilitate recreation opportunities. PCN, who are engaged in active negotiations with Manitoba Hydro, have a lighted ball field, an arena with free electricity, and an ice surface open twenty-four hours. However, the promise to construct new beaches suitable for swimming has not yet been fulfilled. The local community reports that beaches are muddy and infested with weeds, the water has an unpleasant odour, and skin rashes result from exposure. Facts such as these are relevant in determining whether a beach is suitable for swimming, and whether the NFA provision for recreation alternatives are being met.

Physical and mental health. The NFA promises to deal fairly and equitably with all people adversely affected by the project, whether directly or indirectly, for the lifetime of the project. In addition to the eradication of poverty,

Schedule E also promises to improve the physical, social, and economic conditions of the communities. Physical and mental health concerns represent both direct and indirect adverse impacts of the project.

There is a need to address health issues that arise from the mass poverty that the NFA promises to eradicate and the dispossession from the land and a way of life that accompanied hydro development. Health concerns related to poverty and shifts in diet from the disruption of resource harvesting include diabetes and heart disease. Mental health is also a concern in affected communities. High rates of youth suicide persist in the these communities; the notes left behind often say, "We do not want to live this way anymore" (personal communication, Cross Lake 2004). Suicide rates in Aboriginal communities in affected communities are significantly higher than the Canadian national average. In a six-week period in the summer of 2004, three teenagers from South Indian Lake committed suicide.

Local community health officers, nursing stations, and the Manitoba Department of Public Health should be able to provide annual data on mental and physical health issues. Health Canada, the Royal Canadian Mounted Police, and Manitoba Health Services Commission also regularly collect health data. Additional information should be collected on suicide rates, diabetes rates, and infant mortality rates. Funding for traditional physical medical care and mental health services such as suicide prevention hotlines, drug and alcohol treatment, and sex abuse counselling services, could also be monitored.

Cultural health. Articles 7.1 and 7.3 call for funds to protect and preserve objects of cultural significance. Articles 15.3 and 15.8 encourage the continuation of traditional skills. Schedule E calls for the improvement of social conditions in the communities.

Indicators to monitor traditional cultural strength and knowledge can include the number of oral histories completed; the number of traditional activities, feasts, and celebrations; the number of programs that promote learning from Elders; and the number of gatherings (MacPherson and Netro 1994). Respect and caring for Elders could be reflected in the number of community events for Elders, number of Elders involved in decision making, and the living conditions of Elders. The transmission of language to young people is another measure of cultural resilience. In fulfilling article 7 provisions for protection and preservation of objects' cultural significance, maps could be designed to coordinate preservation and record keeping, and funds for these purposes could be monitored.

In Cross Lake, the radio station broadcasts in Cree, and during the week of August 12, 2004, PCN held its first powwow, complete with canoe races and a talent competition, in about 100 years. Regular meetings of the Elders Council and Youth Council provide other indications of cultural health. Manitoba Hydro and the government of Canada through the *Northern Flood Agreement* should be providing annual funds for traditional activities and preservation, and these funds could be monitored.

Aquatic systems. Article 15.4 of the NFA recognizes that "individuals who are permanently resident in or near a Resource Area may habitually hunt, trap, and/or fish within the Resource Area and would expect that both themselves and their progeny should continue to be able to enjoy these benefits from the Resource Area." Article 19.4 agrees to fund and implement "a program to provide for equitable compensation of all adverse effects on fishing activities within the Resource Area, arising directly or indirectly from the Project; which includes fishing rehabilitation and improvement. Article 15.5 calls for the establishment of a Wildlife Advisory and Planning Board, with majority representation of community residents. The board would monitor the wildlife resources, encourage the annual harvest, and formulate and recommend the implementation of programs and works that protect and perpetuate the wildlife in the resource area. The activities of this board could be used to provide information on the state of wildlife within the terrestrial and aquatic ecosystems.

Indicators might include annual catch-per-unit-effort surveys, mercury levels of fish, and population counts. Fishery monitoring data could be obtained from the Manitoba Department of Conservation and Water Stewardship and the Canada Department of Fisheries and Oceans on an annual basis. Information on the mercury levels in fish could be obtained by the Freshwater Fish Marketing Corporation. Additionally, Environment

Canada, Manitoba Environment, Manitoba Natural Resources, and the Canadian Wildlife Services collect data on fish and waterfowl populations.

Environmental water quality. Monitoring the state of environmental water quality is important for meeting the NFA provisions for protecting the aquatic habitat and fisheries, and reducing adverse impacts from hydro development as called for in articles 15.4 and 15.5.

Sampling regimes for environmental water quality are many and consistent in the literature. Parameters to test, from an environmental perspective, include TSS/turbidity, true colour (indicates dissolved and suspended materials in water), dissolved oxygen, water temperature, nutrients (nitrate, phosphate, organic carbon), pH, hardness (calcium chloride concentration), alkalinity, total dissolved solids and conductivity, bacteria and parasites, major ions, metals and metalloids, and hydrocarbons. The results can be compared to provincial and national criteria for the protection of aquatic ecosystems and wildlife. Annual water monitoring data may be obtained from the Manitoba Department of Conservation and Water Stewardship, and Canada Department of Fisheries and Oceans.

Terrestrial system. While the greatest adverse environmental impact of the hydro development is on aquatic ecosystems, terrestrial systems are also affected and covered by articles 15.4 and 15.5. The boreal forest is rapidly declining, and wildlife can be particularly sensitive to the cumulative impacts of development. One indicator might include an update of Manitoba's endangered species populations, their locations, and available habitat. The advances of GIS and other visual-spatial technologies means that mapping could be a powerful tool to fulfill monitoring of some of the provisions of the NFA related to natural resources management, and to the extent that Manitoba Hydro utilizes this technology, appropriate indicators can be developed to communicate the findings.

Capital flows. While implementation of the NFA must be more than financial payments, it is important for the capital flows to be part of the information collected from northern Manitoba. Full public disclosure of all funding arrangements would allow accountability for the amounts Manitoba Hydro reports having spent in the communities. A breakdown of spending is an important consideration, as NFA provisions call for both *specific* appropriations (e.g., article 7.1 calls for funding and supplies necessary to protect the remaining cemeteries from project-related flooding; article 19 calls for fishing and trapping assistance programs to supplement loss in income as a result of adverse affects), and *sufficient* appropriations (article 12.6 provides for an annual review of the capital amount spent on community infrastructure to ensure that reasonable costs can be met). Additionally, community members have expressed concerns that money is being spent on external lawyers and consultants, and that general infrastructure improvements Hydro requires for its operations are being counted in these payment reports.

Audit reports are issued by most of the communities and are available on-line.[9] Manitoba Hydro could also provide detailed appropriations reports. It is also important to compare government funding received in the communities, such as welfare payments, since the NFA payments, as stated in article 2.4, are not supposed to diminish other services the communities are entitled to receive.

Operational considerations. Article 10 of the NFA calls for the minimization of damage, stating that "Manitoba shall have regard to minimizing the destruction of wildlife by controlling the water levels and flows to the extent that it is practical to do so." The flow and retention of water in northern Manitoba to regulate electricity generation create the greatest ongoing disruption to both people and environmental components of the system. PCN cited concerns that approval of Manitoba Hydro's Power Purchase Agreement "will result in changes to the existing hydro system operations that will exacerbate the environmental and associated socioeconomic impacts" (MN PUC 2001).

An important consequence of operational improvements can be mitigation of environmental impacts. Various operational adjustments could have positive results for aquatic systems. Several options can be employed to minimize losses to aquatic species amounts and diversity, including passage facilities like fish ladders, sediment control measures like watershed management, debris dams, sediment flushing and dredging, and minimization of thermal stratification and extreme temperature changes through changes in the configurations of inlet structures, multilevel outlets, and mixing with compressed air or fountains (Goldemberg 2000).

Reporting. Articles 17.3 and 17.5 provide for a reporting structure based on the recommendations of the Lake Winnipeg, Churchill, and Nelson rivers Study Board. Article 20.3 calls for engagement with the communities between Hydro and Manitoba in formulating action plans. Article 16.1 calls for the formulation of a Community Development Plan for each community.

Northern Aboriginal peoples have requested more open communication and dissemination of information. For instance, South Indian Lake water level reports are broadcast on a channel in Thompson that residents in South Indian Lake cannot receive, so the residents receive no warning of water changes. The desire to have documents translated into Cree, particularly so the Elders can be fully informed, has been expressed and is called for by the NFA. The degree to which information is made accessible to all members of all communities is an important component in determining adherence to the NFA, and indicators can be selected to monitor the provision of information through "local workshops; local liaison officers; radio, television, film and any other appropriate medium; and publications in native languages," as called for in article 20.3.

Future development. Article 9.1 of the NFA states that notice will be given to the communities regarding intentions to prepare plans for future development, and article 9.2 states that meaningful consultation must precede any future development.

Indicators should demonstrate that the communities are apprised of future developments well before the plans are prepared, with meetings to discuss future development held in the communities and at convenient times to allow all those potentially affected to participate. The Manitoba Clean Environment Commission in 2003 and 2004 held numerous meetings about a proposed new dam project, but no apparent hearings were held in the communities that would be most affected by the project.

Equitable distribution of funding for participation should also be demonstrated; if meetings are held outside the communities, monitoring should show that funds were provided for both proponents and opponents of future development.

In many respects, not much has changed in the past forty years. Public outcry today resembles that put forth during the early years of development. Indeed, with one exception, all the public correspondence received by the PUC during the Xcel contract review process objected to the commission's approval of the Power Purchase Agreement with Manitoba Hydro. As noted by the PUC, the comments voiced "a concern over the environmental damage caused by the large hydro power development in Manitoba, and with the socioeconomic injury done to the Pimicikamak Cree Nation as a result of the hydro development" (MN PUC 2002). In other respects, however, a great deal has changed. In 1998, the PUC required Xcel Energy to monitor implementation of the NFA; in 2004, it required Xcel Energy to monitor *and* report. The change in wording was small; the change in meaning large.

A further step towards accountability was realized in 2007 when the Minnesota legislature passed the *Environment and Energy Omnibus Bill*. The legislation requires Manitoba Hydro officials to issue an annual report on the median household income and number of residents employed full time; the number of outstanding claims filed against Manitoba Hydro by individuals and communities and the number of claims settled by Manitoba Hydro; and the amount of shoreline damaged by flooding and erosion and the amount of shoreline restored and cleaned (Minnesota Statute, Chapter 57, 216C.052). Accountability is increasingly being demanded and proof is increasingly the litmus test.

The forty years of large-scale hydro development in northern Manitoba have produced a great deal of electricity for Manitobans and Minnesotans, significant profit for Manitoba Hydro and US utilities, and a reliable source of revenue for Manitoba. It has also created overwhelming heartache for northern Aboriginal communities and a fundamental distrust among affected northern communities, southern electricity consumers, corporate shareholders, and state and provincial legislators. A comprehensive, robust, and sincere monitoring plan could potentially create a bridge of trust that would benefit Manitobans and Minnesotans alike.

---

1   "This agreement made as of the 15th day of February, 1966, between: The government of Canada, represented herein by the Minister of Energy, Mines and Resources of the first part and the government of the province of Manitoba, represented herein by the Minister of Public Utilities of the second part." On reserve, Manitoba Legislative Reference Library. Winnipeg, MB. See especially section 17 and section 28 regarding the sale of "non-firm energy" to markets outside the province, and provisions for expansion should markets for power and excess energy inside or outside the province be identified.

2   Fifty-seven percent of the people in northern Manitoba in 2000 were Aboriginal, as defined by the Manitoba Department of Northern and Aboriginal Affairs, compared to 7 percent of the population in Winnipeg and 8.2 percent of the population outside Winnipeg in southern Manitoba. Demographic information from *Aboriginal People in Manitoba 2000*, Aboriginal and Northern Affairs, <www.gov. mb.ca/ana/apm2000/1/e.html>.

3   MN State Statutes 2003, 216B 2422: Subd. 3. "Environmental Costs. a) The commission shall, to the extent practicable, quantify and establish a range of environmental costs associated with each method of electricity generation. A utility shall use the values established by the commission in conjunction with other external factors, including socioeconomic costs, when evaluating and selecting resource options in all proceedings before the commission, including resource plan and certificate of need proceedings."

4   From the March 18, 2003, MN PUC order: "IV. NFA MONITORING Progress made implementing the NFA by four of the five affected Cree Nations testified to by Split Lake Cree Nation and NCN and the prospects for similar use of the NFA by PCN have been key factors in the Commission's determination that the environmental and socioeconomic harms done by the Manitoba Hydro Project have been adequately internalized, taken into account, and considered in this matter. The Commission, therefore, has an interest in the NFA and the ongoing ability of the parties to that treaty to use the treaty and related processes to address the environmental and socioeconomic harms done by the Manitoba Hydro Project. The Commission will direct Xcel to *monitor and report* on the status of the on-going implementation of the NFA in its next Resource Plan."

5   The language of the implementation agreements is clear. There are releases for Canada and Manitoba listed in each community's implementation agreement that are similar in wording to this release of Manitoba Hydro found in the implementation agreement signed by the Norway House Cree Nation: "Norway House Cree Nation hereby releases and forever discharges Hydro of and from any and all actions, causes of action, suits, claims, demands, losses or damages of any nature or kind whatsoever, at law or in equity, which Norway House Cree Nation, its successors, assigns or those it represents, have had, now have or hereafter can, shall or may have, for, or by reason of, any cause, matter or thing whatsoever to the extent attributable to Existing Development or arising out of, or under, the NFA, save and except as set forth in this Agreement, and including claims, if any, of a fiduciary nature which may have arisen in respect of Hydro's obligations to Norway House Cree Nation for anything done or omitted to be done by Hydro to the Date of this Agreement to the extent attributable to Existing Development or arising out of, or under, the NFA, save and except as set forth in this Agreement." Norway House NFA Sub Agreement. Aboriginal and Northern Affairs. The legality under Canadian law of extinguishing treaty rights in subsequent agreements has been called into question and is being examined by Peter Kulchyski, among others.

6   There is generally some discrepancy between the rates reported by Statistics Canada and members from the Aboriginal communities. For instance, Statistics Canada report unemployment rates from between 25 to over 52 percent in the affected communities, while community representatives report up to 75–85 percent unemployment rates. Rather than count only those actively seeking work as being unemployed, as the government does, a PCN member suggested that unemployment be measured as the number of people on welfare divided by the number of people working.

7   The amount of shoreline clogged by debris is reportedly being catalogued by Manitoba Hydro, which then dispatches clean-up crews to remove debris. Debris removal and clean-up has been a major focus of the PCN action plans, which has resulted in employment opportunities and shorelines cleared to the point that, in a few areas, only a maintenance program will be needed to prevent more trees from falling in the water. However, many kilometres of shoreline remain clogged by debris and shorelines continue to slump and erode throughout the system.

8   Real-time and historic hydrometric data are currently available on-line from Environment Canada for some locations. See Environment Canada Real-Time Hydrometric Monitoring Web site: <scitech.pyr.ec.gc.ca/waterweb/formnav>.

9   First Nations' community info and financial audits are available at
    <www.turtleisland.org/news-accountable.htm>.

PART III

TOWARD A CHANGE OF PARADIGM IN QUEBEC

THE *PAIX DES BRAVES*: AN ATTEMPT TO RENEW RELATIONS WITH THE CREE

Romeo Saganash
Jurist and Director
of Governmental Relations
and International Affairs
for the Grand Council of the Crees

IN 2002, QUEBEC PREMIER Bernard Landry and Grand Chief Ted Moses signed a major agreement, which has since become known as *Paix des Braves*. It was given this name because it signalled the making of peace between parties that have historically and almost constantly been at odds.

The word "partnership" is often used in cases where true partnership is simply not possible. It is sometimes used to disguise what is really going on, including dispossession. Real "partnership" demands genuine equality of status and equity of outcomes between the partners. No true partnership can exist when one party exerts power over, and possesses rights at the expense of, the other. What characterizes a true partnership is the agreement upon a common set of goals—shared objectives with equitable results, which require the respectful cooperation of the parties in order to achieve.

The Cree Nation's agreement with the Government of Quebec is vastly different from both Canada's federal land claims policy and its treaty policy, and the many oppressive agreements that have been called "partnerships" that have been made and are still being made pursuant to those policies. We believe that *Paix des Braves,* our 2002 agreement with Quebec, is an agreement based upon the significant recognition of the rights of Indigenous peoples to benefit meaningfully on a nation-to-nation basis from the natural resources and wealth of their own traditional lands. Federal land claims policy to this day is based upon Aboriginal surrender and the extinguishment by the Canadian state of Aboriginal rights.

Government cannot legitimately base its relationships with Indigenous peoples upon a policy that forces them to give up all their rights to vast lands and resources in return for some small, fixed amount of compensation. Such policies doom these societies to poverty and eventual extinction, while enriching Canada and the provinces and the companies that are licensed to exploit their lands, waters, and resources.

The Royal Commission on Aboriginal Peoples (RCAP) warned in 1996, with words that are still valid today, that Aboriginal peoples need much more territory to become economically, culturally, and politically self-sufficient. If they cannot obtain a greater share of the lands and resources in this country, their institutions of self-government will fail. Currently on the margins of Canadian society, they will be pushed to the edge of economic, cultural, and political extinction. This was the major conclusion that came out of the Royal Commission on Aboriginal Peoples. Under international law, the right of self-determination, which Aboriginal peoples possess, as do all peoples, includes our right to benefit from the wealth of our traditional lands. The RCAP's conclusion was, in fact, a call for Canada to fully respect its international human rights obligations.

This human right to self-determination as well as the right for a people to benefit from its own natural wealth and resources are not always exclusive rights and must be expressed differently in different contexts. In Canada, Aboriginal peoples, by virtue of their status as peoples under international law and the Canadian constitution, are one component of the sovereignty of Canada and are one of three orders of government in the land. The meaning of this has been made difficult by Canada and the provinces, in former times dominated by now-discredited colonial thinking, having carved up the country for themselves, leaving little or no economic space for Aboriginal peoples.

I note that in a 2004 speech, Prime Minister Martin left out any mention of Aboriginal peoples as being part of the Canadian confederation. Unfortunately, he also made no mention of the words "peoples," "rights," "treaties," "lands and resources," "honour of the Crown," "relationship," or "respect." These concepts, which could be found in federal policy, as recently as in *Gathering Strength* (Canada's Aboriginal Action Plan 1998), are, it would appear, now being erased.

Some do not think that such political or rights issues are involved when we discuss economic development. This is not true; the agreement between the James Bay Cree Nation and the government of Quebec was possible because it did not involve any preconditions. It did not ask the Crees to give up our right to benefit from our natural resources, nor was there any request that we give up or surrender or extinguish our treaty rights, which exist in perpetuity under the *James Bay and Northern Quebec Agreement.*

Both the James Bay Crees and Quebec realized that our new relationship could not be built in a context of power imbalances, hostility, and contention. We built upon the decision of the Supreme Court in the *Sparrow* case that the relationship between governments and Aboriginal peoples is non-adversarial. The willingness of both parties to seek friendly relations explains why our agreement is called *Paix des Braves*—the peace of the courageous. Our agreement is explicitly based upon creation of a community of economic and social interests between the Cree Nation and the Quebec Nation.

The basis of negotiations—the instructions given to the negotiators for each of the potential partners—was to identify the shared objectives and the means to attain them. There had been a standoff between the Crees and the Government of Quebec with regard to the development and exploitation of resources in our traditional territory, Eeyou Istchee. This standoff exists in many places in Canada between Aboriginal peoples and the governments and developers who jeopardize their existence. Aboriginal peoples want to benefit from development on their lands so they can plan the future of their nations.

Although governments and developers see themselves as having interests contrary to those of the Aboriginal peoples, this is a mistaken perception. This perception creates the exclusion of Aboriginal peoples from the long-term security provided by having access to the means to develop themselves. Not only does this constitute a violation of their human rights, but it also creates long-term instability and doubt over the resources and lands in question. Developers and governments often fight the Aboriginal interests, even joining forces in the courts against the Aboriginal parties. Nevertheless, I would like you to entertain the possibility that the national interest would be better served by sharing the resources of this great land for the long term.

Premier Landry took a pragmatic approach and stepped around this impasse to look for practical solutions. Quebec wanted to develop the rich natural resources in Eeyou Istchee and the Cree Nation wanted to escape the cycle of dependency and poverty created by Canada and Quebec's failure to respect the treaty rights contained in the *James Bay and Northern Quebec Agreement*, which is, after all, a social and economic development agreement.

For the past twenty-nine years, the Grand Council has fought in the courts and in the arena of public relations, in Canada and internationally, to have Canada and Quebec respect the *James Bay and Northern Quebec Agreement*, which contains treaty rights guaranteed by the *Constitution*. Canada has been particularly antagonistic and has continued to insist—in keeping with its ongoing policy of surrender and extinguishment of Aboriginal treaty rights—that we surrender our treaty rights in order to have them implemented. Could the Crown take a more fraudulent or oppressive position? I do not think so.

It was a chaotic history of twenty-one years of court cases and public relations battles with Quebec that was resolved in the *Paix des Braves*. The government of Quebec finally understood that without a serious, meaningful and honourable stake in development, the James Bay Cree Nation would never support it. Just as Quebec enjoyed the benefits from development, it understood that the Crees needed to benefit also if they were to survive as a nation. It is on that basis that we achieved a partnership that was unanimously supported by all sides of the Quebec Legislative Assembly. Now the new premier, Jean Charest, who expressed his support for the agreement when he was in opposition, has supported it publicly since his election as premier and is seeing to its ongoing implementation.

The agreement contains numerous groundbreaking commitments and understandings, including:

- a nation-to-nation relationship between the Quebec Nation and the Cree Nation based on cooperation, relationship, and mutual respect;
- industrial development in traditional lands that must be both compatible with our way of life and sustainable;
- a new Cree–Quebec Mining Exploration Board established to facilitate Cree involvement in mining and mining exploration;

- the implementation of Quebec's treaty obligations for development of the Crees *by* the Crees and the establishment of a Cree Development Corporation to invest in Cree and Cree/non-Cree economic enterprises;
- an annual payment of $70 million to the Crees by Quebec with increases in direct proportion to any increase in resource revenues from our Cree traditional territory;
- a commitment to train Cree game wardens; subject to federal government participation, the creation of a Cree regional police force including the hiring of eighteen full-time Cree constables; and the provision of $115 million over fifteen years to train Crees for permanent employment on the operation of the dams and to provide some part-time employment on remedial works as well as the right to negotiate $300 million in contracts for employment on construction of the EM1 project; and
- the settlement of a number of outstanding land issues, including the construction of escape routes for the community of Chisasibi in the unlikely event of a catastrophic break in the LG2 dam, and for a payment of $7 million annually indexed, for as long as the dams exist.

Other elements of the agreement include the creation of five protected areas near Waskaganish and for the creation of a new park, the second largest in Canada, to be in the Albanel–Mistissini area; $24 million to be put aside for the re-establishment of fish as a preferred dietary food by the Cree people; the dismantling of former Hydro-Québec worksites; and the construction of transmission lines to the community of Waskaganish and Whapmagoostui.

It is also important to note what the new agreement with Quebec does *not* contain. Unlike the so-called treaty "implementation" agreements being put in place elsewhere in Canada to this day, the *Paix des Braves* does not contain any extinguishments of treaty rights. It has a duration of fifty years, and provides for substantial benefits to flow throughout that period on an annual and escalating basis. At the end of the fifty years, the treaty on which it is based will still be whole and intact, because all the treaty rights it contains remain untouched. From a political point of view, we formally recognized that the *Paix des Braves* constituted a 'new relationship,' that it was between the Cree Nation and the Quebec Nation, and that the Crees would benefit very substantially from the wealth that can be and is being generated over all our traditional lands.

The agreement is for an initial period of fifty years, and the annual payment of $70 million will be increased based on any and all increases in value of forestry, mining, and hydroelectric production in Eeyou Istchee.

I believe that this is a model for relationships with Aboriginal peoples that will apply more and more in the future, as we come to realize that present policies simply do not work. Our treaties are not being respected by governments, in spite of their constitutional underpinnings. We see this with the *James Bay and Northern Quebec Agreement* that Canada seems to freely disregard. Recently, Canada has signed agreements with other Aboriginal treaty parties to buy out their treaty rights altogether, in exchange for one-time settlements, which in no way respect the Aboriginal treaty provisions. These are agreements based on the desperation of the Aboriginal parties in a crisis of poverty after years of failure by Canada to respect treaty rights. The sacred and perpetual character of the treaties is entirely lost, replaced by agreements that state that even if the supposed 'implementation agreement' is eventually found to be invalid by the courts, the Aboriginal parties agree not to pursue their legal options. Can you imagine—and I know that you can because of what has happened in Manitoba—the government making an end run around its own courts?

Furthermore, Canada demands that the relevant Aboriginal people indemnify the government in the event that any band members or band entities decide to pursue their legal options. Imagine, an Aboriginal nation being asked to indemnify the governments. The poorest and the most dispossessed indemnifying a G-8 country for the G-8 country's failure to keep its promises—this is a travesty of Crown–Aboriginal relations.

In the James Bay agreement with Quebec, the Crees achieve an important responsibility for the course of future development in the region. Rather than watching the resources being hauled out of our lands, the James Bay Crees are empowered and become major participants in resource management. Since the region encompasses the entire traditional territory of the James Bay Crees—Eeyou Istchee—the James Bay Crees become the major players with regard to how, when, and if development takes place.

One very important aspect of the new agreement is the decision not to pursue the NBR hydroelectric megaproject, which would have flooded 4000 square kilometres of land. Instead, the Crees agreed to accept the construction of a project that will flood an additional eighty kilometres, and then only if it passes environmental and social impact review; this is in addition to a project that had already been approved. All the environmental assessment procedures outlined in the *James Bay and Northern Quebec Agreement* apply, but the James Bay Crees are finally part of the economic picture, and so we may be able to balance the positive social impacts created by increased employment and sufficient funding for social services and community infrastructure against the negative impacts of the project on Cree traditional practices.

The new agreement as a whole transfers Quebec's responsibility for many aspects of Cree development in the territory directly to the James Bay Crees; thus we determine how this money will be spent and how development will be conducted. There will be a Cree Development Corporation to invest in development in the territory with a view to meeting both our investment and employment objectives. Also, because of the new agreement, considerable new money will be available to support traditional activities on the land. For example, the Cree Trappers Association, which was to receive funding from the Crees, Quebec, and Canada, is finally being funded by the Crees and Quebec, with only a small contribution from Canada. Canada has still not come near to meeting its treaty obligations to support traditional activities on the land. But we will hold them accountable.

The *Paix des Braves* is essentially an economic agreement to allow us to achieve social development through serious and properly funded mechanisms for economic development in the entire territory. The Cree communities have been plagued by high unemployment and poverty. Now the James Bay Crees will have the means to invest in and steer future economic development. Again from a pragmatic point of view, we feel that social problems must be attacked at the economic level. We must not fool ourselves by thinking that so-called accountability and local government legislation are going to solve the kind of major problems that Aboriginal peoples face. We in Quebec have been outside of the *Indian Act* for almost twenty years and we have a very high level of accounting and financial reporting to our members and to the government of Canada.

However, accounting for the operations and maintenance funding cannot resolve the fundamental issue of economic exclusion. Any approach that does not, as a minimum, recognize Aboriginal peoples' rights to benefit directly from the resources on their lands is doomed to failure. Our approach with Quebec is to establish an adequate fiscal base from which to participate in the economic development of the region. The social consequences, such as increased employment and investment opportunities, will ultimately attack problems due to poverty and disempowerment.

The government of Canada has not been able to understand or refuses to acknowledge that this new approach is in the greater national interest. The Crees got tired after twenty-five years of waiting for Canada to keep its word. The government of Quebec was able to see past the previous conflicts. Other groups are going to get tired of waiting for Canada as well. The provinces are not going to want to wait. If they examine the *Paix des Braves*, they will see that the Crees and Quebec have made a breakthrough of enormous importance. Canada can take no credit for the *Paix des Braves*, even though in international forums it has been taking credit for the agreement. We know from its twenty-eight years of bumbling and attacks on treaty rights that, in fact, the government of Canada's presence at the *Paix des Braves* negotiation table would have doomed the process to failure; as a result, the negotiations took place in strictest confidentiality.

We are proud of what we have done, and we hope that others will be able to do something similar, based on the principles in our agreement. We are paid directly and significantly on a nation-to-nation basis for the value of the resources that originate in Eeyou Istchee. We may invest in whatever development strategies we think will benefit the James Bay Cree Nation and the region.

We believe that this formula has a much better chance of success than previous attempts based on colonialism or policies of extinguishment and/or isolation on reserves. The new approach does a better job of respecting our fundamental human rights, our rights to the resources in our traditional territory, and to the land where we have always lived. This is our conception of building partnerships for the future, ones that are consistent with the right of self-determination, respect for human rights and dignity, and in the interest of all.

Remarks made at Old Relationships or New Partnerships: Hydro Development on Aboriginal Lands in Quebec and Manitoba. University of Winnipeg. February 23, 2004.

9

SHOULD THE *JAMES BAY AND NORTHERN QUEBEC AGREEMENT* SERVE AS A MODEL AGREEMENT FOR OTHER FIRST NATIONS?

Renée Dupuis

THE 1975 *JAMES BAY AND NORTHERN QUEBEC AGREEMENT* (JBNQA) was, at the time of its signing, not discussed in terms relating to colonial–Aboriginal relations or as a new social contract between the state and Aboriginal peoples. Rather, it was seen as the resolution of a dispute resulting from a legal action brought by several First Nations against the Quebec government and its plans for a major hydroelectric development project. Thirty years on, it is possible to look back at the agreement with a perspective informed by both its causes and ensuing effects. Armed with the advantage of hindsight, an assessment can be made of the relative successes of the agreement in achieving the goals and ideals set out at the time of its signing. In carrying out this evaluation, this essay first recalls the overall political context of Quebec in the 1970s. The rationale for the agreement, recognized as the first "modern treaty" nego-tiated in Canada with Aboriginal peoples,[1] is also examined. In addition, governance structures established through the agreement are shown to corre-spond to traditional decentralized structures common across Canada. More fundamentally, it is argued that the agreement must be examined in refer-ence to improving Aboriginal people's quality of life as well as improving the nature and accountability of Aboriginal governance structures.

BACKGROUND

Robert Bourassa was elected premier of Quebec in the early 1970s on a platform that included a promise to create 100,000 jobs through a major hydroelectric development project on the James Bay in the northwest region of Quebec. This "project of the century" would be Quebec's proudest display of collective success and prosperity since the nationalization of electrical utilities in Quebec (Martin 2003).

The court challenge brought by the Quebec Association of Indians against the proposed project sent shock waves through Quebec that have continued to reverberate to this day. The legal claims made by those bringing the suit were at first considered illegitimate and unfounded in law. How could an obscure statutory provision from approximately sixty years ago, the origins of which dated back a further 100 years, constitute a real obstacle to the construction of an important development project and potential driving force behind the redefinition of Quebec society? And how could Aboriginal people continue to claim rights to Quebec in the twentieth century? Despite the odds, a tribunal of first instance recognized that Aboriginal people had at least the appearance of legal rights (Malouf 1973). An appeals tribunal, however, ruled that this appearance of legal rights could not jeopardize such an important development project and that the rights and interests of the Aboriginal minority could not interfere with the rights and interests of the general population of Quebec.

It was in this emotionally charged environment that the premier of Quebec proposed to begin negotiations with Aboriginal residents living within the proposed project area. An agreement among the parties halted legal actions and allowed work on the project to progress. This agreement, the *James Bay and Northern Quebec Agreement*, was concluded between the federal government, whose involvement was necessary due to its legal and constitutional jurisdiction, the government of Quebec, Cree First Nations, and Inuit peoples.

THE JBNQA: A TWENTIETH-CENTURY AGREEMENT IN THE SPIRIT
OF EIGHTEENTH-CENTURY BRITISH COLONIAL POLICY

Although signed only thirty years ago in the last quarter of the twentieth
century, the agreement stems directly from an Order-in-Council of the British
Crown promulgated in the nineteenth century. In 1870, Great Britain transferred to Canada an enormous territory generally, referred to as Rupert's Land,
which the Hudson's Bay Company had relinquished two years earlier. The
action coincided with the establishment of Canada as a dominion by virtue
of the *Constitution Act* of 1867. In accepting the land transfer, both the Canadian House of Commons and the Senate assured Great Britain that Aboriginal
"claims" would be resolved "in compliance with the principles of equity which
have unvaryingly guided the British Crown in its relations with the Aboriginals."[2] The primary source for "the principles of equity" prior to the *Constitution
Act* was the *Royal Proclamation* of 1763, an imperial order adopted following the
"Traité de Paris," after the cession by France of all its colonies in North America
and the establishment of British sovereignty. According to this policy, the treaties signed by the British Crown in Canada and elsewhere required that the
Aboriginal people cede their rights to large segments of territory in exchange
for the creation of reserves, financial compensation, and guarantees allowing
them to pursue their traditional activities such as hunting, fishing, gathering,
and trapping. Canada continued to apply this British policy after its constitution was enacted, signing various treaties of this type between 1867 and 1930.

The 1870 Order-in-Council that provided for the transfer of rights stipulated that all compensation due to Indians[3] for lands earmarked for colonization should be paid by the Government of Canada together with the
imperial government. The Canadian government transferred this obligation
for compensation to the Quebec government in 1912 when the Parliament
adopted the *Act to Extend the Boundaries of the Province of Quebec*.[4] Section 2
stipulated, among other things, that Quebec would recognize the rights
of the "Indian inhabitants" in Rupert's Land and that it would obtain the
"surrender" of these rights in the same manner as had the Canadian government. The obligation would only be fulfilled by Quebec more than sixty years
later with the signing of the JBNQA (Quebec 1976).

This historic settlement was reached following legal actions taken by Quebec Aboriginal people against the Government of Quebec, which in 1970 had unilaterally initiated an important hydroelectric project.[5] It was a tripartite agreement (Inuit–Cree/Quebec/Canada) since the Act of 1912 stipulated that Aboriginal people must remain under federal jurisdiction, by virtue of category 24 of section 91 of the *Constitution Act* of 1867. In their report, which appeared in 1971, the commission studying Quebec's territorial integrity reminded the provincial government of its obligations in accordance with the Act of 1912 and recommended that it "honour" them (Quebec 1971, recommendation no. 16, vol. 4.1, p. 392). No other authority had done so, at least not publicly, between 1912 and 1971.

As mentioned above, the obligation was first enumerated by Britain in the nineteenth century and was integrated into the Canadian legislation of 1912 in the same spirit; that is, in the context of developing the land required for colonization of the Canadian territory by non-Aboriginal people. For Canada's part, the policy was carried out in conjunction with the implementation of a trusteeship system for Indians and Indian communities in the first consolidated version of the 1876 *Indian Act*.[6] The federal government considered it had no other obligations regarding Aboriginal peoples or the ancestral rights of Aboriginal peoples.

The 1973 *Calder* ruling by the Supreme Court of Canada led the federal government to radically modify its position on the issue of land surrender and sovereignty. In a departure from previous jurisprudence, *Calder* established that Aboriginal people had legal title on Canadian territory due to the sole fact of their previous occupation and use, a title that survives in Canadian law unless it has been surrendered by the Aboriginal people or extinguished by successive governments. In the aftermath of this ruling, the federal government adopted in the same year a policy that consisted in settling, through negotiation, Aboriginal territorial claims (Canada 1981).[7] In cases where claims involve territories located within the boundaries of a province, federal policy requires the involvement of the provincial government in the negotiations and in a possible settlement.

The JBNQA was the first agreement concluded within the context of this federal policy. Stemming from the British policy to conclude historical treaties (pre- and post-confederative) signed by the Crown and based on the surrender of rights, the agreement was used as a model in the negotiation of subsequent agreements concluded up to this day, such as in the 1998 agreement with British Columbia's Nisga'a.

The scope of the agreement far exceeds that of historic treaties. While the text of historic treaties usually covers only a few pages, the JBNQA is 481 pages long, divided into thirty-one chapters, and covers a variety of federal and provincial jurisdictions. According to the provincial negotiator, the agreement provided an opportunity for Quebec to "extend its administration, its legislation, its public institutions and its services to all of Quebec, in the end affirming the integrity of our Territory" (Quebec 1991, XIV).[8] The structures created by the agreement confirmed the role Quebec expected to play in this part of the province. For Quebec, Aboriginal communities were expected to "arrange their local administration in the same manner as Quebec municipalities, while regional organizations [would] exercise municipal functions in regions located outside of communities that have been long established" (Quebec 1991, 12). It therefore appears that one of the objectives of the Government of Quebec at the time was to link up with its network of decentralization structures the Indian and Inuit communities in northern Quebec.

The willingness to obtain authority over the First Nations communities, affirmed once again at the beginning of the 1970s by Quebec, coincided with the willingness expressed the year before by the federal government to abandon its constitutional jurisdiction. This was to be done by transferring authority to provincial authorities and by abolishing the trusteeship system of the *Indian Act* and the Indian reserves. Presented by the then Minister of Indian Affairs, Jean Chrétien (who became prime minister of Canada in 1993), in a *White Paper* published in 1969, the proposal was met with strong opposition from First Nations, who were demanding that any transfer of federal authority be done through the reclaiming of authority by the communities themselves. Ultimately, the federal government abandoned the proposal, at least officially.

THE MECHANISMS OF GOVERNANCE IN THE JBNQA:
FEDERAL AND PROVINCIAL DECENTRALIZATION STRUCTURES

The JBNQA established several types of local or supra-local administrative structures among the Inuit and the Crees, including certain provincial structures that coincided with areas of federal jurisdiction in regards to the Indians and Inuit. All parties ultimately accepted in the agreement, including the Cree First Nations and the Inuit, a transfer of power from the federal authority to the Government of Quebec. For the Cree communities (and for the Naskapis, after the signing of the *Northeastern Quebec Agreement* in 1978), this represented a radical change in that they became subject to provincial authority while remaining under federal authority. For the Inuit, however, the situation constituted a virtual confirmation of the status quo, insofar as they are excluded from the *Indian Act*,[9] which *de facto* placed them under Quebec authority well before the signing of the agreement. The agreement also provided the First Nations and the Inuit an opportunity to create regional administrative structures that superimposed themselves on the local authorities, which had not existed until then.

Thus, the JBNQA created both provincial structures of territorial decentralization—i.e., local and regional administrations—as well as functional decentralization through the creation of corporations in the fields of health, social services, education, economic development, environment, public health, and justice notably (see Dupuis 1999 for more details). The agreement also generated the creation of a new governance system in which the band councils act as local administrators whose authority stems from both provincial laws on part of the lands (category 1B) and federal laws for another section of the lands (category 1A). Thus, Cree local provincial administrations now have authority over category 1B lands[10] while the Inuit, at least in northern villages, have jurisdiction over category I lands.

In parallel fashion, the federal government adopted, in 1984, a special local administration scheme that almost completely replaced the *Indian Act* regime. By virtue of the *Cree-Naskapi (of Quebec) Act*,[11] the federal system of territorial decentralization granted more authority to the local band councils over category 1A lands, namely the former settlements over which they had authority prior to 1975 under the *Indian Act*. It should be noted, however, that these new powers remain subject to the federal government's approval and regulatory power.[12]

Between the signing of the JBNQA in 1975 and the adoption of the 1984 federal law, there was also a major change in the Canadian constitutional regime. As a result of this regime change, rights stemming from the agreement acquired constitutional status with the adoption of the *Constitution Act* 1982, which repatriated the *Constitution* to Canada and marked the official recognition of the existence of Aboriginal peoples in Canada and their specific rights—i.e., Aboriginal and treaty rights.

The constitutional conference of 1983, the first in a series of conferences meant to define these newly recognized rights, modified the *Constitution* to specify that rights stemming from land claim agreements would be protected as though they were treaty rights. In that the JBNQA and the *Northeastern Quebec Agreement* are included in this category of agreements, the analysis of what constituted a guaranteed constitutional right to the Crees and Inuit became a major issue, notably on the issue of governance.[13]

The constitutional conferences were also an opportunity for Aboriginal peoples to express their desires to have their inherent right to self-government explicitly recognized. For many within the Cree communities, the JBNQA was wholly inadequate on these grounds. They argued that rather than self-government, the agreement simply imposed new varieties of federal and/or provincial structures, which Aboriginal peoples had little choice but to accept. This has put the JBNQA under challenge and has led the Crees to initiate a series of legal challenges contesting the validity of the surrender of their Aboriginal rights and affirming that their inherent right to self-government had not, in fact, been ceded. It became clear that the signatories of the agreement had been replaced by a generation of Cree spokespeople who vehemently rejected both the content of the agreement and its context, which, in their opinion, had forced the Crees into signing an essentially unjust document.

Many supplementary agreements have been signed since 1975. Few agreements, however, have been as important as the recent accord negotiated discreetly by the Chief of the Grand Council of the Crees, Dr. Ted Moses, and the Premier of Quebec, Bernard Landry. Referred to as the *Paix des Braves*, the deal commits the Grand Council of the Crees to a fifty-year agreement with the Quebec government to enable new hydroelectric projects to be carried out in their territories in exchange for the abandonment of a series of legal proceedings intended by the Crees. The agreement also calls for Cree participation in the development of this territory and of fees of $3.5 billion dollars to be paid by the government and the utility in exchange for the right to exploit resources in this region. Negotiated directly by the Chief of the Grand Council in the name of the Crees, contested for various reasons, and finally ratified by a Cree majority, the agreement represents a nation-to-nation understanding that, according to then-Premier Landry, will secure new, more harmonious relationships between the Quebec government and the Crees of Quebec.

Despite the new perspectives opened by the *Paix des Braves*, it is important to note that this new deal does not supplant the JBNQA. Thus, whatever social changes might be associated with the *Paix* will occur within the context of the JBNQA. Furthermore, questions that have arisen during the almost thirty years since the agreement has gone into effect remain relevant. While significant issues regarding delays in the application of its provisions or the lack of a specific schedule in the implementation of this agreement might be taken up, the concern here is with certain aspects of governance, which should be closely examined by both the parties involved in this agreement and by society as a whole. Among the most important of the governance-related questions are the following.

- Do the administrative structures created as part of the agreement represent more than a transfer of federal authority on the part of the Canadian government to the government of Quebec? Have we truly allowed for a form of responsible government to be implemented in Cree, Naskapi, and Inuit communities, accountable to their population and operating in a real transparent manner?
- Did the creation of supra-local Cree and Inuit structures in the context of the agreement diminish local authority to the benefit of regional authorities that are not directly accountable to the local population, or did it contribute to the increased efficiency of the local authorities?

- Did the creation of functionally decentralized structures meant to provide various services for the population, such as health or education, improve the quality and quantity of services?
- Have the services ensured over the last thirty years, through these various structures, made it possible to sensibly improve living and health conditions among the Cree, Naskapi, and Inuit populations in comparison to other Aboriginal communities in Canada?
- Section 67 of the *Canadian Human Rights Act*[14] denies all recourse to Indians who are victims of discrimination caused either by the *Indian Act*, by the federal government, or by a band council. This provision was applicable to Cree and Naskapi communities governed by the *Indian Act*. Did the 1984 adoption of the *Cree-Naskapi (of Quebec) Act*, which almost completely replaced the *Indian Act* in the case of the Crees and the Naskapis, remove this problem?
- What has been the effect of the recognition, in the *Constitution Act* 1982, of the status of Aboriginal peoples and their Aboriginal rights on the administrative structures created by the agreement?
- Does the current form of the structures created by the agreement mean a constitutionally protected right stemming from a land claims agreement, in accordance with paragraph 35(3) of the *Constitution Act* of 1982?
- How can the claim by Crees, Naskapis, and Inuit of their inherent right to self-government be reconciled with the structures created by the agreement?
- What are the effects, on the structures created by the agreement, of an eventual regional government in Nunavik being negotiated for the section of Quebec territory north of the 55th parallel?

Many of the foregoing questions indicate a need to evaluate, more than thirty years after its signing, the governmental structures created by the JBNQA. It seems preferable that such an examination be undertaken by all the signatories to the agreement and that it be conducted in a parallel manner by the Inuit, the Crees, and the Naskapis, and the provincial and federal governments. If the parties do not agree on the necessity of such an examination, the Quebec government and the federal government especially, because of its particular fiduciary obligation, should proceed with it. This examination would make it possible to evaluate the effectiveness of federal policy, and not only insofar as it affects the Crees, the Naskapis, and the Inuit; in fact, the two governments are currently negotiating, and will continue negotiating in the future, agreements similar to the JBNQA with other First Nations in Quebec and elsewhere in Canada, including the Atikamekw, the Innus-Montagnais, and the Quebec Algonquin. It would be advantageous to conduct such an evaluation before applying the model almost in full to other First Nations, as is currently proposed.

Such an evaluation must especially consider the results of the agreement in improving Cree, Naskapi, and Inuit socio-economic conditions and the role played by the new governance structures in bringing about these results. It must also be committed to determining whether these structures have improved the operations of local and regional political authorities from the point of view of the responsibility, accountability, and transparency that are expected today from government administrations. Finally, this evaluation could enable the content of the agreement to be measured against Aboriginal peoples' constitutional rights recognized since 1982.

---

1   Aboriginal peoples here refer to Métis, Inuit, and First Nations as referred to by the law or legal documents. First Nations refers to all "Indian communities" with or without reserve status.

2   Order-in-Council by His Majesty admitting Rupert's Land and the Northwest Territory, schedule (A) p. 9, reproduced in the R.S.C. 1985, app. II, no. 9.

3   During a dispute between the federal and Quebec governments, the Supreme Court of Canada decided in 1939, in its ruling *Re Eskimos* [1939] R.C.S. 104, that the expression "Indians," described in category 24 of section 91 of the *Constitutional Act of 1867,* includes the "Eskimos," which is to say the Inuit. The Inuit, therefore, fall under the federal jurisdiction as do the Indians.

4   S.C. 1912, 2 Geo. V, c. 45. The Quebec counterpoint of this federal law is *An Act Respecting the Extension of the Province of Quebec by the Annexation of Ungava,* S.Q. 1912, 2 Geo. V, c. 7.

5   To the agreement would be added in 1978 the *Northeastern Quebec Agreement,* an accessory agreement concluded between the parties in the agreement and the Naskapis in the Schefferville region. That agreement amended the agreement to adapt it to the recognized rights of the Naskapis.

6   S.C. 1876, c. 18.

7   Adopted in 1973, this policy was reviewed and later published by the federal government under the title: *In all fairness: a native claims policy—general claims* (Ottawa, Supply and Services, 1981).

8   The philosophy of the agreement from Quebec's point of view was presented by the provincial negotiator, MNA John Ciaccia, on November 5, 1975, at the Quebec National Assembly, before the draft agreement to be concluded was studied. This presentation is reproduced in Quebec (1991).

9   *Indian Act*, 1985, L.C. c. I-5, par. 4(1).

10 Category 1B lands are adjacent to federal Indian settlements existing before the agreement, which have become category 1A lands.

11 *An Act respecting certain provisions of the James Bay and Northern Quebec Agreement and the Northeastern Quebec Agreement relating principally to Cree and Naskapi local government and to the land regime governing Category 1A and Category 1A-N land*, 1984, L.C. 32-33 Éliz. Ch.18. As indicated by its name, this act also provides a follow-up to the commitments made by the federal government and taken towards the Naskapis, who signed the *Northeastern Quebec Agreement* in 1978. This agreement amended the James Bay agreement to include the Naskapis.

12 See, notably, paragraphs 45(2) and (4) and paragraph 66(2) of the act.

13 It will be interesting to follow the attitude of the courts in regards to the qualification of governance mechanisms created by the agreement. If they are qualified as a right stemming from a territorial claim agreement, they will be doubly protected, not only as a contractual right but also as a constitutional right, which is more limiting to legislators and governments (federal and provincial) who must now justify any infringement of these rights according to the criteria developed by the Supreme Court since 1990.

14 *Canadian Human Rights Act*, L.R.C., 1985, c. H-6.

10

THE END OF AN ERA IN QUEBEC: THE GREAT WHALE PROJECT AND THE INUIT OF KUUJJUARAPIK AND THE UMIUJAQ

Thibault Martin

HYDRO-QUÉBEC'S GREAT WHALE HYDROELECTRIC PROJECT, also known as James Bay Phase II, was never realized despite several years of preparatory studies and negotiations. Though little has been researched or published on the project to date, its preliminary stages did produce a number of significant social impacts on populations settled within the project area. In these pages, the legacy of the Great Whale Project will be examined through its social and other human impacts on the Inuit population, such as the partial resettlement of the Kuujjuarapik community.[1] The most significant aspect of the Great Whale Project is that it marked a turning point in the historical relationship between Hydro-Québec and Aboriginal groups in Quebec. Indeed, at a moment when Hydro-Québec had achieved a measure of success in imposing its prescription for development on Aboriginal peoples in the North, a campaign of concerted opposition from Cree and Inuit leaders contributed to the postponement of the project. In addition, this episode gave rise to a large-scale mobilization of Inuit and Crees to negotiate an equal partnership with the modern state.

A MODERN PATH TO DEVELOPMENT

Robert Bourassa, premier of Quebec, launched the James Bay Project in the belief that hydroelectric development would provide a means to secure Quebec's economic independence. For the premier, it was necessary to "uproot" the wealth of the North for the benefit of all Quebec (Bourassa 1985, 27). The symbolic intent of the James Bay projects was to show the world, and Québecers themselves, the capacity of Quebec to achieve great things. As indicated in the following comment from Bourassa, this sentiment was at play during the very first phases of hydroelectric development on James Bay:

> First, it was necessary to motivate and inspire a deep sense of commitment. We had to convince ourselves that we had the knowledge, technical skills and managerial proficiency to construct the world's most advanced and efficient production facilities. We had to firmly believe in the future of the project if we were to succeed in dispatching the required materials and expertise to such a remote wilderness area and harsh climate. We had to divert rivers by constructing kilometres and kilometres of dams [and] we had to locate the millions of dollars necessary to finance the project and respond to the needs of the Aboriginal peoples of the region with fairness and compassion. (21; author's translation)

These remarks reveal several of the ideas underlying the development of the James Bay Project, and to a certain extent the Quiet Revolution itself. First, a need felt by Québecers to create a national identity was channelled into a project that could unite and engage the entire population. Also, the project itself would support a shift away from the rurality characteristic of traditional French Canadian society, in favour of a technological and technocratic vision of a modern society overseen by managers, executives, and planners of megaprojects. As indicated in the final lines of the above-cited excerpt, also behind the project was the desire to occupy, vis-à-vis the Aboriginal population, the role of colonial protector so familiar to the modern state.

The way in which the project was conceived reflects a typically modern vision of development, in the sense that the words "modern" and "development" would have carried during the Industrial Revolution. As Bourassa wrote, following the completion of Phase I of the James Bay Project:

> In fact, because of its climate and unique terrain conditions, we could almost say that Quebec is an immense hydroelectric plant that is only being partially utilized. Every day, millions of potential kilowatt-hours are flushed out to sea. What a waste! (18; author's translation)

In order to minimize this waste, Hydro-Québec's engineers undertook a systematic plan of development for the region's hydroelectric resources. Their preliminary studies led to the conception of three distinct hydroelectric complexes. The first complex, the La Grande Complex, was constructed on the river of the same name, immediately following the signing of the *James Bay Agreement*. This complex included eight reservoirs: Caniapiscau (4275 km²), Robert Bourassa (2835 km²), La Grande-3 (2420 km²), Laforge 1 (1288 km²), Opinaca (1040 km²), La Grande-4 (765 km²), Laforge 2 (260 km²), and La Grande-1 (70 km²). Many of these reservoirs are classed among the most significant dams in the world. The accumulated surface of all these reservoirs totals 12,285 km², which corresponds to 40 percent of the area of Belgium, a country with a population of ten million. In fact, La Grande Complex necessitated the flooding of a territory larger than the Akosombo Reservoir, which was at the time the largest constructed water retainer in the world.

With the La Grande project realized, Hydro-Québec next envisioned the development of the Great Whale Complex, which would exploit the electric potential of the Great Whale River and its tributaries. A third complex, Nottaway–Broadback–Ruppert (**NBR**), was also in the pipeline, and would cover the southernmost rivers of the James Bay basin. This latter project, suspended for several years, was relaunched at the beginning of 2002 with construction to begin shortly thereafter. Once construction on all three complexes was completed, Bourassa intended to incorporate these structures into an even more grandiose plan for the exploitation of Quebec's water resources. This plan would have transformed the James Bay into an immense lake, effectively separating it, via a system of dikes, from the Hudson Bay. The waters from this lake, once desalinated, would have been redirected toward large metropolitan areas in the south of the country or toward agricultural lands in the US and Canada. The following quote from Premier Bourassa illustrates the hyperbolic nature of the project, as well as the definition of development espoused, at that time, by the government of Quebec.

> This new and entirely man-made Canadian body of water will harness the streams of the James Bay basin, which totals an average volume approximately twice that of all the Great Lakes basins. Plans for this first step are for the recycling (and not the diversion) of one part of this enormous volume of new waters, to control the volume of the international hydrographical system of the Great Lakes and Saint Lawrence River. This will allow us to provide aid to agricultural regions most under threat of drought in the Canadian West and the United States. . . . We are talking here of a "recycling" plan. This project does not entail the diversion of Canadian waters. Exported water would be only that which had served its purpose in Canada and would be otherwise flushed out to sea unutilized. Once accumulated in a new artificial lake . . . these 'used' waters could be recycled to be used for new purposes in the south of Quebec, in Ontario, as part of the hydrographical system of the Great Lakes and Saint Lawrence River and, finally, in Central/Western Canada and the United States. (182–83; author's translation)

Although this final recycling scheme was never realized, it illustrates the profound desire on the part of the Quebec government to control the forces of nature for its own benefit. Not surprisingly, perhaps, all these projects were devised without having consulted the First Nations and Inuit peoples who would have been affected.

However, a concerted campaign of resistance mounted by First Nations, Inuit, and environmental groups, combined with significant fluctuations in demand for hydroelectricity, obligated Hydro-Québec to re-evaluate its priorities so thoroughly that the Great Whale and NBR projects were postponed. Though the La Grande Project was never realized, preliminary

studies, which would form the basis of construction plans, required significant research and the mobilization of hundreds of people, and led to social
and environmental impacts on Inuit communities. In fact, the scale of the
preliminary studies on the Great Whale Project carried impacts comparable
to medium-sized projects realized elsewhere. The following section briefly
recalls the nature of this preliminary work, and attempts to estimate its larger
impacts on the affected communities. The position of the Inuit communities toward the project is then analyzed with particular attention being paid
to the strategies developed by these communities. Finally, it is argued that
the Great Whale Project was an important step, at least symbolically, in the
redefinition of relations between Quebec and Aboriginal peoples.

THE GREAT WHALE PROJECT

As shown in Table 10.1, work on the Great Whale Project began in two
distinct phases between 1971 and 1992. Studies on Phase I of the project
were undertaken from 1975 and 1981, and those for Phase II from 1989
to 1992. The goal of these studies was to outline possible work plans and
establish their economic and technical feasibility; they would also allow for
evaluation of the impacts of the project on the biophysical and human environment in order to propose future mitigating measures.

This research led to a significant increase in activity on Inuit land—the
construction of camps to serve as accommodations for employees of Hydro-
Québec and its consultants. The provincial utility constructed, at Kuujjuarapik, a winterized camp with a 150- to 200-person capacity. This camp
remained open until 1981; though consisting mainly of tents, several buildings (housing for executives, canteen, washhouse, games room, workshops,
etc.) were also built. The settlement, which served as the project's base camp,
was located within a ten-minute walking distance from the village. Another
camp with a 250- to 300-person capacity was constructed thirty kilometres
north of Kuujjuarapik. Smaller camps were also erected at various locations
within the study area. During the summer months, up to 500 technicians
and specialists stayed in the study area (a number roughly equivalent to
the population of the Inuit residents of the community.) In addition to these
camps, Hydro-Québec maintained several other sites for storing materials,

TABLE 10.1

Great Whale Project Main Events

Preliminary Studies and Feasibility Study, Phase I (1964–1981)

YEAR	EVENTS
1971	Quebec announces a project to harness the hydroelectric potential of the James Bay area.
1972	Cree and Inuit representatives file a motion for interlocutory injunction.
1973	The Quebec Superior Court orders suspension of the work in the James Bay area. One week later, the Court of Appeal suspends the injunction. Work resumes. Quebec and Ottawa begin negotiations with Aboriginal peoples.
1974	A base plan is developed for construction of three separate complexes: the La Grande, Great Whale, and Nottaway–Broadback–Rupert.
1975	The James Bay and Northern Quebec Agreement is signed.
1976	A series of exploration camps are built, including one in Kuujjuarapik and several inland camps.
1978–81	During the summer peak of research activities, there are as many as 500 employees of Hydro-Québec and its consultants in the study area.
1981	The final report on the feasibility study is published.
1982	The Great Whale project is put on hold.

Feasibility Study, Phase II (1989–1992) and Later Events

YEAR	EVENTS
1988	The Great Whale project is relaunched.
1989	Field research begins.
1992	Public hearings on the environmental impact assessment directive and public consultation. End of phase II research.
1993	The feasibility study report is published.
1994	The Great Whale project is suspended.
1995	The project exploration camps are dismantled.

mainly barrels of oil. Some of these sites were located within Kuujjuarapik, one at the mouth of the Great Whale River, and another on the grounds of the airport. In addition, between 1975 and 1982, Hydro-Québec established a helicopter base at Kuujjuarapik.

The Great Whale Project also gave rise to a series of public relations exercises, which took place at Kuujjuarapik and other localities affected by the project. Officially, Hydro-Québec maintained that these activities were intended to inform the public of the project. Though not addressed publicly, Hydro-Québec was also keen to sell the project to audiences at the local, national, and even international levels. As an employee of Hydro-Québec commented to us in private, "[W]e have learned through scientific studies that people are most afraid of the unknown. We therefore had the idea to educate the Inuit on hydroelectric dams. We thought this would lessen their anxiety and opposition to the project."

Hydro-Québec organized a number of workshops to allow First Nations members to voice their perspectives, concerns, and hopes for the project. The corporation also organized visits to the La Grande reservoir, including surveys of the region by helicopter. Most of the tours at La Grande were aimed to seduce the Inuit, especially the Elders. The corporation always paid for the travel of all the participants. The people we interviewed in Kuujjuarapik commented that it was only people chosen by Hydro-Québec who were invited to take part in the "trips" to La Grande, and that "only the leaders were invited to this sort of thing." It would therefore appear that Hydro-Québec did attempt to leave an impression on certain community members, especially on Inuit leaders who would be more likely involved in subsequent project negotiations.

Another important element at this stage of the project was the government-run public consultation on the Great Whale Project, which took place in January 1992. Public hearings were held, from January to March 1992, at Val D'Or, Montréal, and at five northern locations, including Umiujaq and Kuujjuarapik. The Inuit participated in the public hearings and in the environmental assessment process; in addition, several working groups and negotiating groups were established. An Inuit representative was appointed to each of these groups, whose responsibilities were to study the pre-project reports published by Hydro-Québec and assess the project's potential to generate a variety of environmental and social impacts. In this way the Inuit people, from community and regional leaders to the population at large, were deeply involved, in very diverse ways, in the preparatory phase of the Great Whale Project.

Concurrent with the participation of certain Inuit leaders in the preparatory process, other Inuit formed with the Crees a common front of resistance to the project. These two groups mounted joint public actions, most notably the Odeyak tour of the northeastern United States, which involved forty or so Crees and Inuit. The word "Odeyak" is a contraction of two words, one Cree and one Inuit, one meaning "canoe" and the other "kayak." From March to April 1990, the expedition traversed Quebec and a corner of the United States, stopping in several cities to rally opposition and challenge elected officials to boycott electricity from Hydro-Québec. This action received significant media attention, and several Canadian and American newspapers published, in feature articles, the photo of the Odeyak gliding at the feet of the Statue of Liberty. A second tour was organized for the autumn of the same year. Though it took place only in Quebec, the tour did achieve a comparable level of media attention, and culminated with the delivery of a petition signed by several hundred Québecers to the National Assembly. The Inuit people were participants in other protests organized or supported by environmental pressure groups (National Audubon Society, Greenpeace, Earth First, Sierra Club, etc.) that took place in large cities across Canada and the UK, as well as the northern communities of Chisasibi, Kuujjuarapik, and Inukjuak. In addition to its media activism, the Makivik Society supported legal challenges mounted by representatives of the Crees. The aim of such legal actions was to delay or indeed inhibit the Great Whale Project by forcing Hydro-Québec to revise its environmental assessment procedures (Massot 1993, 22).

Inuit employed throughout this period a remarkable dual strategy. When acting in partnership with the Crees, the community was openly and forcefully opposed to the project, while consistently maintaining a measure of dialogue with Hydro-Québec. This strategy of engagement and resistance differed from the approach of the Crees, who, from 1988, had cut ties with the public corporation. The Inuit leaders, on the other hand, chose to negotiate with Hydro-Québec because it was felt that, were the project to go ahead, the Inuit should at least be at the table to participate in pre-project studies or negotiate favourable terms to any subsequent agreement. On April 14, 1994, the Inuit signed with Hydro-Québec the *Kuujjuarapik Agreement-in-Principle*. As part of this agreement, Inuit and Hydro-Québec representatives articulated the basics for the negotiation of a convention on the construction of the Great Whale Complex. The agreement also specified the terms of several development funds and the amounts Hydro-Québec would contribute. However, once the project preparations were completed, the government of Quebec announced, at the end of 1994, that the project had been suspended, and to date it has not been resurrected.

Studies undertaken by Hydro-Québec and its consultants had three main impacts: economic, environmental (including effects on Inuit hunting practices), and social. First, with respect to its economic impacts, it should be noted that the project stimulated significant economic activity, notably at Kuujjuarapik. The figures that would allow an evaluation of the expenditures of Hydro-Québec and its consultants, during Phase I, are no longer available, and thus it is not possible to make precise economic estimates for that period. However, existing information and documents collected on Phase II of the project would allow for a fair assessment of Phase I economic returns. Hydro-Québec's expenditures, in the region and toward Inuit organizations, total some $7.5 million (in 1995 dollars). This amount represents funds injected directly into the Nunavik economy. Not included in this total are Hydro-Québec's expenditures outside the region that covered the salaries of engineers, executives, and technicians working to research plans. Hydro-Québec's total injection of funds represented 4.7 percent of the regional GDP of Nunavik for the year 1995. Of this amount, $820,000 was spent on salaries and $6.7 million went toward the purchase of goods and services. However, among these expenditures, $1.25 million was used to purchase products from outside the region. Expenditures on imported products, notably fuel, cannot be said to have contributed directly to the local economy.

A team of researchers from Laval University (Duhaime et al. 1998) calculated, from these data, the economic returns generated by this injection of funds. According to their estimates, it stimulated direct, indirect, and inferred returns equivalent to $4.5 million in the production of goods and services (**GDP** at 1995 market price). Minus taxes and imports, the value added to the region by the Phase II studies is estimated at $3.6 million. On this amount, $2.6 million represent salaries paid within Nunavik.

Expenditures related to the Great Whale Project were therefore significant, representing an estimated injection of funds roughly equivalent to the potential investment in a winter Olympic Games for the region of Quebec City. However, following such a significant investment in the local economies of Kuujjuarapik or Umiujaq, the two villages most affected by the project, did not experience any real economic sustainable growth during or after the project. The reason for this result stems from the type of expenditures made by Hydro-Québec: the largest portion of funds was spent to transport materials or personnel, buy fuel, or erect temporary settlements, which had very little permanent effect on the local economy. More troubling still was the "boom and bust" cycle engendered by the significant but ephemeral injections of funds to the local community. Witnesses have estimated that uncertainties in the planning stages of the project, together with two suspensions of work in 1982 and 1994, may have had a detrimental effect on many local businesses. For instance, one entrepreneur in Kuujjuarapik, owner of a local hotel that significantly expanded its operations to meet with seasonal demand, was forced to close down once the project was postponed as its business became too expensive to maintain.

In contrast to the organization of an event like the Olympic games, this project did not endow the region with any new infrastructure. Hence, Hydro-Québec did transfer to the Inuit community a small number of prefabricated buildings, which for the most part have not been utilized. In fact, several residents consider these to be dangerous structures in need of demolition. According to municipal officials in Kuujjuarapik, the Great Whale Project may have, in fact, hindered the development of infrastructure in the village. The public bodies responsible for Aboriginal and northern community development actually pushed back certain necessary infrastructure work in the village of Kuujjuarapik (such as improvements to the airport, installation of an aqueduct and sewer system, construction of a generating station, etc.) in anticipation of Hydro-Québec's investment in the region. According to those community members surveyed, the suspension of the project had the effect of unduly prolonging this anticipation and hindered the development of much needed and overdue investments in infrastructure in the community of Kuujjuarapik.

In terms of employment, the impacts of the project were less negative. New income generated by the pre-project studies totalled $2.6 million. This represents approximately $370,000 in salaries, per year, for seven years (the duration of the feasibility studies), the equivalent to forty-eight full-time jobs. As the project was in existence for a period of seven years, about seven full-time jobs were therefore created during the pre-project study period. Since the majority of economic after-effects were generated in the community of Kuujjuarapik, where the number of full-time jobs hovered at around 165 at this time, it is possible to say that the project stimulated a 4 percent increase in the number of jobs in the community. Considering the community's high rate of unemployment, it could be said that any new jobs created by the project would constitute a positive effect. However, according to those community members surveyed, the jobs on offer were seasonal, of little interest to applicants, and did not include any professional training. Excepting those jobs related to project negotiations, employment was offered mainly in the service sector as guides, interpreters, cooks, security guards, and camp maintenance workers, none of which afforded the Inuit people much opportunity to gain new skills.

However, the project did also allow for the creation of a certain number of quality jobs, such as those on negotiating committees or advisory boards. Hydro-Québec was itself responsible for absorbing the cost of running and paying out the salaries or honoraria to participants. Several Inuit people were engaged on these committees as negotiators or experts on the regional environment. Those who occupied such positions gained important political knowledge, or were able to hone their negotiating skills. Some became veritable experts on the text of the *James Bay Agreement*, thoroughly employing and integrating the logic of the Canadian bureaucracy. Involvement in these committees also undoubtedly affected the careers of these individuals, who were afforded the opportunity to leverage their experience to obtain employment or to get involved in the local administration or community politics. As articulated by the mayor of Kuujjuarapik in 1996:

> Because of this job on the Inuit Task Force, I learned to speak (English) better, and I learned a lot about the environment. It gave me experience. I learned to know people and to negotiate. And because of this experience, I learned to do my job as mayor better and more quickly.

It is also quite possible that, after a bit of time, committee members had acquired enough experience to negotiate better compensatory measures for the benefit of their community or to increase the number of obstacles to the project in order to slow down its progress.

Generally, the experience gained allowed committee members to feel a measure of control when negotiating face-to-face with Hydro-Québec. Instead of feeling obligated to submit silently to the state's will, some Inuit people gained the sense that they could influence decisions and outcomes on the project. This sense of power led to defiance not in evidence at the time the *James Bay Agreement* was signed. As indicated, with irony, by a leader in Kuujjuarapik involved in the negotiations after the signing of the *James Bay Agreement*, "[A]t that time, we didn't know how to negotiate with Whites. We were nomads, living in the bush. That's why we signed the JBNQA . . . but since then we've learned how to make better deals."

Inuit representatives have thus been able to boost their confidence as leaders and negotiators through this process. When the project was suspended in 1994, Inuit leaders demanded that Hydro-Québec complete a study to evaluate the impact of the project's cessation on their communities. This request might appear ironic, given that the Inuit supported the suspension of the project, but this stance shows to what extent they had become staunch negotiators, willing to fire all their guns even when involved in a situation deemed favourable to their interests.

On the other hand, according to those Inuit residents surveyed, it would seem that the pre-project studies had significant and direct adverse impacts on life in their communities. The pre-project research activities brought with it diverse frustrations: noise, pollution, and increased movement on the land. These activities would have affected traditional migration routes of certain animal species, especially geese. These stresses on the land and environment would undoubtedly have led to a loss for hunters, who would be forced to compensate for their losses by buying food in the marketplace. They would have also obligated the Inuit, for whom hunting is the principal economic activity, to displace their routes in order to maintain their yields. Research activities also brought about the displacement of Crees' hunting routes toward the coast. The Crees of the neighbouring community of Whapmagoostui, who hunt traditionally inland in an area not used by the Inuit, were forced to change their regular hunting practices in order to avoid the problems caused by project-related work. This state of affairs was reported by all the hunters in the village; even non-Aboriginal residents observed the change, to the point where many such non-Aboriginal people in the community spoke of an "invasion" of Inuit territory by the Crees.

The Great Whale Project also generated significant social impacts on the community. First, tensions were heightened between the Crees and Inuit communities. According to certain community insiders, the Cree population disapproved of Inuit engagement in the pre-project studies. This provoked a number of disputes, on both institutional and individual levels. Above all, the presence of Hydro-Québec employees in the community, whose numbers, as non-Aboriginal temporary residents, in Kuujjuarapik at times almost surpassed the Inuit population, led to certain social stresses such as an increase in consumption of alcohol and drugs brought into the community by workers from the south, either for personal use or for trafficking within the community. Secondary effects were also felt, including an increase in violence within the community or the incidence of parental neglect. In addition, during Phase I of the project, workers housed in the camp at Kuujjuarapik were in the practice of luring young Inuit women by offering them drugs, alcohol, or money. It should not be overlooked that the majority of residents in this camp were young men, living far away from their spouses or companions, and several young local women became pregnant. Children born of extramarital relations were then left without fathers or means of material support, which came to represent a significant strain on the community.

The presence of this camp and the interest it held for many Inuit people contributed to tensions within the community, notably between young people and Elders. All those surveyed in the community had observed this tension. The project appeared to have triggered the spread of both positive and negative aspects of modern life within the community, distracting attention from traditional practices and leading to an increase in social problems. As remarked by one Inuk of Kuujjuarapik:

> We learned to sell alcohol under the table. We learned to smoke dope. Because of all this, people have begun to eat less and to eat food of poorer quality. This has led to other problems. New illnesses have appeared. Our community is falling apart, physically and socially.

The list of impacts related to the Great Whale Project would not be complete without the matter of the Inuit relocation to Umiujaq. The issues surrounding this affair are vastly more complex than can receive proper treatment here, and the reader is invited to refer to other works that examine the subject in detail (Martin 2002). In brief, in 1986, at the height of work on the Great Whale Project, 286 Inuit people moved from Kuujjuarapik to establish the new village of Umiujaq. While these members of the community moved for historical reasons, resettling an area their ancestors had once occupied, it would appear that the Great Whale Project contributed indirectly to the decision to relocate the community. Social problems, resulting from the presence of Hydro-Québec workers in the community, together with the project's negative effects on the traditional hunt, convinced a number of Inuit that a relocation of the community would be necessary in order to preserve any semblance of a traditional way of life on their ancestral lands.

This return to traditional lands and lifestyle was made possible under the *James Bay Agreement*, which anticipated the construction of a new village in the Lac Guillaume–Delisle area (where Umiujaq is now located) to resettle the Inuit people of Kuujjuarapik in case the community members chose to distance themselves from the Great Whale Project and its impacts. Therefore, while the Great Whale Project was not the sole cause of this community schism, it did provide an institutional and material basis for the creation of a new village (Martin 2002). In triggering the realization that this type of modern development could endanger the community's traditional ways of life, the project was, to an extent, responsible for the separation of the community of Kuujjuarapik into two geographically separate and distinct entities. This did not come without significant consequences for the community. Most of the residents of Kuujjuarapik lost at least one family member to the new community, which brought about a palpable sense of frustration among those who felt abandoned by those who chose to settle in Umiujaq. Residents of Umiujaq, in turn, were disappointed that their cousins, brothers, and sisters had not followed their lead in moving to the new village to escape the effects of the Great Whale Project.

ANALYSIS: A MIXED BAG

Conflicting visions of traditional and modern development. The Great Whale Project illustrates the dichotomy that exists between locally and globally defined notions of development. For the state, Québec in this case, development would be held synonymous with "growth"; for local actors, notably the Inuit, it signifies the development of tools necessary to ensure the preservation of their ways of life. These fundamentally diverging perspectives lead to ever more conflicts as the phenomenon of globalization progresses. To respond to the growing demand for energy and resources by industrialized regions of the globe, states—both in industrialized and industrializing countries— have put more and more pressure on regions yet untouched by the process of industrial development. This is not a completely new state of affairs for the Inuit people, who have dealt with global influences since the first European whale hunters scoured the Arctic waters. Beginning in the twenty-first century, however, these pressures arose not only from private interests, but from the state as well. By its authority over the society at large, the state therefore legitimizes the development of Aboriginal lands for the profit of external or foreign interests.

In studies examining the subject of development projects, this dichotomy is well known and recalls a very simple concept: the interests of the collective whole versus those of the individual. The whole, or at least the majority, can exercise virtually unrestricted authority over the assets of minorities. In the same way, industrialized regions, in the name of globalization, can exercise jurisdiction over local actors in order to further their own vision of development. The Quebec Court of Appeals expressed this idea when it overturned the *Malouf* injunction, which had temporarily halted construction of the La Grande Complex.

> The interests of the public, and of the Quebec population at large, are therefore pitted against those of about two thousand of its residents. We are of the opinion that there is no comparison between these two sets of interests; at this stage in the process the needs of these populations are not similar. (cited by Malouf 1973, 205)

Following this decision from the Court of Appeals, the federal and provincial governments, lawfully representing the interests of the majority, negotiated the *James Bay Agreement* along with the Crees, Inuit, and Naskapis. This had the effect of institutionalizing the rights of the majority to use sovereign lands to service their own interests. Hence, the agreement did include compensatory provisions that addressed the rights of Inuit and First Nations to follow their own model for development and recognized the need to afford them the necessary tools to preserve their ways of life. Without fundamentally reshaping the Western perspective on development, the *James Bay Agreement* did, however, represent a breach in the hitherto unshakeable faith of the West in its vision of progress and "modern" development. In a way, the *James Bay Agreement* served as a milestone for later deals such as the Nunavut Accord and the recently signed Nunavik Accord. Indeed, both agreements devolved a certain degree of legislative power to the Inuit in order that they might decide, for themselves, on the type of development to pursue.

The *James Bay Agreement* itself carries a measure of ambiguity, as it simultaneously created the legal conditions for a modern approach to development whilst affirming the legitimacy of the Aboriginal perspective and alternative to growth-led development. It is precisely this ambiguity that Cree and Inuit protesters exploited to mount a guerrilla campaign in the media and the courts, which was ultimately successful in halting further work for the Great Whale project. Since the project was never constructed as planned, one could almost say that the Great Whale saga ended in a victory for the Aboriginal perspective on development. Of course, the official version of this episode is that Hydro-Québec abandoned the project as a result of decreases in international demand for hydroelectricity, and not that the utility had bowed to pressure mounted by Quebec's Inuit and Crees. This version might hold as long as international demand for hydroelectricity remained weak. The resumption of energy-intensive policies in the United States completely changed the landscape and would have given Hydro-Québec every justification to relaunch those hydroelectric projects it held on standby (Great Whale and NBR). However, though the design and pre-project studies had already been completed and refined, the Great Whale Project was never resurrected. Instead, Hydro-Québec preferred to canvass other areas and start other projects, such as that on the Sainte-Marguerite River in Innu territory. This would indicate that the demand-driven argument does not hold, but rather that Hydro-Québec preferred to opt for a new series of projects and negotiations with Cree and Inuit peoples.

In the context of these new negotiations Aboriginal peoples are treated as equals and partners, not as adversaries to be manipulated or co-opted. The symbolic victory of the Crees and Inuit peoples, evidenced by the suspension of the project and their capacity to bear upon the execution of projects in exploiting international opinion, is certainly the origin of the *Paix des Braves*, a veritable alliance between Quebec and First Peoples. Further, one could suggest that if the Crees and Inuit are from this point forward treated as equals by Quebec, this would not be the unique result of a provincial government decision to anoint them with this status, but rather because they had fought for this status through their guerrilla campaign against the Great Whale Project.

The quiet skill of the Crees and Inuit. This victory for the Crees and Inuit lies first with their capacity to win over public sympathies by orchestrating actions that stress the importance of environmental protection and cultural diversity. To this it should be added that they were able to assemble in support of their cause a collection of pressure groups with diverse and at times opposing agendas. Supporters of the Crees and Inuit constituted quite a diverse patchwork of civil society. Among these were ecologists fiercely opposed to the commercialization of animal furs, who may not have been natural allies with traditional hunters and trappers, as well as students of both sovereigntist and federalist camps. The coalition also included American politicians opposed to the Great Whale Project: moderates such as Robert Kennedy Jr. who opposed the project for environmental reasons and conservatives from various states in New England (notably New Hampshire and Massachusetts) who were not motivated by environmental imperatives so much as the desire to support their own energy-producing sectors, namely the coal industry. It should also be noted that while the Inuit took pains to present a common front with the Crees throughout their campaign, their strategies did often diverge. For example, the Inuit did participate in the Phase II pre-project studies, while the Crees refused all forms of engagement with Hydro-Québec. Nevertheless, on the national and international scenes, the Inuit always gave the impression of working hand in hand with the Crees.

Another success for the Crees and Inuit in this conflict was in having succeeded in attracting the attention of the media, intellectuals, and leaders of Western countries. Their approach, which included not only the Odeyak expedition but also delegations of representatives to The Hague, Washington, and Geneva, as well as advertisements in influential American dailies, effectively spread their message and rallied international support for their cause. Above all, by exposing to the world the colonial will of the modern Quebec state, they offered to Quebec civil society a mirror reflection of itself. The image revealed was not that of the society that Québecers dreamed of creating. Even leaders of the sovereigntist movement, for whom the quest for economic self-sufficiency was closely aligned with the goal of political autonomy, were not prepared to see their emancipatory agenda transformed to suit an obsolete colonial regime. In addition, the heavy-handed treatment to which the Crees and Inuit were subjected tarnished the image of the Quebec government, and threatened to detract from the sovereigntist cause. It is, therefore, not surprising that Premier Jacques

Parizeau, as a gesture of goodwill toward the Inuit and First Nations of Quebec, announced the postponement of the Great Whale Project. Moreover, to begin a new era in relations between Quebec and Aboriginal peoples, he further specified that this suspension would be "forever."

This decision was as well received by the Quebec population as had been news of the *Malouf* injunction. Indeed, whatever the feelings held by the majority of Québecers toward First Nations and Inuit peoples, a number of influential intellectuals, artists, and politicians held that the emancipation of Quebec could not be to the detriment of its Aboriginal citizens. It is quite possible that this attitude was in part the result of the actions of the Crees and Inuit who were able to show the importance, both for themselves and for the cause of cultural diversity, of maintaining their traditional ways of life. The Crees and Inuit also developed greater connections with other Aboriginal nations of the Americas, a strategy that helped to show that Quebec's goal was not a simple error in judgment, but rather part of a paradigm for development with negative implications for Aboriginal peoples.

Local democracy over colonial elitism. It is important to note that the Great Whale Project highlighted a particularity of the Inuit mode of governance. The issue of governance here is central, since the heart of the dilemma faced by colonized societies rests in the destruction of their traditional political structures and their replacement with foreign institutions. These new structures, often proven ineffective in their inability to adapt to the new social context in which they operate, contribute to the alienation of the subordinated group. Nunavik, however, is an example that diverges from the classic colonial experience. In the colonial model, as described by Albert Memmi (1972), the central power aids the emergence of a new local elite comprised of young natives of the region, educated in the mores and at the institutions of the colonial society, and primed to occupy important positions in the local administration. Once in place, the local elite acts as a direct link to the central administration; having obtained power, prestige, and economic advancement, this new elite eventually sides with the interests of the colonial power and adopts its values and customs. Members of this elite end up increasingly resembling the non-natives with whom

they most often associate, distancing themselves from their native coun-
trymen. In the case of Nunavik, it is clear that the *James Bay Agreement*
did contribute to the establishment of new institutions, which in turn
formed a basis for a new technocratic elite whose actions would support
the central power. For example, the Makivik Society—the corporation
that manages the indemnities paid out to the Inuit—was for a long time
located in Montréal. Among those Inuit community members surveyed,
several remarked that the directors of Makivik, surrounded by lawyers and
consultants, seemed by outward appearances to have been controlled by
their handlers. This would also hold for the majority of other institutions,
such as Kativik School Board, Kativik Regional Social Services, and Cree
Regional Health, Regional Development Council, and the regional police
corps whose mandates are to enforce laws and regulations or to administer
local programs set out by the provincial and federal governments.

In this context, the Great Whale Project negotiation process should have
served to consolidate ties between the new elite—servicing in these new
institutions—and the provincial government. Well-paying jobs on negotiating committees or advisory boards, travel, expense accounts given
to a handful of Inuit interlocutors, in addition to the personal linkages
made over the years of negotiations, should have led to the harmoniza-
tion between the views of Inuit leaders and representatives of the modern
state. Actually, Hydro-Québec tried to seduce the members of this new
elite by always maintaining decorum and by sending high-ranking officials to negotiate with them. We have had the opportunity to participate
at several meetings between representatives of the Inuit communities of
Kuujjuarapik and Umiujaq and Hydro-Québec, and have observed at each
meeting the service of a private plane to transport participants between
villages. Inuit interlocutors were invited to travel this way freely from one
village to another. Inside the plane, a certain camaraderie could develop,
aided by consumption of aperitifs. Relations between the two groups were
certainly unequal, however, as evidenced by Hydro-Québec's choice to
travel by private plane rather than charter flights around the region. This
type of behaviour would serve to show their Inuit hosts Hydro-Québec's
economic superiority and largesse.

It is quite remarkable that this strategy, so clearly aimed at co-opting a new elite to serve the ambitions of the state, did not work in Nunavik. This holds true even though the comments of several witnesses, including the following quote from an Inuk involved in the Great Whale Project, reveal that Western ideas had insinuated themselves into the outlook of many Inuit people:

> I wouldn't say go ahead, build it, because I love the land too much. But as a man, you have to adapt to your environment and climate. For thousands of years, men, Inuit as well as Whites, have proved they can adapt. I have confidence we will continue to adapt. We'll adapt to the dam. I don't think the environment can change so quickly that man can't adapt to it. Our mother, the Earth, watches over us. I said to myself, if Hydro-Québec wants to go ahead with this project, I don't have the power to stop them, but I know that as human beings the members of this community are going to be able to adapt. . . . We are not as threatened as we sometimes think. We can always adapt to a new situation. If the compensation and the mitigation measures are acceptable, we can agree to the project.

This is not an isolated attitude; among those Inuit surveyed, several in fact blamed their leaders for having been unduly influenced by Hydro-Québec.

> The leaders did not defend our interests. . . . In my opinion, they were only thinking about what they were going to get out of it. . . . Money is what got the Inuit to agree to participate in the studies. But it wasn't the people who wanted it, it was the leaders.

Just as revealing is the following testimonial, which shows that a number of residents of Kuujjuarapik believe that the negotiators may have taken the negotiations as ends unto themselves.

> I know some who must be disappointed the project has been suspended. I think the members of the Inuit Task Force didn't like the suspension of the project because they lost their jobs. I bet they're hoping the project will be resumed.

The preceding testimonials should be taken in context in order not to be misunderstood. They are, of course, reflections of the pressure the community exerts on its leaders as a way of ensuring they continue to act for the public good, more than they are an indication of any hidden agenda on the part of Inuit leaders. In reality, there is no evidence to show that Inuit leaders involved in the negotiations supported the project; their actions would indicate quite the contrary. That they were tempted to personally profit from their involvement in the project is not impossible, nor that a prolongation of negotiations would not be seen to be personally favourable, but we did not collect any evidence indicating that these considerations actually influenced the behaviour of these actors and, on the contrary, it appeared that these leaders were indeed consistently working for the collective interest.

Public pressure was exerted not only on negotiators from the community, but on regional negotiators based in Montréal. Testimonials, both from community leaders and the population at large, demonstrate some form of dissatisfaction with the actions of the Makivik Society in the context of the Great Whale Project. One community member after another vocalized complaints about how Inuit funds were managed to serve priorities that did not correspond with the wishes of the community but, rather, the corporation and its directors. Some believe that Makivik did not support the activities of protestors enough, preferring instead to support the negotiations with Hydro-Québec. According to many of those surveyed, it was in response to its critics that Makivik became associated, at the last minute, with the Odeyak project. One is left to wonder how the population became so informed and tuned into the process of negotiations, to the point of sensing that their leaders were at risk of being influenced by Hydro-Québec. The answer lies in the Inuit model of democracy, rooted in a type of "agora," where debates and decision making take place simultaneously.

The Inuit Agora: between traditional and modern forms of governance. This public forum, the home of Inuit democracy, takes place not in the physical environment but rather over the airwaves. Each village in Nunavik maintains a community radio station that broadcasts music, news, and messages among local residents. Hunters phone the station to report the capture of game; the town hall makes announcements on matters of interest to the public, such as employment vacancies and community projects. The radio also serves to maintain personal ties within the community. Those wishing to make contact with a friend or relative have only to phone the radio station and broadcast this fact over the airwaves, as virtually the entire community is connected via this medium. The radio bridges distances created by modern life and makes it possible to maintain close ties characteristic of traditional societies. This interchange over the airwaves allows community members to stay connected to one another, which creates a forum for public exchanges and debate on important issues.

According to those community members surveyed, the Great Whale Project sparked intense debate on the radio, which became the main forum for expression of dissent or discontent with Inuit leadership in their handling of the project. The interchange on the subject of the Great Whale Project had a wide reach and thus gave rise to structured debate on the issue. According to those surveyed, the populations of both Kuujjuarapik and Umiujaq seem to have belonged to one of two camps. Some citizens supported a compromise with Hydro-Québec and participation in the pre-project studies, and others supported a more radical strategy of non-engagement with the corporation. Both camps confronted each other in this way throughout the lifespan of the project; every decision made by the community leadership was thoroughly debated over the airwaves. The strategy employed by the Inuit community—which saw them participate in both negotiations for the project and protests against it—was a reflection of the often contradictory wishes of the community. It would appear that the Inuit leadership, instead of favouring one option over another, chose to simultaneously pursue the different options put forth by different segments of the community. This would indicate the extent to which the radio, as a public forum for expression, contributed to the creation of a unique form of governance that values consensus and compromise over the will of the majority.

If we dig deeper into the issue of Inuit governance, we would see that the Western democratic model employed in Nunavik has integrated traditional forms of governance. While Inuit communities in Nunavik are governed by officials elected by universal suffrage, it should be noted that Western methods of governance have not totally supplanted traditional governance structures. Local elites tend to belong to "grand" traditional families (grand both in number and prestige, due to the charisma of a number of their members). In this way a certain family will control the town hall, just as another may control the local cooperative or community clinic. According to several Inuit community members surveyed, elections were won based on candidates' successful mobilization of friends and family members, and thus social ties were more important than 'political ideas' in affecting electoral outcomes. One respondent in Kuujjuarapik suggested that candidates had only to hand out jobs or housing for their family members in order to be re-elected. When asked if this troubled her, she answered with laughter:

> A bit, because my family is small. That means I probably will never have better housing. But, people who belong to a large family have many relatives who ask for a lot of services. They need to have important jobs so they can help their family. Me, I don't have a lot of people counting on me. In a way, it's easier.

Democracy, therefore, is in part subjugated to traditional ways of thinking founded on ideas of reciprocity. This co-optation of democracy seems acceptable to the Inuit people, not because they do not value democracy as such, but because they see in their system a built-in mechanism for compromise between the demands of their society and the rational mode of governance imposed on their community from the outside. One could also hypothesize (and several insiders surveyed would agree) that the public agora, where democratic debates free from familial influences are held, serves to balance traditional influences over politics. This is made all the more effective by leaders who are willing to act according to the opinions expressed by the community. Inuit leaders and negotiators who, for personal or economic reasons (as some have indicated), might have favoured the continuation of the project, chose despite this to adopt the community's stance in opposition to the project.

The effectiveness of such a model can be appreciated through the results it has achieved. In the case of the Great Whale Project, the existence of a public forum most certainly helped leaders avoid undue influence from

Hydro-Québec. The Inuit model does not necessarily translate into victory for the ruling party, as is often the case in the Canadian parliamentary system. In the latter model, the voice of the opposition—even if acknowledged—has little chance of influencing real outcomes. In the Inuit model of governance, democratically held debate is able to influence those in power. Hence, there are limits to this phenomenon and the sheer diversity in public opinion might place constraints on leaders' efforts. Representatives of government or its agencies, in the context of negotiations with the Inuit, have attempted to discount this and encourage the adoption of one monolithic approach. The state expects that the stance of the community represents the voice of the majority and that this majority acts as a one undifferentiated mass. While this might work well for societies of millions, the Inuit still live within a relatively small community. In this context, to impose the will of the majority would be perceived as tantamount to an abuse of power. This is indicated in the following comment from one Inuk:

> For us, the Aboriginal people, when we talk about issues, the most important opinions are those of the smallest group of people. The opinion of the majority of people, everybody knows that already. It is more important to discuss the opinion of those who don't think like everyone else. White people only think the majority is important, but if we only listen to the majority, who will address the issues of the minority?

This idea, characteristic of the traditional consensual form of governance, would appear to have survived modern influences such as those brought in by the Great Whale Project. The public debates throughout this period served to help institutionalize the agora as a forum where differing perspectives on the world's issues are reconciled. Unfortunately, the growth of modern institutions, increasingly complex bureaucracies within Nunavik, and assorted external pressures threaten to transform the Inuit leadership into administrative technocrats over public representatives. Nevertheless, despite the burden of change, the Inuit continually value a system of governance that remains directly linked to its constituency. In this vein, the Makivik Society recently moved its operations from Montreal to Kuujjuaq in a significant and symbolic attempt to affect a rapprochement between elected officials and public administrators.

The stance adopted by Hydro-Québec vis-à-vis the Inuit and First Nations has greatly evolved since the launch of the James Bay Project. A number of factors would help explain this evolution; notably, as indicated in this chapter, sovereigntist leaders hoped that a new relationship with Quebec's First Peoples would serve to reduce their resistance to the idea of Quebec's independence. The study of the Great Whale Project presented in this chapter reveals, by contrast, that the tenacity and resistance of the Inuit and Crees forced the provincial government to treat First Peoples as equals. This resistance also contributed to a redefinition of relationship between Hydro-Québec and the province's Inuit and Cree populations. In short, the *Paix des Braves* would never have materialized without the resistance of the Braves.

Opposition to the Great Whale Project served to strengthen the legitimacy of Inuit leadership, as well as develop within the affected communities a mode of governance incorporating both modern and traditional methods of consultation and decision making. While the economic benefits derived from the Great Whale Project are minimal compared to the social impacts that resulted from its pre-project phase, the one positive impact of the project—and it is a major one—was that it allowed the Inuit to exert their demand to be treated as equals by Quebecers, and no longer as colonial subjects in need of protection by the state.

---

1   This paper was derived from my doctoral research (Martin 2001a) and from Martin (2002 and 2003), from which I extracted the raw materials for this work. For the purposes of simplicity and clarity, I have chosen not to burden the existing text with detailed descriptions of methodology. For more on this I would suggest the reader seek out the above-cited works. I will note here that research was conducted during two field studies in 1996 and 1998 at Kuujjuarapik and Umiujaq (Nunavik, Québec). Background information was collected during a series of semi-structured interviews of Inuit residents in these two communities. The first field study took place as part of research, funded by Hydro-Québec, which sought to measure the impacts of the Great Whale hydroelectric project on both communities (see Duhaime et al. 1998).

The second field study was conceived as a follow-up to test the hypotheses generated during the analysis of information gathered during the first study. I would like to thank the community members of Kuujjuarapik and Umiujaq, and particularly Anthony Ittoshat, Noah Inukpuk, and Alec Tukaluk. Thanks also to my interpreters Alice Meeko, Jessie Araguterk, Okoya Muktu, and Lizzie Tooktoo. I would also like to acknowledge here several organizations who offered financial support for my research: Association of Canadian Universities for Northern Studies (ACUNS), Social Sciences and Humanities Research Council of Canada (SSHRC), Fonds pour la formation de chercheurs et l'aide à la recherche (Fonds FCAR), Department of Indian Affairs and Northern Development. I would especially like to thank Shauna Troniak for her help in translating from the original French an earlier text that served as the basis for this chapter.

11

More Dams for Nitassinan: New Business Partnerships
between Hydro-Québec and Innu Communities

Paul Charest

IN JUNE OF 2003, THIERRY VANDAL, the president of Hydro-Québec
Production, described the Province of Quebec as "the land of large dams"
(Francoeur 2003). A more honest description would have noted that it is
Aboriginal lands, in particular those of the Innu and Cree peoples, that
have become "the land of dams and reservoirs," thanks to Hydro-Québec's
efforts to harness as many large rivers as possible for the production of
hydroelectricity at a profitable cost. A quick estimate shows that approximately 80 percent of its hydroelectric production capacity comes from
the dams and reservoirs located in the territories of the Quebec Innu and
Crees, or about 24,000 MW out of a total of 29,000 MW (Hydro-Québec
2001, 108). Add the 4000 MW generated in Labrador's Innu lands and
this percentage climbs to 90 percent. Even this figure does not take into
account the production equipment located in Innu country and belonging
to private companies such as Alcan, Abitibi-Price, and Iron Ore, which
have a combined capacity of more than 1500 MW. Altogether, about one
third of all Hydro-Québec's hydro energy production, or 10,000 MW,
comes from Innu lands in Quebec and Labrador.

The exploitation of rivers flowing in Innu and Cree country has resulted
in a hydro-dependent province; indeed, some 40 percent of the total energy
consumed in Quebec in now supplied by hydroelectricity, compared

to only 19 percent in 1951 (Francoeur 2003). Whether willingly or not, since the 1950s, the Innu and Cree peoples have been intimately involved in the economic transformation of Quebec in that their traditional lands are the site of hydroelectric production facilities that now represent some 92 percent of all the electricity generated by Hydro-Québec. Since 1968, this government-owned enterprise has been one of the motors of economic development in the province, a role that the recently elected Liberal government would like Hydro-Québec to continue, as evidenced by the discussion on the utility's strategic plan for 2004 to 2008 that took place during the hearings held by the Parliamentary Commission on Economy and Labour (Hydro-Québec 2003). The utility seems to be in agreement with this stance, in that it foresees investments of about three billion dollars per year for the next ten to fifteen years for the construction of dams and associated infrastructure.

The great majority of hydroelectric projects in Innu territory shown on Map 11.1 were completed before 1975. Some were considered technological feats of their time, like the Manic 5 dam, the Daniel Johnson dam, or the 735 kV power lines, which were often used as examples of the new know-how acquired by Quebec engineers. When the big works moved to James Bay in the 1970s, the rivers of the North Shore region were largely forgotten by Hydro-Québec planners and engineers, except for projects intended to increase the production capacity of the powerhouses of the Bersimis, aux Outardes, Manicouagan watersheds, and the small station of Robertson Lake. But a new phase of large construction projects began with SM-3 in 1994 and Toulnoustouc in 1999. Moreover, construction is well advanced on a new dam and reservoir unit (a fourth one) on the Peribonka River following the authorization by the Quebec government. Preliminary studies are also being pursued on two large rivers located on the middle and the lower north shore, the Romaine and the Little-Mecatina, of which the energy production capacity is estimated at 3000 MW.

Table 11.1 provides a list of the new hydroelectric projects completed or planned in Innu territory and Nitassinan, and their energy production capacity. This paper focuses attention on these recent projects, the larger economic and political context in which they have and will be realized, the

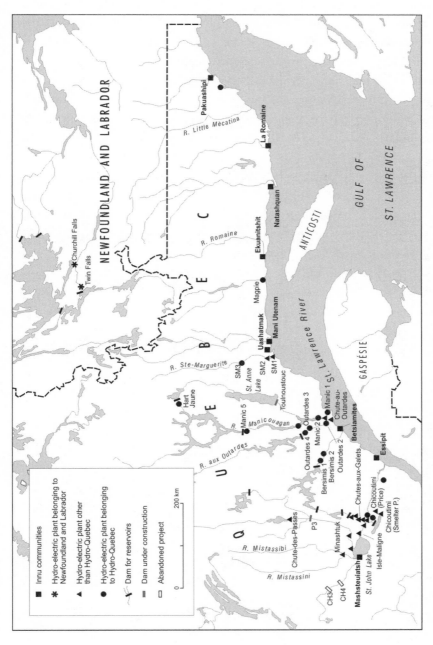

MAP 11.1 Hydroelectric Dams and Reservoirs in Innu Territory

TABLE 11.1

Hydroelectric Power Stations in Innu Territories

Owner	Quebec generating station	Type of station	Hydro system	Year of completion	Capacity in MW
Hydro-Québec	Outardes-2	Run of river	Aux Outardes River	1978	472
Hydro-Québec	Outardes-3	Run of river	Aux Outardes River	1969	891
Hydro-Québec	Outardes-4	Reservoir	Aux Outardes River	1969	630
City of Jonquière	Jonquière n°1	Run of river	Aux Sables River	1996 (after renovation)	4.5
Abitibi-Consolidated inc.	Jonquière	Reservoir	Aux Sables River	1998 (after renovation)	4.85
La Société d'énergie Belle Rivière inc.	Belle Rivière	Run of river	Belle Rivière	1993 (after renovation)	1
Hydro-Québec	Bersimis-1	Reservoir	Betsiamites River	1956	1125
Hydro-Québec	Bersimis-2	Run of river	Betsiamites River	1959	845
Hydro-Québec	Lac Robertson	Reservoir	Ha! Ha! River	1995	21
Hydro-Québec	Toulnustouc	Reservoir	Manicouagan River	2005	526
Hydro-Québec	Manic-3	Run of river	Manicouagan River	1975	1244
Hydro-Québec	Manic-5-PA	Reservoir	Manicouagan River	1989	1064
Hydro-Québec	Hart-Jaune	Reservoir	Manicouagan River	1960	50
Hydro-Québec	Manic-2	Run of river	Manicouagan River	1965	1024
Hydro-Québec	Manic-1	Run of river	Manicouagan River	1966	184
Hydro-Québec	Manic-5	Reservoir	Manicouagan River	1970	1528
Société Minashtuk inc.	Minashtuk	Run of river	Mistassibi River	2000	12
Hydro Morin Inc.	Chute-Blanche	Reservoir	Peribonka River	1998	1.5
Société d'énergie Petites Bergeronnes Inc. / Axor	Petites Bergeronnes	Run of river	Petites Bergeronnes River	1994 (after renovation)	4.2
Innergex Inc.	Portneuf-1	Run of river	Portneuf River	1996	7.5
Innergex Inc.	Portneuf-2	Run of river	Portneuf River	1996	11.75
Innergex Inc.	Portneuf-3	Run of river	Portneuf River	1996	7.5
Pouvoir Riverin Inc. (société en commandite)	Pentecôte	Run of river	Riverin River	1999	2
Hydro-Québec	Sainte-Marguerite-3	Reservoir	Sainte-Marguerite River	2004	884
Hydrowatt SM-1 Inc.	Sainte-Marguerite-1	Reservoir	Sainte-Marguerite River	1993 (after renovation)	8
Hydro Morin Inc.	Anse Saint-Jean	Run of river	Saint-Jean River	1995 (after renovation)	0,45
Fiducie Boralex énergie	RSP-1	Run of river	Sault aux Cochons River	1993 (after renovation)	1
Fiducie Boralex énergie	RSP-3	Run of river	Sault aux Cochons River	1995	5,5
					10,512

(Note: Private dams are not included in the table.)

role of Hydro-Québec as a state enterprise and in its new policy of partnership with Aboriginal people, more specifically with the Innu, and the negotiation of a settlement of land claims that has been going on for the last twenty-
five years.

THE INNU AND NITASSINAN

The Innu are the most populous of the ten Amerindian nations living in the
province of Quebec, having a total population of 15,000 persons, just a few
hundred more than the Crees (Canada, Affaires Indiennes 2002). There are
about 2000 residents in Labrador living in two villages. In Quebec, the Innu
form nine local communities (or bands), living on nine reservations and one
settlement, extending from Lake St-John and all along the North Shore (Map
11.2). The population of the Innu local communities varies, the larger ones
(Mashteuiatsh, Betsiamites, Uashat mak Mani-Utenam) having more than
3000 members each, being located closer to the main urban and industrial part

MAP 11.2 The Nitassinan (Territory) Claimed by Quebec Innus, 1979

of the province. A number of the communities have signed agreements with Hydro-Québec for the purpose of hydroelectric development. Their location in regions heavily touched by the industrial development of resources (forestry, mining, hydroelectricity production, and transportation) and the urgent need for job creation can explain the reluctant acceptance of continuing resource exploitation.

The development of the dams was followed by a series of claims by the Innu communities located within the region affected. The first of the claims was made in April of 1979, when the Conseil Attikamek–Montagnais (CAM) presented a statement of comprehensive claims to the minister of Indian Affairs. The claim was made in accordance with the policy of the federal government that was adopted in 1973 (CAM 1979). In January of the following year, the same statement was sent to the premier of Quebec, René Lévesque. From 1981 to 1983 a research project on use and occupancy by the Innu showed that the total superficies of the traditional and actual Innu territory, for which the recognition of a land title was claimed in Quebec and Labrador, was about 600,000 square kilometres (Deschênes and Dominique 1983). This situation and the extent of this Innu territory are shown on Map 11.2.

Nearly twenty-five years later, after scores of meetings, discussions, exchange of documents, propositions, and counter-propositions, no final agreement has yet been signed. During this time period, the CAM has disappeared and been replaced by three different political entities, which are now negotiating separate agreements in the name of the communities they represent. Two years ago, the Mamuitun tribal council, representing four Innu communities and about 8000 Innus, signed an Agreement in Principle with the negotiators of the governments of Quebec and Canada (Anonymous 2002), which was examined during public hearings of the Quebec Commission of the Institutions at the beginning 2003. It was ratified by the Legislative Assembly two years later. Mamit Innuat, the other Innu council, representing three other Innu communities, is also negotiating with the representatives of the provincial and federal governments, but the pace of negotiation is slower because of its more radical positions concerning land rights and rights on the exploitation of natural resources, water in particular. However, Hydro-Québec's intentions to build many dams, reservoirs, and power plants on the Romaine and Little-Mecatina rivers should put more pressure on the pace of negotiations in the months and years to come.

HYDRO-QUÉBEC, THE GOVERNMENT OF QUEBEC, AND ABORIGINAL PEOPLES

The new wave of hydroelectric development in Innu country is occurring in a very different context from that in the 1950s, 1960s, and 1970s, the decades during which the Bersimis, aux Outardes, and Manicouagan structures were built. The ancestral rights of the Aboriginal groups can no longer be ignored as it was in that time (Charest 1980). The *Calder* and *Malouf* court decisions in 1973, the federal policy concerning comprehensive claims, the *James Bay and Northern Quebec Agreement*, and others that followed, have created an obligation for development promoters like Hydro-Québec to negotiate with Aboriginal leaders and communities still having land titles and other Aboriginal rights that have not been extinguished.

More than thirty years ago, however, things happened differently with the Innu of the North Shore region. The first large hydroelectric and mining developments were carried out before the adoption of the federal comprehensive claims policy. Consequently, the Innu and their rights were ignored and they received very few benefits from the many large construction works, the billions of dollars spent, and the thousands of jobs created. On the other hand, since the 1994 disappearance of the CAM, the Innu no longer have a central political organization to represent them and, as no agreement has been signed, they have no legal framework allowing them to have a greater control over the decisions concerning the development of their lands. This is why discussions and negotiations with Hydro-Québec as well as other developers of natural resources are made on a project-by-project and band-by-band basis. This style of negotiation has been adhered to since the beginning of the 1990s and has included negotiations for the three large new hydroelectric projects of SM-3, Toulnoustouc, and Peribonka, as well as with smaller projects for the restoration of power plants and some river diversions. In all cases, Hydro-Québec has negotiated separately with the leaders of three different Innu communities, even if they were members of a central organization.

It is an open question, of course, whether this practice flows from a principle of 'divide to reign' or is the result of the division of the Quebec Innus into two separate political councils (Mamuitun and Mamit Innuat) and two autonomous communities who themselves are not negotiating. To some extent both explanations are valid since Hydro-Québec profits from a situation where a local community wants to keep all the advantages of a project on its territory for itself without sharing with other Innu communities of the same organization. In this respect, the ancestral value of sharing seems to be put aside here. Yet, the local communities argue that sharing must be done inside the local community rather than at a national or provincial level. This is particularly true since the Innu nation is divided into two groups separated by the Quebec-Labrador boundary. Thus, the millions in compensation money, the contracts, and the jobs can be divided among members of the different communities affected by a particular project more than those who live farther away, such as the Innu of the lower North Shore who are mostly opposed to hydroelectric projects.

The other major change now facing Hydro-Québec is the displacement of its traditional goal of selling electricity at the lowest cost possible to its individual clients, who receive a personal rent from the exploitation of a very abundant natural resource. Instead, it is now obligated to pay larger and larger dividends to its only owner, the Quebec government, in order to help balance the province's annual budget, a goal that is always difficult to achieve. As of 2002, the utility was required to transfer some $1.5 billion to the treasury, a figure that has now risen to $2 billion. The sale of electricity in the lucrative North American energy market, and in particular the exportation of energy to the United States, and even price increases to consumers, as was done recently, are now part of the strategies used by Hydro-Québec to fulfil the new political order. Indeed, the pressure is high on the managers of the state company to accelerate the pace of construction of new production units, especially hydroelectric ones, in order to increase the quantity of energy exported and generate larger profits. Most of the new projects considered by Hydro-Québec for the next ten to fifteen years will be located in Innu country on the Peribonka, Romaine, and Little-Mecatina rivers on the Quebec side, and eventually at Gull Island on the Churchill River in Labrador. The primary beneficiaries of this type of large-scale and low-priced energy production are, of course, the inhabitants of the St. Lawrence Valley, where the great majority of Quebecers live. But those who are the most affected by this kind of energy choice are the Aboriginal inhabitants of the northern part of the province, mainly the Innu and the Crees discussed above.[1]

It is not, of course, solely the decision of Hydro-Québec to proceed with these new initiatives. The provincial government of Quebec generally follows Hydro-Québec in its electricity policy, particularly in the fields of production and distribution of electricity, the exception being when prices are increased beyond that considered reasonable by the general public. Hydroelectric energy is also generally considered by Quebec citizens and most of their economic and political elites as a clean energy source in line with sustainable development, and is presented as such by Hydro-Québec. Further, hydroelectric energy is understood to give the province a compara-tive advantage relative to other provinces, which benefit from large deposits of oil and gas. These perceptions explain the public's opposition to the construction of the Suroît gas power plant, proposed by the managers of Hydro-Québec, as well as the quiet agreement, for the moment at least, to the many large hydroelectric projects mentioned in Hydro-Québec's Stra-tegic Plan 2004–2008.

Given the continued preference for traditional large-scale and central-ized power generation schemes,[2] the question of whether there exists a new sort of relationship between Hydro-Québec, the provincial government, the citizens of Quebec, and Aboriginal populations is absolutely critical. To some extent, at least, there seems to be. In 1998, for instance, the govern-ment of the Parti Québécois published a document entitled "Partnership/ Development/Action," explaining its policy concerning the relations with Aboriginal peoples (Quebec SAA 1998). The idea of partnership is central, according to Premier Lucien Bouchard:

> I understand how important it is to respond rapidly and adequately to the priorities of these communities. This is why I repeat the commitment of Quebec to try its best to help Aboriginals for proj-ects in partnerships which fulfill rightful aspirations. I sincerely believe that, together, we will succeed in making economic and

social development the key factor for a larger autonomy and Aboriginals' control of their own destiny. (Quebec **SAA** 1998, 3; author's translation)

The exact character of the partnership was further elaborated by Bouchard in the following terms:

By the conclusion of the agreements between local Aboriginal and non-Aboriginal authorities, for example, band councils and regional county municipalities, between Aboriginal and non-Aboriginal entrepreneurs and enterprises, between Aboriginal and non-Aboriginal institutions with social, economic, and cultural interests like economic development corporations, community organizations, etc. (Quebec **SAA** 1998, 23; author's translation)

While these words are indeed reassuring, the fact remains that economic development made possible through access to resources through the settlement of land claims, the establishment of an economic development fund to finance projects in and by Aboriginal communities and individuals, and the carrying out of business partnerships between Aboriginal peoples and non-Aboriginal peoples are at the heart of both the orientation and the proposed actions. It is unclear whether the new Liberal government will go on with the same policy, but up until now the results of this policy have been largely praised by Aboriginal leaders and managers, especially by those working in the sector of community infrastructure. Moreover, the idea of partnership has become very popular when speaking about relations between Aboriginal and non-Aboriginal people, as shown by the agreements between the Quebec government and the Crees of Quebec (Quebec and Grand Council of the Crees 2001) and the Inuit of Nunavik. For example, a folder explaining the *Paix des Braves* presents this agreement as "innovating in many ways: negotiated from nation to nation, it establishes a partnership for the management of resources and enlarges the responsibilities allocated to the Crees communities" (Quebec and Grand Council of the Crees 2001, 3; author's translation). In the same manner, the recent agreements between Hydro-Québec and the Innu communities of Betsiamites and Mashteuiatsh for the hydroelectric development on the Toulnoustouc and the Peribonka rivers are also marked by the idea of partnership. However, as will be illustrated below, they are not directly involved with the Quebec government because no land claims agreement has been signed with the Innu thus far.

HYDRO-QUÉBEC AND THE INNU

In order to answer the question of whether a new relationship is emerging, it is useful to look at the way in which the relationship between Hydro-Québec and the Innu has evolved. In essence, three overlapping but distinct phases in this relationship can be identified: a) ignorance and silence; b) opposition, confrontation, and reconciliation; and c) agreements and partnership.

Ignorance and silence. Ignorance was the attitude of Hydro-Québec towards the Innus in the 1950s, the 1960s, and the beginning of the 1970s when many large construction projects transformed a large portion of the Bersimis, aux Outardes, and Manicouagan river watersheds. The Aluminium Company of Canada (Alcan) showed the same ignorance in the case of the Peribonka River with the building of three dams and powerhouses in the 1950s. In fact, ignorance regarding the environmental and socio-cultural impacts of these huge works (fourteen power plants and six large reservoirs) was common in an era before both an ecological consciousness and environmental legislation came to oblige the promoters of large development projects to perform impact studies and take measures to better protect the ecosystems and the people living in the areas affected.

By 1975, some 10,000 MW of hydroelectricity production capacity had been installed in Innu country (Charest 1982).[3] The Innu suffered the harms created by these projects in silence and without public opposition. Positive impacts were limited to a few seasonal and poorly paid jobs (Charest 1980 and 1982). For example, half the family hunting territories of the Betsiamites community were totally or partially drowned, and hunting and trapping activities dropped to a new low; significant recovery is still not visible. On the other hand, the easier access to family territories due to the construction of road networks has given an advantage to the forest industry, the sport hunters and fishers, and country camps owners, a situation that discouraged even more of the Innu from practising their own traditional activities. The Innu of Betsiamites finally received compensation of $150, 000 in 1975, an amount that can be considered as symbolic compared to the $225 million for the James Bay agreement negotiated at the same time for all "the damages caused outside the reservation and to buy peace" (Charest 1980, 335). More than twenty years later, in 1997, the same community filed a lawsuit of $500 million against Hydro-Québec for the same damages. It has been suspended, but not abandoned, during the negotiation of the agreement on the Toulnoustouc project.

Opposition / confrontation / reconciliation. In 1975, with the establishment of the CAM, the relationship with Hydro-Québec began to improve, as illustrated by the circumstances surrounding the construction of the Betsiamites facility. However, by the beginning of the 1980s, the political position of the council was one of opposition to the hydroelectric projects as Hydro-Québec refused to recognize the Aboriginal rights of the Innu. This opposition was first publicly manifested during two public hearings: the first in 1985 on the Robertson Lake project to built a small power plant of 21 MW and the second in 1986 on a 315 kV Radisson–Nicolet–Des Cantons power line (BAPE 1985 and 1987). The latter case was finally settled when the Atikamekw communities decided to negotiate and sign a separate agreement with Hydro-Québec (Anonymous 1988). The Innu of Mashteuiatsh pursued a similar path a few years later (Anonymous 1990).

In each case, the main components of the agreements were similar: financial compensation, contracts and jobs for clearing the vegetation associated with the passage of the line, and the connection of one Atikamekw community to the Hydro-Québec electricity network. At the time, these agreements represented a new model of cooperation rather than confrontation between Hydro-Québec and some of the member communities of the CAM. The same kind of agreement was signed by the community of Mashteuiatsh in 1994 concerning the passage of the twelfth 735 kV power line through their hunting and trapping family territories (Anonymous 1994). In the years before, beginning in 1987, joint committees composed of representatives of the CAM and Hydro-Québec were formed to examine the social and cultural impacts of the new projects on the Innus communities concerned. This measure helped to facilitate the accepting of certain projects in particular, including the two power lines just mentioned. However, the following quotation tells us much about the kind of power relationship existing between Hydro-Québec and local communities when it comes to the decision-making process:

> As we cannot and would not stop this kind of development in the ancestral territory of the Lake St. John's Montagnais, the council has decided that it is wise to negotiate arrangements with Hydro-Québec for the mitigation of the environmental and social impacts of the project, in an effort to obtain economic advantages for the Montagnais, and to compensate for their inconveniences. (Anonymous 1994, 1; author's translation)

In the same document, it is also written that "[T]his agreement breaks new ground, up to a certain point, in opening the door for perspectives of partnership in many fields." In addition to the usual economic advantages in terms of contracts and jobs, and the creation of a fund for community development, the main point of the agreement was, in fact, the possibility of a partnership with Hydro-Québec to develop a joint project for a small hydroelectric power plant (Anonymous 1994, 6). This project, called Minashtuk, was effectively realized.

But the strategy designed by Hydro-Québec to buy the consent of some Innu communities for its power line projects did not work in the case of a small power plant at Robertson Lake on the lower North Shore. The project, initiated in 1985 and then postponed for some years following a negative report by the Bureau des Audiences Publiques sur l'Environnement (BAPE), was reformulated at the beginning of the 1990s. But the two communities in this region did not accept this unilateral decision, twice going to court to block the project and twice losing. As a result, a small power plant of 21 MW was built and began production in 1995, replacing the old, expensive, and noisy diesel plants that had previously supplied electricity to twelve small fishing communities along the Quebec North Shore and Labrador coast. In October of 2003, the community of Pakua Shipi, whose hunting lands were affected by the project, finally accepted a financial compensation of $1.5 million from Hydro-Québec for the "loss of access to this part of their territory and the loss of their traditional hunting and fishing activities" (Radio-Canada, Est du Québec, 16 October 2003). Their original claim was for $10 million.

The fortunes of the Innu took on a more positive character in the case of the Ashuapmushuan River. In the early 1990s, Hydro-Québec had worked on a project to build two power plants on this river named CH 3 and CH 4; the original plan called for four facilities. However, the Innus of Mashteuiatsh, concerned by the project, declared their firm opposition during a public press conference in January of 1992 (Conseil des Montagnais 1992). With the help of many environmental groups also opposed to the project, in 2002 they succeeded in blocking the project and having the Ashuapmushuan classified as a patrimonial river.

The battle was more epic in the case of the Sainte-Marguerite-3 (or SM-3) project, the first major dam proposed for the North Shore by Hydro-Québec since the end of the Manic-Outardes works. The communities of Uashat mak Mani-Utenam, members of the same administrative band, were deeply divided over whether to accept the project. A referendum was held in February 1992, with those in favour obtaining a small overall majority of the votes. However, if the majority was in favour of the project in Uashat, the opposite sentiment prevailed in the case of Mani-Utenam. Reacting to this divided vote, some members of the Coalition Nitassinan, which was opposed to the project, tried unsuccessfully to officially separate the two bands. In their frustration, they occupied the local school, broke the furniture of the band administrative building during the night, and, finally, blocked the access road to the future sites of the dam and power plant for a few weeks. Some of them were arrested, brought to court and sentenced to jail (Charest 1994). In spite of this fierce opposition, the band council (also called Innu Takuaikan) signed an agreement with Hydro-Québec in 1994 (Anonymous, *Uashat mak Mani-Utenam* 1994), which brought major economic and social benefits for the two communities. Despite the still controversial nature of the agreement, it nonetheless initiated the series of partnership agreements that marked the new relationships between Hydro-Québec and some of the Innu communities during the 1990s.

Partnership agreements. The report of the BAPE environmental commission
on the Sainte-Marguerite-3 hydroelectric project was the first to make reference to partnership:

> The partnership formulas desirable and desired for the concep-
> tion of the development and exploitation of the resources of this
> territory are still to be defined, either in the context of the nego-
> tiation process going on with the Aboriginals, or according to a
> collaboration mechanism suitable to the MRC. But carefulness is
> a rule for Hydro-Québec which cannot assume the responsibili-
> ties of other governmental institutions. (BAPE 1993, 233)

The call for 'carefulness' was surely heard by Hydro-Québec, for in the
1994 *Uashat mak Mani-Utenam Agreement*, while the terms "partnership" or
"partners" are not used, others terms quite close to the same reality are used:
"to collaborate," "to participate," "to sustain community development,"
"to conciliate respective interests," "to harmonize relations," "to favour the
granting of contracts," and "to favour the hiring of Innu workers." The part
of the agreement closest to a partnership is the creation of a Society for Reme-
diatory Works (SOTRAC), financed by a fund of $10 million from Hydro-
Québec, whose activities will be done in collaboration with the Aboriginal
communities (Anonymous 1994, art. 13.1). Missing from the agreement are
firm commitments on the part of Hydro-Québec for the granting of contracts
and the hiring of Innu workers other than a rather vague commitment to
'favour' these two measures. The main economic clause of the agreement
is the payment by Hydro-Québec of a sum close to $34 million over a fifty-
year period, the purpose of which is to set up a community economic development fund entirely under the management of the Innu Takuaikan (band
council), subject to certain conditions concerning its use and a verification of
its conformity to the agreement by Hydro-Québec.

The first real partnership agreement between Hydro-Québec and an
Innu community involved the small 9.9 MW Minashtuk power plant built
on the Mistassibi River in the territory of the Mashteuiatsh community. The
station, which began to produce electricity in the year 2000, is owned by
Hydro-Ilnu and has only two shareholders: the band of Mashteuiatsh with

50.1 percent of the shares, and Hydro-Québec with 49.9 percent. According to the agreement, the profits are shared at the same proportion. The project has raised some negative comments from persons familiar with the environmental regulations of the Quebec Department of Environment. First, by fixing the production capacity of the plant at 9.9 MW, the partners of Hydro-Ilnu avoided the obligation to make a detailed impact study and a public examination by a BAPE commission. Also, the capacity of the reservoir was three times the limit of 50,000 square metres, beyond which public hearings are also necessary (Francoeur, "Hydro-Ilnu" 2000). For many critics, it is particularly disturbing that an Innu community has worked hand in hand with Hydro-Québec to avoid a detailed analysis of the project and public hearings with the help of the Quebec Department of Environment, which must examine and recommend each project for its final acceptance.

A similar sort of mini-power station on the Escoumins River, proposed by the Essipit community a few years after that of Minashtuk, has been put aside for the moment because the price at which Hydro-Québec was buying the energy produced by the private firms dropped from five cents per kilowatt/hour in the case of Hydro-Ilnu to only three cents for the new projects. As the Escoumins is a salmon river that has been restored at considerable cost, work required to protect this species made the project unprofitable. Other Innu communities are also interested in becoming the owner of mini-power stations, often as a way of generating some financial capital to invest in other community projects. These include the Betsiamites, who are planning the construction of two mini-stations at the Sault-au-Cochon River, a site that has been put aside especially for the Innu by the government of Quebec.

Perhaps the best example of the new partnership between Hydro-Québec and an Innu community also involves the community of Betsiamites. On 21 June 1999, the president of Hydro-Québec, André Cailler, and the chief of the band, René Simon, signed a Partnership Agreement between Hydro-Québec and the Band Council of Betsiamites; the agreement was subject to approval by the members of the community in a referendum that took place in September of that year. The agreement called for two very different projects: a) the building of a new dam and powerhouse just below the existing Ste-Anne reservoir used to regulate the water flow for the Manic 2 power station; and b) the construction of dikes on the upper part of the Portneuf and Sault-au-Cochon rivers for the diversion of their waters towards the Bersimis River to increase the flow of this river and subsequent energy production for the Bersimis-1 and Bersimis-2 power plants built in the 1950s. A true business partnership was established in the case of the diversion project, with the financial participation of the Betsiamites band for 17.5 percent of its total costs, estimated to be $82 million, for an investment of $14.35 million on the part of the band. In exchange, the band was to receive an equivalent percentage of the surplus of energy generated by the diversions and bought by Hydro-Québec "at a minimum guaranteed price of 3 cents for a KW indexed in function of the electricity fares increase in Quebec for the 'production' component of the energy price" (Conseil de Bande de Betsiamites and Hydro-Québec 1999, 8). For the first fifty years of the ninety-nine-years agreement, the minimum amount of band income is estimated at not less than $100 million.

Morevover, 12.5 percent of the total of jobs, "calculated in full time year/persons equivalence" and 10 percent of the total value of the contracts are reserved for Innu members and enterprises of Betsiamites (Conseil de bande de Betsiamites and Hydro-Québec 1999, 11–12). Also, as in the case of the *Uashat mak Mani-Utenam Agreement*, three different funds were created with money allocated by Hydro-Québec: a) a community fund of over $10 million; b) a Innu Aitun fund or traditional activities support fund of close to $2 million; and c) a $11 million fund for remediation works to be executed by a SOTRAC–Betsiamites joint enterprise entity (Conseil de Bande de Betsiamites and Hydro-Québec 1999, 9–10).

The two contracts granted to Betsiamites, in the amounts of $35 million and $20 million, were granted to the Peshamiu Ilnuts Enterprises, a fully band-owned enterprise. The first concerns the installation of the workers' camp; the second, the operation of the cafeterias and the houseworks. The jobs filled by the Innu workers were mainly non-specialized and less well paid, due essentially to the lack of formal education on behalf of the Innus. In addition to the operation of the cafeterias and the housework, the band is associated with the multinational company Sodexho, which specializes in the management of workers, camps and food services, and has experience in these sectors. Still, the execution of the contract ran into problems due to work absenteeism and the high turnover of the workers, resulting in lower productivity than expected and a higher cost of operation. These problems were resolved by a modification of the contract to take into account the lack of experience of the band with this kind of work on a large scale and by better organizing the Innu employees (Raphaël Picard, oral communication, June 6, 2004). Regarding the work of the SOTRAC, its first annual report in 2002 does not say much other than a description of the beginning of its operation and the financial support granted to two projects linked with the use of the hunting territories by young Innus (Conseil de Bande de Betsiamites 2002).

This kind of financial partnership seems to be lacking from the agreement signed between the representatives of the Mashteuiatsh community and those of Hydro-Québec for the project Peribonka-3 (BAPE 2003). In this case, the main components are the financial compensations to create the same three funds as for the Betsiamites agreement, for a total sum of just under $113 million, of which the community development will receive $100 million. As the management of this fund will be 'exclusive' to the Innu council of Mashteuiatsh, there is no real partnership involved here. However, according to the Hydro-Québec Web site, ten contracts (for a total of forty-six) have already been 'reserved' for the band-owned Developement Piekuagami Ilnuatsh enterprise (Hydro-Québec 2004).[4]

In one of the sections in its report, titled *To Work in Partnership*, BAPE expands the practice of partnership to the whole Saguenay-Lake St. John region with the following recommendations:

> In the opinion of the commission, the creation of a working group including representatives of regional economic development institutions and of the promoter seems to be essential in a process aiming to maximize the economic effects of the hydroelectric development projects on the Peribonka River. (Hydro-Québec 2004, 66).

If this proposition is put into practice, we can suppose than one or more Innu will also be members of a 'coordinating' rather than 'partnership' committee.

The difficulties of forging this new relationship should not, of course, be underestimated. A few years ago, for instance, Hydro-Québec seemed to have forgotten the essence of such an arrangement when some of its higher ranked administrators, along with representatives of the government of Newfoundland and Labrador, announced Phase II of the Churchill River development. In only two days, the Innu of Labrador gathered a strong delegation of Aboriginal people, many from the Quebec North Shore, to protest the highly publicized press conference in the small village of Churchill Falls. This Innu resistance was triggered by the fact that they were once again ignored during the discussions between Hydro-Québec and the government of Newfoundland over the planning of the project, and informed just forty-eight hours before the day of the press conference. The Labrador and Quebec Innu took this opportunity, as they had in the case of the low-level flights from the Goose Bay military airport, to "denounce the lack of consideration given when important decisions must be made on issues in which they are directly involved" (Charest 1999, 89).

CONDITIONS FOR A TRUE PARTNERSHIP

It seems, therefore, that the Parti Québécois has put the idea "of development in partnership" at the centre of its policy regarding Aboriginal people. For its part, Hydro-Québec has its own policy regarding business partnership as part of its general policy, the most important components of which are the establishment of mutual respect, an enduring sharing of the risks and benefits, and the realization of a business partnership congruent with its values and strategic orientations in the pursuit of a true mutuality of interests to generate benefits or savings (Hydro-Québec 2004). Consequently, in order to ensure the development and dissemination of advantageous partnerships, Hydro-Quebec pledged to, among other things, allow for business partnerships that are in harmony with the natural and social environment; conclude formal agreements with its partners clearly stipulating the conditions and requirements linking the parts; recognize and respect the degree of autonomy conferred by any partnership agreement; and realize its financial operations and its commercial arrangements with its partners on a business basis (Hydro-Québec 1998, 15; author's translation).

According to Hydro-Québec, therefore, the idea of a partnership is largely a business proposition. Among Innu leaders, however, reference to the notion of partnership seems to be a bit anterior to its use by Hydro-Québec and the provincial government, particularly in light of the Innu's own struggle to give meaning to the term. For instance, in a speech given during the international congress on Aboriginal peoples and the use of water resources, held in Montreal in 1993, René Simon, then president of the Council of the Atikamekw and Montagnais, said:

> Fundamentally, we are not opposed to hydroelectric develop-
> ment in our territory and we have shown that before. But in the
> future the planning and realisation of this development must be
> done with us, respecting our respective preoccupations. . . . For
> example, we believe that in some cases a partnership approach
> with Hydro-Québec or other promoters can lead to a better
> social and environmental integration of projects of common
> interest. Some Montagnais communities have already tried past
> approaches of this sort, but met with a rebuttal, or were proposed
> unacceptable conditions. Unfortunately, things are easy to say
> when the political will is not there. Nevertheless, I personally
> believe that partnership is an avenue of solution because it creates
> links, forces dialogue, and favours compromises. (Simon 1993,
> 7–8; author's translation)

A few years later, René Simon was able to put his thinking into practice when, as chief of Betsiamites, he signed the 1999 partnership agreement
with Hydro-Québec.

The notion of partnership was further elaborated when the Assembly of
First Nations of Quebec and Labrador (AFNQL), of which the Innu communities are members, adopted a strategy for sustainable development in 1997.
According to the Assembly, such development could be attained only in
the situation of a "necessary partnership" with governments and the whole
non-Aboriginal population:

> The First Nations, true to their traditional values of respect,
> sharing and ritual aid, look for a harmonious and peaceful coex-
> istence with the rest of the Canadian population. Coexistence

would necessarily take the form of a partnership based on mutual consent of the parties and on a relationship of lasting trust. . . . The fact of establishing a real partnership in which the First Nations are involved upstream of projects, of the decision making and of the interventions on the territory and through which they satisfy their needs constitutes the real challenge for those who want to have access to sustainable development. . . . The partnership implicates first a mutual recognition, Government to Government, equal to equal. This builds on a lasting trust relationship that develops between partners. Since the respective benefits and interests are taken into account, the partnership allows a better use of each other's strengths, in a measure that serves each one. (AFNQL 1997, 26)

The kind of partnership proposed by the Assembly is much more than just a business partnership. It is a partnership extended to all the political, social, and cultural levels of relations between Aboriginal and non-Aboriginal people, who live together on the same territory. Under this type of partnership, there is an absolute equality of all the partners. Guy Bellefleur, the chief negotiator, expressed the same logic for the Mamit Innuat council in May of 1998. Speaking about the proposed hydroelectric developments in the Quebec and Labrador parts of Nitassinan, Bellefleur argued:

The government of Quebec and Labrador must cease to lie to their population. They must recognize Aboriginals as true political, economic and cultural partners. We propose to the government to be a stakeholder. We want to be true partners in the decision making process in matters of the management of water, lands, and energy. To restore the actual situation of non confidence and avoid those kind of problems occurring when Aboriginals fight against major development projects of governments on their traditional territories, we must truly recognize Aboriginals as unavoidable actors in the decision making process today. (Bellefleur 1998, 571; author's translation)

Bellefleur went on to say that an appropriate partnership is first of all political and that it must be included in any treaty between "Quebec,

Canada, and the First Nations of Mamit Innuat" meant to create a shared jurisdiction "for all environmental matters" (571). This same position is held today by the Mamit Innuat council, namely that an agreement with the provincial and federal governments on the comprehensive land claims, in which exclusive and shared jurisdictions of the Innu will be clearly defined, must be reached before negotiating any particular development project, and, more specifically, the future hydroelectric projects of Hydro-Québec in the area of Nitassinan on the Romaine and Little-Mecatina rivers. The failure to do so explains why the discussion between Hydro-Québec and the leaders of Mamit Innuat about these projects are still in their early stages. Moreover, according to Jean-Charles Piétacho, chief of the Mingan community, the three Innu communities of Mamit Innuat will not negotiate separately with Hydro-Québec, as was the case with the communities of Mamuitun.

The Mamit Innuat council has thus adopted a different political stand from that of the communities of the Mamuitun council, whose more pragmatic individual strategies can be explained by the uncertainty of reaching a final agreement on their land claims, despite twenty-five years of negotiations, and that the only realistic possibility of stopping the projects is a successful court challenge. Up to now the communities of Mamit Innuat were less subjected to the pressures of an impending development project by Hydro-Québec. However, the pressure will be greater and more difficult to resist when the almost completed pre-project impact study will be examined by a BAPE environmental commission during public hearings probably in 2008. A political partnership with the government of Quebec within a treaty or land claims agreement is surely the best solution. However, such a conclusion is highly unlikely, given that the process of negotiating project-by-project and community-by-community has been successful in establishing "business-only partnerships" with other Innu communities in the past ten years.

In light of these considerations, it is apparent that a true partnership concerning the hydroelectric development in Innu country or Nitassinan should include negotiated agreements at two different levels: a) the political level, from nation to nation between representatives of the governments of Quebec, Canada, and Innu political organizations; and b) at the economic level with business agreements and contracts between Hydro-Québec or any other promoter wishing to have access to the resources of Nitassinan, and the appropriate Innu political/economic leaders, and entrepreneurs.

From this perspective, the recent business partnerships completed between Hydro-Québec and the three Innu communities is an incomplete partnership giving a greater advantage to Hydro-Québec, which, as a provincial company, stands to benefit when important environmental and political decisions have to be made concerning the use of natural resources on Innu lands where there are still unsettled land rights. The more time that passes, the more the Innu will be caught between the agenda of Hydro-Québec and its mega-hydroelectric projects supported by the province of Quebec in the name of economic development.

The Innu, being without a negotiated treaty or agreement, and faced with land claim disputes that seemingly have no end, are in a weak position relative to Hydro-Québec. This is true even if the agreements between the company and the Innu communities are more and more generous from a strictly economic point of view. In fact, these very populous communities are finding that their ancestral rights are becoming increasingly eroded by large and small development projects of many kinds, to the point that they have no choice but to maximize their economic gains from the projects chosen and proposed by Hydro-Québec.

Clearly, one of the main strategies that some Innu leaders have adopted is to try to keep some rivers with an important patrimonial value intact, such as the Ashuapmushuan and Moisie, and to negotiate economic advantages from projects on rivers already exploited, including the Ste-Marguerite, the Peribonka, and the Toulnoustouc. Another short-term strategy, one related to the difficult state of the local economies, is to get at least their fair share of the jobs and contracts from each project to alleviate the situation. A third strategy for the long term is to accumulate financial capital to create their own enterprises and invest in profitable projects (Picard 2004).

On the other hand, Hydro-Québec has not come back haphazardly to the North Shore for its great hydroelectric works. The international campaign of the Crees to block the Great Whale River project is surely one of the reasons, as is the political weakness of the Innu, who, at least relative to the Crees, demonstrate a weak level of political cohesion. Thus, the political division of the Innu as well as the absence of agreements with the Quebec and federal governments favours the strategy of Hydro-Québec, which is to negotiate the future hydroelectric developments on the North Shore on a project-by-project basis without a general vision or plan for the long term. In this regard the company's development strategy harkens back to the 1970s-era James Bay projects.

As seen above, Hydro-Québec wants to maintain its status as principal decision maker for all its projects and partnerships. In particular, the company wants the right to choose projects according to its own criteria and agenda. It is true that the government has something to say, but it is primarily motivated by the dividends it can get from a higher production of energy and increased exports on the continental energy market. The local population also has something to say, and while it may sometimes succeed in modifying or delaying a project, very seldom can it block a project completely. As a result, at least for the time being, the Innu are not really involved in the political and economic decision-making process concerning the development of their lands and resources according to their own needs and priorities. Perhaps some day this situation will be reversed, at which point the Innu will at least share decision-making powers in the development of Nitassinan, their communities, and populations who have lived here for countless generations.

---

1   At the time of this printing, discussion between the representatives of Hydro-Québec and Mamit Innuat about these hydroelectric facilities has begun.

2   Many in the environmental and energy-efficiency movements criticize Hydro-Québec for not investing very much in either energy efficiency or alternative sources of energy like windmills. This criticism seems warranted, particularly given that Quebec is one of the highest energy- and electricity-consuming societies in the world. While Hydro-Québec says that it is only responding to the demand, its first and main role is to produce and sell more and more energy.

3 See Charest (1982, 60) for an analysis of the generic and specific impacts of these works on the Innu hunting groups and families, their economic activities, social relationships, cultural practices, and so on.

4 An important fact must be mentioned: for the sake of equity between the Aboriginal and non-Aboriginal inhabitants of the Lake St-John region, the two MRC of Maria-Chapdelaine and Fjord-du-Saguenay have claimed and finally obtained the same total amount of $113 million to be divided in two parts and paid over the same period of fifty years.

12

GOVERNANCE AND HYDRO DEVELOPMENT IN QUEBEC AND MANITOBA

Brian Craik

CANADA'S ABORIGINAL NATIONS have long been organized societies with distinct conceptions of land use and resource ownership. These guiding social principles allowed them to space individuals and communities over their traditional territories in ways that would maximize success in using the resources on which they depended. These patterns of life and resource exploitation ensured their survival and the sustainability of the lands that supported them.

When treaties were signed with newcomers, the right to continue to govern and exploit resources in traditional ways was not recognized (Frideres 2000; Dupuis, *Quel Canada* 1999). The great problem in these arrangements, aside from the legal issues, is that they not only contained a static view of Aboriginal societies, but also inevitably led to the reduction of the area available to maintain Indigenous economies and traditional modes of life. In other words, the relationships forged with Aboriginal nations by the colonial newcomers were processes of displacement and dispossession that, over time, left the Aboriginal nations with little, or nothing. Certainly the areas with the resources necessary to generate the types of revenues needed to maintain today's communities with even a moderate lifestyle are most often not included in the present land bases. Helen Buckley (1992) has given a detailed account of the process that led to the almost total dispossession of the

First Nations of the prairies. After they were forced to surrender the majority of their land to the settlers and, as a result, could not maintain their hunting practices, several First Nations turned toward agriculture for survival. Once they achieved even a modicum of success, however, they were soon expelled by a new wave of settlers from the best and most productive agricultural lands, again to be left with almost nothing. The last step in that process of dispossession, at least in provinces such as Manitoba and Quebec, has been hydro development (Waldram 1988).

As a result, a very strange and artificial situation has been created where 700 Aboriginal communities across Canada now face the profound challenge of how to solve a developmental problem that was created and is being perpetuated by federal and provincial policies. This paper explores the question of what can be done to offset the negative effects of the treaties that purportedly extinguished rights and consequentially reduced the areas on which these communities are able to pursue economic development. The treaties have, in effect, been a major cause of displacement and dispossession of these Aboriginal communities and of their consequent exclusion from the growing regional economies that surround them.

The question of how to deal with the practical situation "on the ground" is vital to any resolution of the situation. Governments should not be surprised if some Aboriginal peoples, because they do not see any end to the cycle of poverty, turn to desperate measures. Indeed, such measures are understandable and are justified to the degree that they are within the confines of what is legal. However, when they go over the edge of legality, at least here in Canada, they serve only to deepen the problems for all involved.

The answer to Aboriginal economic development is not simple and involves many different strategies. The Royal Commission on Aboriginal Peoples (1996) has identified a number of options, some of which involve opening the door for increased interaction and cooperation among Aboriginal peoples as nations and the governments, municipalities, and corporations that drive the regional economies in the traditional territories of the Aboriginal peoples. Others require increased funding for youth education and increased funding for the training of those who now find themselves unqualified to seize existing employment opportunities.

Most importantly, any new plan must involve Aboriginal peoples having a stake in development that extends to having a very important word on whether and under what terms specific development projects may proceed. The stake that they have in development must not be a payoff or compensation for continued exclusion but a fundamental entitlement consisting of development, education, training, jobs, revenue streams, and contract opportunities based on the decisions that are freely made by the Aboriginal peoples involved.

THE PRELUDE TO THE *PAIX DES BRAVES*

The socio-economic situation in Manitoba is, in many respects, comparable to the James Bay, Quebec, situation. Northern Manitoba is a boreal forest environment that historically supported a fur economy as well as an Aboriginal fishery on Southern Indian Lake. In the South, this sort of land-based economy was, to some degree, supplanted by an agricultural-based economy. It continued to thrive in the North, however, and sustained a largely traditional form of social organization. Today, both northern Quebec and northern Manitoba support a forestry industry, some mining, and large mega-hydroelectric projects.

When the James Bay Crees signed the *James Bay and Northern Quebec Agreement* (JBNQA) in 1975, they hoped to turn their backs on historic treaty policies supporting colonial practices of displacement and dispossession. At the time they were criticized by some Aboriginal leaders for doing so because their plan involved making a deal not just with the Crown in Right of Canada but also with the Province of Quebec. Under the agreement, services such as education, health and social services, and income security for trappers are now operated under provincially established institutions rather than under the jurisdiction of the federal government.

The land regime embedded in the JBNQA also tried to make a break with the historic colonial "reserve-Crown land solution" (Morin 2002). The agreement provided some recognition that Cree interests continued throughout their traditional territory, a fact that was used as a foundational element a quarter of a century later in the *Paix des Braves*.

The *Indian Act* had no place in the JBQNA since membership in the agreement goes to anyone who is recognized by a Cree community as having ancestry stemming from the community. In order to maintain an active membership, an individual must have been domiciled in the territory during the last ten years. Note, again, that it is the whole territory that is recognized as important in this regard, not just the Cree community lands.

The same inclusive principle holds with regard to development; that is, it is recognized that the Crees in Quebec have the right to the contracts and employment benefits anywhere on the territory. The governments of Quebec and Canada both committed to these measures for federal and provincial contracts and jobs and, since the beginning of the treaty period, have considered regulations to strengthen the enforcement of these obligations. Unfortunately, neither the Province nor the federal government made good on their promises. Employment training designed to make the Crees eligible to qualify for jobs created by development on the territory suffered a similar fate. Thus, while groundbreaking promises were made in 1975, the actual progress on the ground was minimal. Indeed, the first fifteen years of the JBQNA implementation were characterized by court case after court case as both Canada and Quebec fought to diminish the Cree rights in the agreement, while the Crees fought to make their institutions function in the best way possible.[1]

In 1989, partly in response to the difficulties of implementing the JBQNA, the nine James Bay Cree First Nations decided to launch an all-out campaign against the proposed Great Whale and Nottaway–Broadback–Rupert hydroelectric projects. The decision to oppose the projects came from a review of their experience with the JBNQA that pointed to its failure to bring about Cree economic and community development.

The history of the long, hard, international campaign against the hydro projects is complex; suffice it to say that this effort required enormous Cree unity, discipline, determination, and commitment. The result of the struggle was that Quebec's proposed hydro megaprojects were eventually frozen in 1994. The fight against the dams, and the simultaneous fight for Cree political rights that followed, helped to politicize the residents of the Cree communities and to make them aware of the economic and political forces that were the backdrop to their situation.

To appreciate what motivated the resistance of the Crees in Quebec, it is necessary to understand the situation of the Quebec Crees at the time of the struggle. First, the population was increasing dramatically through the period of 1989 to 1995 when the Great Whale fight took place. Approximately 200 new job entrants were coming out of school each year, few of whom were able to find a job. One third of the Cree workforce (about 1800 people) was employed by local and regional governments, the Cree School Board and Cree Board of Health and Social Services, and in the administration of other social service agencies. Another third hunted, fished, and trapped full time, and sought part-time employment in the summer months to augment the low cash incomes derived from the trapper program. The final third was unemployed or only casually employed. Few were employed in the private sector, though most would have taken such jobs had any existed. This lack of opportunity had other equally deleterious social effects; for example, depressing student performance in school. After all, reasoned the youth of the Cree communities, why go to school if there will not be any jobs available when you finish?

Meanwhile, the government of Quebec was extracting many billions of dollars' worth of resources from the traditional lands of the James Bay Crees. Thousands of direct and permanent jobs were linked to the hydro projects and many thousands more were dependent on the cheap source of electricity associated with the dams. The huge bulk of these jobs was, of course, filled by non-Aboriginal workers within the territory and in the South. The government of Canada was also earning hundreds of millions of dollars in tax revenues resulting from the project.

Significant promises of economic and social development had, of course, been made to the Crees that were not being honoured. The situation of the Inuit of Nunavik, who also signed the JBNQA, illustrates the situation. A 1998 study by Robichaud, Duhaime, and Fréchette showed that during the Great Whale project, Inuit of Nunavik had an annual income of $15,765—far below the national average of $21,511. Even more striking was the income realized by the non-Aboriginal residents of Nunavik, which stood at a remarkable $82,269. It is important to note that the non-Aboriginal population living in the region was and still are working for the institutions created by the JBNQA (Martin 2003).

Equally problematic was the structure of the labour force. While the James Bay Cree people represented at least one third of the population in the region, they still had less than 1 percent of the permanent jobs in hydroelectric development, fewer than 5 percent in forestry, and about 10 percent of the jobs in mining. Resource development since the signing of the JBNQA had simply not created much employment for them. Indeed, the exclusion of the James Bay Cree people from the regional economy was actually increasing at the time if the population increase over the period is factored into the equation. The exclusion had, not unexpectedly, significant local consequences. By the end of the 1990s, for instance, the Crees faced a housing shortfall of at least 1400 housing units and of the related community facilities.

Relations with the government of Quebec after the 1995 referendum on Quebec separation were strained in light of the continued Cree efforts to assert their rights also in that context, including their right to self-determination. In spite of, and some would say *because* of, the growing James Bay Cree Nation political strength in Canada and internationally, the government of Quebec and the Crees met in the mid-1990s to discuss ways of improving their relations.

Accordingly, Hydro-Québec opened discussions with the Cree communities on a possible new project, the Eastmain 1A–Rupert Diversion Project. As proposed, the project would have brought 80 percent of the waters of the Rupert River at the diversion point into the previously approved Eastmain 1 Project, which is part of the La Grande Project, requiring the construction of the new EM1A powerhouse. The new water would have also increased the output of the existing La Grande Project at La Grande-1 and La Grande-2 powerhouses. Under the scheme, Waskaganish, at the mouth of the Rupert River, would have lost about 45 percent of the river's flow. The community used the river as its source of water and also took fish at a long-established weir upstream. The river was also an historic fur trade travel route.

After an initial review, all nine James Bay Cree communities met in assembly in Waskaganish in 2001 to consider another key aspect of the proposal: a new sort of commercial relationship between the Crees and the utility. Under the terms of the proposal, the Crees were to borrow, with

Hydro-Québec's backing, funds sufficient to invest in the construction of the project in return for which they would receive a proportionate part of the profits over a specified period of time. Despite certain positive aspects, the Crees of Quebec rejected this proposal at the Waskaganish meeting, without much consideration of the commercial aspects. Indeed, many of the participants took issue with the need to borrow such significant sums. From their perspective, they had already "invested" in the project since it was to go forward on their traditional lands.

In addition to this fundamental point of contention, three other factors led the participants to reject the proposal: first, the potential loss of the fishing place in the river and the other damages to the river; second, the belief that this transaction would not resolve the problems the Crees were having with the implementation of the JBNQA; and third, the very important feeling that the deal favoured some James Bay Cree communities over others. The deal, in other words, would harm the sense of unity that had prevailed to that point among the various James Bay Cree communities. This, then, was the context that ultimately laid the foundation for the 2001 *Paix des Braves*.

DIVERGENT PATHS

Hydro-Québec and the Government of Quebec are to be credited for coming to the understanding that Aboriginal peoples must have a fundamental economic stake in all their traditional lands *and* that they have a nation-to-nation relationship with other governments in Canada. Contrary to the ongoing pronouncements of federal government representatives that these things are unimportant, the parties to the *Paix des Braves* understood the foundational principles required to reach agreement on a new developmental model. Indeed, these principles provide the basis upon which Canada and the provinces can create a respectful and sustainable relationship with Aboriginal peoples that also will ensure their survival as viable cultural entities (Saganash 2002).

At some basic level, the situations in Quebec and Manitoba are quite similar. In Quebec, the Crees have a four-way relationship with the federal and provincial governments, and the hydroelectric Crown corporation that built several megaprojects in the 1970s. The traditional boreal forest lands of the original Cree owners of the mid-northern portion of the province were subjected to significant resource exploitation by governments and corporations from the South, but for twenty-five years or more, the Crees were short-changed by the deals they had signed. A similar situation continues to prevail in Manitoba.

In both provinces, the federal and provincial governments were forced by the courts and other factors to enter into two very similar flood treaties, the 1975 JBNQA in Quebec and the 1977 *Northern Flood Agreement* (NFA) in Manitoba. In both cases, the governments and hydro corporations solemnly promised that the serious adverse effects on the economies and societies of the Aboriginal peoples would be mitigated and/or remediated and that compensation would be provided for the harms caused by the flooding and dam construction. The same governmental bodies also promised that social and economic benefits to come from the hydro projects to the provinces and Canada would accrue to the affected Aboriginal peoples through community infrastructure, education and training, economic development, and self-government.

The next twenty-five years in both Quebec and Manitoba established that these governments and Canada had lied or at least acted in bad faith (Hoffman 2002). In both cases, once the governments had what they wanted and once the hydro megaprojects were built and the enormous revenues were flowing south, the governments looked to their treaty obligations mainly to try to diminish them, and not to bring about the development of these northern Aboriginal communities and their integration into the regional economies. As stated in 1995 by the Cree–Naskapi Commission in its annual report to Parliament, "[I]n the course of Canadian history, a notion persists that governments make promises to induce natives to surrender their lands and other rights and then routinely break these promises, frequently hiding behind legal technicalities. Regrettably, the evidence supporting this notion is extensive" (Cree–Naskapi Commission 1995).

In both Quebec and Manitoba, the environmental and socio-economic consequences of the hydro projects were extremely serious. In both provinces, there was extensive flooding, increased mercury contamination, and massive social and economic displacement. A recent Interchurch Inquiry referred to the situation in Manitoba as a "moral and ecological catastrophe" (Manitoba Aboriginal Rights Coalition 2001). Certainly, on the basis of their own experience through the 1980s and 1990s, the James Bay Crees would agree, although things, at least on the Quebec side, are starting to change very significantly for them with the new agreement.

At least partly in response to claims arising out of the broken promises evident in both Quebec and Manitoba, the federal government began deliberate efforts in the 1980s to bring about the extinguishment of the two modern flood agreement treaties. The roots of these efforts can be found in the same document, the Mulroney government's Nielsen programs review of the mid-'80s. The Nielsen report established that liability for the ongoing treaty obligations to the Aboriginal signatories of the two flood agreement treaties from Quebec and Manitoba was reaching billions of dollars. In recognition of this fact, the report, without any serious thought about the future of the affected societies, recommended that the two treaties should be terminated in favour of lump-sum settlements. It also recommended that in the future, treaties containing ongoing obligation like the two flood agreement treaties should never be entered into again by Canada. Essentially, the recommendation represented a denial of constitutionally protected promises of northern development by southern Canadians. Nonetheless, the substance of this report became national policy that endures to this day, even though the Mulroney Conservative government is long gone, as is the Chrétien Liberal government.

By 1991, in the midst of the fallout from the Neilsen-directed policy, the Northern Flood Committee, which consisted of representatives from Cross Lake, Split Lake, York Factory, Nelson House, and Norway House, was pleading with the Royal Commission on Aboriginal Peoples for assistance due to the duress caused by the government's 'divide and conquer' and 'starve them out' strategies. The strategies were, according to the committee, destroying the strong sense of unity that had characterized the Aboriginal North up to that point and were undermining the fundamental premises of the *Northern Flood Agreement*. In lieu of the sustainable strategy of long-term growth contained in the agreement, the government was seeking a once-and-for-all-time payment. The demand raised important questions. Would, for instance, the leadership of these communities be any more capable than the professional managers of Crown corporations to invest one-time payments to create economic growth with the funds? Further, and perhaps even more importantly, when the lump-sum payments were exhausted, as they surely would be, what would sustain these communities in the future?

Despite the unanswered questions, between 1992 and 1997, four out of five of the NFA First Nation signatories succumbed to this federal strategy. The federal pressure to terminate the NFA treaty reputedly included bribery of entire community electorates. In the case of these four NFA First Nations signatories, their perpetual NFA rights were extinguished in return for the very modest one-time payments. The First Nations signatories were also forced to indemnify the Crown for any future breaches of the settlements. Shortly after the signing, special treaty termination legislation was enacted in Parliament.

The very same federal officials who were involved in the extinguishment of the NFA in Manitoba came to the James Bay Crees and suggested that they also accept a similar "Comprehensive Implementation Agreement." The agreement again was based on a tiny, once-only buy-out of all the promises made in the JBNQA. Fortunately, in a major departure with the events that unfolded in Manitoba, the unity among the leadership and people of the nine James Bay Cree First Nations and within the Inuit communities of Nunavik remained strong (see Martin 2003; Salisbury 1986), perhaps in part due to the successes that the Quebec Crees and Inuit had with the education, health care, trapper income security services (Crees), and the hunting support program (Inuit) that they were able to provide to their people. Both the Inuit and the James Bay Cree leadership and people understood that in order to survive as a people, it was and remains to this day essential to maintain unity, and that in the absence of this unity, the long-term federal scheme to assimilate the First Nations and the Inuit and extinguish and disperse them as nations and as peoples will succeed.

A singularly important consequence of the continuing demonstration of unity among the Quebec Crees on all fronts—i.e., hydro projects, forestry, mining, and Quebec independence—is the *Paix des Braves*. Once provincial officials realized that the Cree Nation would not go away and that room had to be made for them, the need for serious negotiation became obvious. The alternative was several more decades of conflict in the courts, in the press, in the international forums and, of course, in James Bay. As a result, the JBNQA and its perpetual promises are still intact and have not been surrendered for once-only buy-out payments, and should remain in effect for generations to come. At the end of the *Paix des Braves* agreement period of fifty years, during which time the James Bay Cree Nation receives substantial government-to-government fund transfers every year, the JBNQA treaty will still stand as it did before and the terms of its fulfilment will once again be renewed. The government of Quebec's obligations to the Crees will remain unchanged, constitutionally protected, and available to ensure that future generations of Crees have a perpetual basis for a stake in their traditional lands and resources.

APPLYING THE LESSONS OF THE *PAIX DES BRAVES* TO MANITOBA

An examination of basic demographic and economic statistics from Quebec and Manitoba reveals that on most levels the provinces of Manitoba and Quebec are very similar. In respect of all these key statistics, the Quebec-to-Manitoba ratio is about 7:1. That is, Quebec's and Manitoba's economies are proportionally the same size for the size of their overall populations and their GDP-per-capita is essentially the same.

However, there are a few major relevant differences. First, in proportion to overall population and the size of the economy, there are almost fifteen times as many Aboriginal people in Manitoba as in Quebec. Second, Manitoba Hydro's net revenue was, in 2002, one-twentieth that of Hydro-Québec's. This will undoubtedly be a major factor in how big an "engine of development" Manitoba Hydro might be for a local *Paix des Braves*. Third, the James Bay Crees' *Paix des Braves* beneficiary population is only 0.2 percent of the Quebec population. In contrast, the equivalent in Manitoba is, proportionally at least, twenty-five times bigger in Manitoba than in Quebec.

In my view, these numbers lead to three important conclusions. First, in Manitoba, the scale of the Aboriginal economic development challenge is much greater than in Quebec. Second, the size of the provincial economic engine available to meet this challenge is proportionally smaller in Manitoba than in Quebec. Finally, the statistics suggest that even if Manitoba Hydro and the government of Manitoba now actively wish to make a *Paix des Braves*-like arrangement with flood-affected Aboriginal people in Manitoba, they have only a small fraction of the capacity of Quebec to do so.

It is also true that Manitoba benefits enormously from having the lowest electricity rates of any Canadian province. It is economic folly and one of the key elements of the social tragedy of Aboriginal conditions in Manitoba that the electricity rates have not been increased for years. The beneficiaries of these low rates are, of course, the companies and the residents of the large cities located in the southern part of the province. Those who pay for these low rates are, on the other hand, the residents of northern Manitoba whose traditional lands have been flooded and who are failing to receive the benefits that were supposed to flow to them under the NFA. They pay day-to-day in the poverty that they face and in the unemployment, poor health conditions, and disempowerment that they experience.

Despite the differences in the underlying conditions, it is nonetheless the case that the basic principle of the *Paix des Braves*, namely equitable sharing with Aboriginal peoples of the benefits derived from the exploitation of their traditional lands and resources, is fully applicable in Manitoba. This could take the form of job and contract commitments, training, revenue sharing, and other special commitments, as in James Bay, Quebec. It is also true that these measures can gradually be increased and built into the cost of doing business. Indeed, higher electricity rates in Manitoba should be one way of evening out the social inequality that exists between affected communities and the beneficiaries of today's low rates in the South.

It would be a major error if one focused only on the government of Manitoba and Manitoba Hydro as the engine for Aboriginal development. In that the federal government has constitutional jurisdiction for Aboriginal peoples and lands reserved for "Indians," it too bears a share of the responsibility. The federal government, as the Crown signatory to both historic and modern treaties, has both the obligation *and* the economic capacity to undertake the developmental effort required to make a difference in Aboriginal development in Manitoba. The federal government has also the responsibility to protect the

First Nations from any provincial government's exactions. Ottawa took this duty seriously in the case of Quebec, including extending support to the Crees of Quebec when the province started the works for the James Bay's hydro project without consulting with Aboriginal communities. Partially thanks to this support, the Crees were able to organize resistance to the project, which forced Quebec to negotiate the JBNQA.

There is absolutely no reason why federal equalization should not now put its G-8 shoulder to Aboriginal economic development, just as it always has with respect to non-Native health care and non-Native economic development. Nor is there is any reason that Aboriginal people in Manitoba should be poor. Manitoba must decide to include in its calculation of the equalization deficit the cost of bringing its Aboriginal nations into the social and economic future of the province. As part of this exercise, it and the relevant Aboriginal nations should agree on, and make public, the size and cost of redressing Aboriginal exclusion from the Manitoba economy and the size of the inequity in housing, education, and health care. This would be a first step in finding the solutions.

Imagine if the *Northern Flood Agreement*, which is still alive in at least one NFA signatory First Nation, became a 90 percent federal responsibility. Imagine if all the terms and spirit and intent of Treaty 5, for example, were fulfilled by the federal Crown. Imagine also if s. 91(24) meant something for the dozens of federal reserve towns in Manitoba that need paved roads, housing, much more funding for education and social programs, and on and on. Isn't it about time that the government of Manitoba changed sides on the extinguishment of the treaties in Manitoba, and went to court *with* First Nations, as co-plaintiffs and *against the federal Crown*, to enforce the terms of these treaties? It would be a first.

The government of Manitoba needs to realize that every federal dollar that flows into Indian Country in Manitoba is actually a transfer dollar from Ottawa into the Manitoba economy. The government of Quebec was once a successful plaintiff against the federal government in respect of hundreds of millions of federal education funding for the James Bay Crees. Quebec understands that the JBNQA of 1975 is an engine with a large federal obligation for Quebec regional economic development. That was the deal in 1975; and it could be so again for Manitoba today.

The author gratefuly acknowledges the assistance of Andrew Orkin and Jessica Orkin for their help in verifying the socio-economic data for Manitoba. Any errors or omissions are, of course, the sole responsibility of the author.

1   Despite the difficulties associated with the implementation of the JBNQA, some positive outcomes did result, particularly in regard to education, health care, and income security for trappers. In the cases of education and health care, the services that they provide through the Cree-Quebec institutions as a result of the agreement are vastly superior to what the federal government provides elsewhere and follow Cree-controlled Quebec standards. A recent study from British Columbia, for instance, confirms that federal education standards in Aboriginal communities in BC are well below what the provinces provide. According to the study, for a school of 100 students, BC provincial standards produced 70 percent more funding than did those of DIAND (Matthew 2000).

Contributors

Ken Bradley has been the JustEnergy Program Director for Minnesotans for an Energy-Efficient Economy (ME3) since February 2002. He has coordinated the work of the JustEnergy advisory committee and has spoken about energy and justice issues at dozens of universities and colleges, churches, and community organizations. He has co-authored a report with the University of Minnesota Human Rights Center that outlines a monitoring and reporting process using the *Northern Flood Agreement* as the mechanism.

Paul Charest retired in 2004 after thirty-five years of teaching at the Department of Anthropology of Laval University. He remains Associate Professor at this department and an active researcher of the Centre interuniversitaire d'études et de recherches autochtones (Ciéra). He has been working with the Innu nation since 1976 and was research director and scientific advisor of the Conseil Attikamek–Montagnais (CAM) until 1990. He is the author of many papers concerning the exploitation of natural resources on Innu land and its impact. In 1995, he received the Weaver–Tremblay Award in Applied Anthropology.

Brian Craik is Director of Federal Relations for the Grand Council of the Crees. He has been an applied anthropologist and political strategist for thirty years. He played a central role in both the 1989 to 1994 campaign that stopped the Great Whale River hydroelectric project and the implementation of the 2002 agreement with Quebec.

Jules Dufour is Professor Emeritus of the Université du Québec in Chicoutimi. For the past thirty-five years, his research has focused on the development and conservation of natural resources in Canada and Quebec. He has collaborated in numerous inquiries, with a particular emphasis on the assessment of hydroelectric development projects and their impact on the environment. He sat on the Commission de toponymie of Quebec from 1990 to 2002, was President of the Estates General for the Environment of the Saguenay-Lac-Saint-Jean region, and sat on the Nunavik Commission for the creation of self-government. Professor Dufour received the 1995 and 2000 Canada Goose Awards, the environmental certificate of merit, Gens d'action, awarded by the Union for Sustainable Development, the Provancher Society of Natural History of Canada, and the Fondation de la faune du Québec. He has been a member of the Universal Ambassador Peace Circle since 2006, and in 2007 he was named Chevalier de l'Ordre national du Québec.

Lydia Dobrovolny has a Master of Science in Science, Technology and Environmental Policy from the University of Minnesota and a Bachelor of Science in Biology from Whitworth College in Spokane, Washington. She has travelled throughout the United States, Canada, Kenya, and Japan. She recently completed a 1200-mile solo bike-camp trip around Lake Superior. Her career goals include implementing renewable energy solutions that will contribute to a sustainable and just future.

Renée Dupuis is a lawyer who has been in private practice in Quebec since 1973. She has served as Chief Commissioner of the Indian Claims Commission since June 2003. A specialist in human rights and Aboriginal rights, she is the author of several works, including *Quel Canada pour les Autochtones, La fin de l'exclusion* (Boréal, 2001), published in English by Lorimer (2004) as *Justice for Canada's Aboriginal Peoples,* and *Le statut juridique des peuples autochtones en droit canadien* (Carswell, 1999). She has acted as legal advisor for several First Nations and as a consultant for federal and provincial departments. She has been a member of the Canadian Human Rights Commission (1989 to 1995). She has taught administrative law at the École nationale d'administration publique and was appointed commissioner of the Indian Specific Claims Commission by the federal Cabinet in March 2001.

Steven M. Hoffman is Professor of Political Science at the University of St. Thomas in St. Paul, Minnesota. He received his PhD from the University of Delaware in 1987 and has published several books and numerous journal articles and technical reports on a variety of topics related to energy and environmental policy. He has also served as a director for several state-wide environmental policy and advocacy organizations.

Peter Kulchyski is a professor in the Department of Native Studies at the University of Manitoba. He is currently engaged in research on Aboriginal self-government and resource stewardship in four northern communities. He published several books about Aboriginal peoples, most recently *Like the Sound of a Drum: Aboriginal Politics in Denendeh and Nunavut* (University of Manitoba Press, 2006) and, with Frank Tester, *Kiumajut (Talking Back): Game Management and Inuit Rights* (University of British Columbia Press, 2007).

Thibault Martin is Professor of Sociology at the Université du Québec en Outaouais. He also taught for four years at the University of Winnipeg. For the last ten years, his research has been in the field of social impacts of hydro-electric developments. His book, *De la banquise au congélateur*, discusses the efforts of the James Bay Inuit to cope with hydro development and social change, and was awarded a prize for Best First Sociology Book by the Association internationale des sociologes de langue française.

Gabrielle A. Slowey is an Assistant Professor in the Department of Political Science at York University, Toronto, Canada. Her research interests include Canadian politics, with a focus on indigenous development in Canada and New Zealand neo-liberalism and globalization; public policy, federalism, land claims, and self-determination; treaties; resource development; and Aboriginal-state relations. She has conducted research at numerous field sites, including the Northwest Territories, Yukon, northern Alberta, northern Quebec, and New Zealand. Her new book, *Navigating Neoliberalism: Self-Determination and the Mikisew Cree First Nation*, will be published by University of British Columbia Press in 2008.

Marc-Adélard Tremblay is Professor Emeritus at Laval University, Quebec City, where he founded the Department of Anthropology in 1970. He is a pioneer in cultural anthropology in Quebec. His interests include health methodology and applied research, ethnicity and Aboriginal peoples, and rural communities and socio-economic changes.

Romuald Wera studied geography in France (University of Caen and the Sorbonne University of Paris) and Finland (University of Oulu and University of Rovaniemi). He worked for two years as a visiting researcher at the Arctic Centre of Rovaniemi. In 2002 he wrote two reports on the Barents Euro-Arctic Region, focusing on Sámi adaptation to global changes. In 2003, he undertook doctoral studies in Finland, focusing on socio-spatial transformation of Nenets culture and territories due to global changes and energy development. In 2005 he moved to Canada to work on relocation and social impacts related to hydroelectric development. He is currently working as a private consultant.

APPENDIX: SELECTED WEB SITES

General Information and National Institutions

The Assembly of First Nations
<http://www.afn.ca/>

Native Women's Association of Canada
<http://www.nwac-hq.org>

Indian and Northern Affairs Canada
<http://www.ainc-inac.gc.ca/>

Aboriginal Canada Portal
<http://www.aboriginalcanada.gc.ca/>

Statistics Canada
<http://statcan.ca/start.html>

Quebec

L'Institut de développement durable des Premières Nations du Quebec et du Labrador/Assembly of First Nations of Quebec and Labrador Sustainable Development Institute
<www.iddpnql.ca/an/mainFreameset-4.htm>.

Femmes Autochtones du Québec/Quebec Native Women
<www.faq-qnw.org>

Secrétariat aux Affaires autochtones (Quebec)
<www.autochtones.gouv.qc.ca/index_en.asp>

Aboriginal Quebec
<http://www.panorama-quebec.com>

Grand Council of the Crees
<http://www.gcc.ca/>

Makivik Corporation
<http://www.makivik.org/eng/index.asp>

The Naskapi Nation
<http://www.naskapi.ca/>

Hydro-Québec
<http://www.hydroquebec.com/comprendre/histoire/faits_saillants.html>.

Manitoba

Assembly of Manitoba Chiefs
<http://www.manitobachiefs.com/>

Manitoba Metis Federation
<http://www.mmf.mb.ca/>

Manitoba Aboriginal and Northern Affairs
<www.gov.mb.ca/ana>

Manitoba First Nations Profile
<http://www.communityprofiles.mb.ca/first_nations.html>

Nisichawayasihk (Nelson House) Cree Nation
<http://www.ncncree.com/>

Agreements

Comprehensive Claims Policy and Status of Claims
<http://www.turtleisland.org/news/comp.pdf>

Role of the Canadian Courts in Aboriginal Rights
<http://www.waseskun.net/roleof.htm>

Agreement concerning a new relationship between le Gouvernement du Québec and the Crees of Quebec
<http://www.autochtones.gouv.qc.ca/relations_autochtones/ententes/cris/20020207_en.htm>

Agreement in principle of a general nature between the First Nations of Mamuitun and Nutashkuan and the governments of Quebec and Canada
<http://www.autochtones.gouv.qc.ca/relations_autochtones/ententes/innus/20040331.htm>

Amiqqaaluta — Let us Share Mapping the Road Toward a Government for Nunavik Report of the Nunanik Commission. March 2001
<http://www.ainc-inac.gc.ca/pr/agr/nunavik/lus_e.html>

Labrador Inuit Land Claim Final Agreement
<http://www.nunatsiavut.com/en/agreement.php>

Nisga'a Final Agreement Act
<http://laws.justice.gc.ca/en/N-23.3/>

Sanarrutik Agreement
<www.saa.gouv.qc.ca>

Northern Flood Agreement
<http://www.nfa-arb.org/agmnt>

James Bay and Northern Quebec Agreement
<http://www.gcc.ca/pdf/LEG000000006.pdf>

Cree-Naskapi (of Quebec) Act
<http://www.canlii.org/ca/sta/c-45.7/sec2.html>

Canada's Aboriginal Action Plan 1998
<http://www.ainc-inac.gc.ca/gs/index_e.html>

Bibliography

Abele, Francis. "Understanding What Happened Here: The Political Economy of Indigenous Peoples." In *Understanding Canada: Building on the New Canadian Political Economy*, ed. Wallace Clement. Montreal and Kingston: McGill-Queen's University Press, 1997.

_____, Graham, Katherine A., and Allan Maslove. "Negotiating Canada: Changes in First Nations Policy over the Last Thirty Years." In *How Ottawa Spends: 1999–2000*, ed. Leslie Pal. Don Mills: Oxford University Press, 1999.

Adams, Howard. *A Tortured People: The Politics of Colonization*. Penticton: Theytus Books Ltd, 1995.

Agreement in Principle to guide discussions and arrangements concerning the Wuskwatim/Notigi Projects and the Wuskwatim/Notigi Transmission Facilities. Agreement between the Nisichawayasihk Cree Nation and Manitoba Hydro. 25 September 2001.

Albo, Gregory, and Jane Jenson. "Remapping Canada: The State in the Era of Globalization." In *Understanding Canada: Building on the New Canadian Political Economy*, ed. Wallace Clement. Montreal and Kingston: McGill-Queen's University Press, 1997.

Alliance Autochtone. <http://www.allianceautochtone.com/judgments.html>. Accessed August 2005.

Anderson, Robert B. "Corporate/Indigenous Partnerships in Economic Development: The First Nations in Canada." *World Development* 25, 9 (1997): 1483–1503.

Anonymous. *Convention Atikamekw/Hydro-Québec*, 1988.

_____. *Convention Mashteuiatsh/Hydro-Québec*, 1990.

_____. *Convention Mashteuiatsh/Hydro-Québec*, 1994.

_____. « Entente Mashteuiatsh-Hydro-Québec 1994. » *Info Ligne* 12, 12 (1994): 1–12.

_____. *Entente Uashat mak Mani-Utenam*, 1994.

_____. *Proposition d'entente de principe d'ordre général entre les Premières Nations de Mamuitun et de Natashkuan et le gouvernement du Québec et le gouvernement du Canada*, 2002.

Asch, Michael. "The Dene Economy." In *Dene Nation: The Colony Within*, ed. Mel Watkins. Toronto: University of Toronto Press, 1977.

_____. *Home and Native Land*. Toronto: Methuen, 1984.

_____. "Indigenous Self-Determination and Applied Anthropology in Canada: Finding a Place to Stand." *Anthropologica* 43, 2 (2001): 201–207.

_____. "Self-Government in the New Millennium." In *Canada*, ed. John Bird and Lorraine Land. Toronto: Irwin Publishing, 2002.

Assembly of First Nations. *The Story*. <www.afn.ca/search.asp?lang=1&search query=The+story>. Accessed September 2003, 2005.

Assembly of the First Nations of Quebec and Labrador. "Sustainable Development Strategy for the First Nations of Quebec and Labrador." *Canada Indian Affairs and Northern Development: Towards Sustainable Development*. Ottawa, Public Works and Government Services 2, 4 (1997): 1–39.

Atwood, Charles, H. *The Water Resources of Manitoba*. Winnipeg: Economic Survey Board, 1938.

Axworthy, Lloyd, and Ken Arenson, Chairs. "Edited Proceedings of Council's Special Meeting, 19 January 1973, at Legislative Building, Winnipeg." Manitoba Environmental Council, September 1984.

Bakker, Isabella, and Katherine Scott. "The Post-Liberal Keynesian Welfare State." In *Understanding Canada: Building on the New Canadian Political Economy*, ed. Wallace Clement. Montreal and Kingston: McGill-Queen's University Press, 1997.

Barnsley, Paul. "Interim Overhaul of Indian Act Planned." *Windspeaker* 18, 10 (2001): 1.

Bateman, Leonard. *A History of Electric Power Development in Manitoba*. Winnipeg: IEEE Canadian Review, Bateman and Associates Ltd, 2005.

Bellavance, Claude. *Shawinigan Water and Power, 1898–1963, Formation et déclin d'un groupe industriel au Québec*. Montréal: Boréal, 1994.

Bellefleur, Guy. « Mémoire du Conseil des Innu du Nitassinan (Organisation non gouvernementale). » In *Evaluation d'impacts et participation publique : tendances dans le monde francophone*, ed. Claude E. Delisle and Michel A. Bouchard. Montréal: Secrétariat francophone de l'Association internationale pour l'évaluation environnementale, 1998.

Berger, Thomas R. *Village Journey*. New York: Hill and Wang, 1985.

Binette, André. « Le droit à l'autodétermination. 1. Les Peuples paraissent de plus en plus résolus à assumer le risque de l'incertitude pour maîtriser davantage leur propre évolution. » *Le Devoir*, 17 November 1993, p. A7.

_____. « Le droit à l'autodétermination. 2. L'un des défis du XXIème siècle sera de reléguer aux oubliettes de l'histoire le principe des nationalités et d'inventer un nouveau mode de coexistence entre les Peuples. » *Le Devoir*, 18 November 1993, p. A7.

Bishop, Carol, and Susan Bigelow. "Leo Panitch Award Canada Research Chair in Comparative Political Economy." *York University Communications Gazette* 32, 16 (17 April 2002).

Boldt, Menno. *Surviving as Indians*. Toronto: University of Toronto Press, 1993.

Bouchard, Serge. « Faux Combats, tristes arènes: Réflexion critique sur l'Amérindianisme d'aujourd'hui. » *Recherches Amérindiennes au Québec* 9, 3 (1979): 183–193.

Bourassa, Robert. *L'énergie du Nord. La force du Québec*. Montréal: Québec-Amérique, 1985.

Brattle Group. *Survey of Transmission Siting Practices in the Midwest*. Prepared for the Edison Electric Institute and Organization of MISO States. November 2004.

Braun, Will. Personal interview conducted by Steve Hoffman, April 2005.

Brennan, R.B. "Hydro's Future Vastly Different from its Past—New Projects Face 'Excruciating' Environmental Assessments." Letter, *Winnipeg Free Press*, 26 August 2004.

Brodie, Janine. "Meso-Discourses, State Forms and the Gendering of Liberal-Democratic Citizenship." *Citizenship Studies* 1, 2 (1997): 223–242.

_____. *Politics on the Margins*. Halifax: Fernwood Publishing, 1995.

Brody, Hugh. *The Other Side of Eden*. Vancouver: Douglas and McIntyre, 2000.

Brunetti, Wayne. "The Promise and Challenge of Renewable Energy." Remarks delivered to the World Renewable Energy Congress, 1 September 2004.

Buckley, Helen. *From Wooden Ploughs to Welfare: Why Indian Policy Failed in the Prairie Provinces*. Montréal: McGill-Queen's University Press, 1992.

Bureau des Audiences Publiques sur l'Environnement (BAPE). *Aménagement hydroélectrique Sainte-Marguerite-3*. Québec: The Author, 1993.

_____. *Projet d'aménagement hydroélectrique de la rivière Péribonka par Hydro-Québec*. Québec: The Author, 2003.

_____. *Projet de centrale hydro-électrique sur la Basse-Côte-Nord (lac Robertson)*. Québec: The Author, 1985.

_____. *Projet de ligne à courant continu à + - 450 kV. Radisson-Nicolet-des Cantons*. Québec: The Author, 1987.

Cairns, Alan C. *Citizens Plus: Aboriginal Peoples and the Canadian State*. Vancouver: University of British Columbia Press, 2000.

Canada. *Aboriginal Self-Government. Ottawa: The Government of Canada's Approach to Implementation of the Inherent Right and the Negotiation of Aboriginal Self-Government*. Ottawa: Department of Indian and Northern Affairs, 1995.

_____. *Accord de principe entre les Inuit du Labrador et sa Majesté la Reine du Chef du Canada et sa Majesté la Reine du Chef de Terre-Neuve*. Ottawa: The Author, 2000.

_____. *In All Fairness: A Native Claims Policy—General Claims*. Ottawa: Supply and Services, 1981.

_____. *Comprehensive Claims Policy and Status of Claims*. Ottawa: Department of Indian and Northern Affairs, 2002.

_____. *Distribution of Legislative Powers: Powers of the Parliament, Exclusive Powers of Provincial Legislatures*. Ottawa : The Author, 2000.

_____. *Entente définitive de la Première Nation des Nacho Nyak Dun*. Ottawa: Approvisionnements et Services Canada, 1993.

_____. *Entente définitive des Premières Nations de Champagne et de Aishihik*. Ottawa: Approvisionnements et Services Canada, 1993.

_____. *The Indian Policy of the Government of Canada—1969*. Ottawa: Indian and Northern Affairs Canada, 1969.

_____. *Les Inuit du Canada*. Ottawa: Inuit Tapirisat du Canada et Ministère des Affaires Indiennes et du Nord Canada, 1995.

_____. *People to People, Nation to Nation. À l'aube d'un rapprochement. Points saillants du Rapport de la Commission royale sur les peuples autochtones*. Ottawa: Ministère des Approvisionnements et Services Canada, 1996.

_____. *La politique indienne du Gouvernement du Canada*. Présentée à la Première Session du 28ème Parlement par l'Honorable Jean Chrétien, Ministre des Affaires Indiennes et du Nord canadien, 1993.

_____. *Politiques sur les revendications territoriales globales et état des revendications*. Ottawa: Ministère des Affaires indiennes et du Nord Canada, 2000.

_____. *Population indienne et inuite au Québec*. Ottawa: Travaux publics et Services gouvernementaux Canada, 2001.

_____. *Population indienne et inuite au Québec 2002. Indian and Inuit Populations in Quebec 2002*. Ottawa: Travaux publics et services gouvernementaux Canada, Affaires Indiennes et du Nord, 2002.

_____. *Rassembler nos forces. Le Plan d'action du Canada pour les questions autochtones*. Ottawa: Ministère des Travaux publics et Services gouvernementaux, 1997.

_____. *Réforme des dispositions constitutionnelles concernant les Autochtone : la démarche fédérale*, Ottawa : Conférence des Premiers Ministres, Questions constitutionnelles intéressant les Autochtones, 1987.

_____. *Report of the Royal Commission on Aboriginal Peoples*. Ottawa: Communication Group Publishing, 1996.

CBC News. *Eyebrows Raised over Hydro Payments to First Nation*. <winnipeg.cbc.ca/regional/servlet/>. Accessed April 2005.

Canadian Energy Board. *Electricity Exports and Imports. Tables 2A and 3A*. <www.neb.gc.ca>.

Canadian Hydropower Association. "Hydropower: A Response to Canada's Climate Change and Air Quality Challenges." <http://www.owa.ca/pdfs/CHABrief.pdf>. Accessed 26 October 2007.

Cans, Roger. *La bataille de l'eau*. Second edition. Paris: Le Monde Editions, 1997.

CASIL Agreement. An Agreement between the Community Association of South Indian Lake, the Manitoba Hydro-Electric Board and Her Majesty the Queen in Right of the Province of Manitoba. 10 August, 1992.

Cassidy, Frank. "First Nations Governments in Canada: An Emerging Field of Study." *Canadian Journal of Political Science* 23, 1 (1990): 73–99.

Charest, Paul. « Les barrages hydro-électriques en territoire montagnais et leurs effets sur les communautés amérindiennes. » *Recherches amérindiennes au Québec* 9, 4 (1980): 323–338.

_____. "Hydroelectric Dam Construction and the Foraging Activities of Eastern Quebec Montagnais." In *Politics and History in Band Societies*, ed. Eleanor Leacock and Richard Lee. New York: Cambridge University Press, 1982.

_____. « Les Innus et la Phase II de l'aménagement hydroélectrique de la rivière Churchill au Labrador. » *Recherches amérindiennes au Québec* 29, 2 (1999): 88–95.

_____. *Dans l'ombre de la Baie-James : Les Innus montagnais du Québec et les nouveau projets hydroélectriques sur leurs terres ancestrales.* Paper presented at the Congrès international de l'Association des américanistes, Stockholm, Sweden, 8 July 1994.

_____. « Recherches anthropologiques et contexte politique en milieux Atikamekw et Montagnais. » *Culture* 11, 3 (1982): 11–23.

Chilboyko, Jim. "Ontario, Manitoba May Revisit Power Project. Provinces Take First Step to Send Electricity East." *Business Edge* 1, 23 (11 November 2005). <www.businessedge.ca/article.cfm/newsID/11296.cfm>.

Chodkiewicz, Jean-Luc, and Jennifer Brown, eds. *First Nations and Hydroelectric Development in Northern Manitoba.* Winnipeg: Centre for Rupert's Land Studies, 1999.

Churchill, Ward. A *Little Matter of Genocide : Holocaust and Denial in the Americas 1492 to Present.* San Francisco: City Lights Books, 1997.

_____. *Struggle for the Land: Indigenous Resistance to Genocide, Ecocide, and Expropriation in Contemporary North America.* Munroe, ME: Common Courage Press, 1993.

Clapp, Jennifer, and Peter Dauvergne. *Paths to a Green World: The Political Economy of the Global Environment.* Cambridge, MA: The MIT Press, 2005.

Clark, Christopher. Testimony before the Minnesota Public Utilities Commission by Xcel Counsel, 19 December 2002. From PUC tape copies 02-155, 02-156, and 02-157.

Conseil Attikamek–Montagnais. « Nishastanan Nitasinan. Notre terre nous l'aimons et nous y tenons : Revendication territoriales des bandes atikamègues et montagnaises. » *Recherches amérindiennes au Québec* 9, 2 (1979): 171–182.

Conseil de Bande de Betsiamites et Hydro-Québec. *Entente de partenariat entre Hydro-Québec et le conseil de bande de Betsiamites.* Betsiamites: The Author, 1999.

_____. *Premier rapport d'activités de la SOTRAC-Betsiamites : Septembre 2001 au 31 mars 2002.* Betsiamites: SOTRAC, 2002.

Conseil des Montagnais du Lac St-Jean. *Étude d'impact du projet de l'Ashuapmushuan. Analyse du Conseil des Montagnais du lac St-Jean.* Mashteuiatsh: The Author, 1992.

_____. *La rivière Ashuapmushuan serait irrémédiablement bouleversée.* Communiqué de presse. 21 January 1992.

Craik, Brian. "Breaking with Colonialism: The Crees of James Bay and Their New Relationship Agreement with Quebec." *Canadian Dimensions* 38, 3. <http://www.canadiandimension.com/>. Accessed 25 September 2004.

Cree-Naskapi Commission. "Annual Report submitted to the Quebec Government." Unpublished document. Quebec : The Author, 1995.

Cruikshank, Julie. *The Social Life of Stories.* Vancouver: University of British Columbia Press, 1998.

Culp, Joseph. "Integrated Assessment of Ecosystem Integrity of Large Northern Rivers: The Northern River Basins Study Example." *Journal of Aquatic Ecosystem Stress and Recovery*, 8, 1 (2000): 1–94.

Cummins, Bryan D., and John L. Steckley. *Aboriginal Policing: A Canadian Perspective.* Toronto: Pearson Education Canada Inc., 2003.

Davis, Robert, and Mark Zannis. *The Genocide Machine in Canada: The Pacification of the North.* Montréal: Black Rose Books, 1973.

DeBrou, Dave, and Bill Waiser, eds. *Documenting Canada: A History of Modern Canada in Documents.* Saskatoon: Fifth House Publishers, 1992.

Department of Fisheries and Oceans, Central and Arctic Region. *Federal Ecological Monitoring Program: Final Report.* Volume 2. Ottawa: The Author, 1992.

Deschênes, Jean-Guy, and Richard Dominique. *Nitassinan.* Village-des-Hurons: Conseil Attikamek-Montagnais, 1983.

Dickason, Olive P. *Les Premières Nations du Canada. Depuis les temps les plus lointains jusqu'à nos jours* [1992]. Quebec: Éditions du Septentrion, 1996.

_____. "Reclaiming Stolen Land." In *Nation to Nation: Aboriginal Sovereignty and the Future of Canada*, ed. John Bird, Lorraine Land, and Murray MacAdam. Toronto and Vancouver: Irwin Publishing, 2002.

Dominique, Richard. « L'évaluation de la politique québécoise envers les Autochtones. » Manuscrit. Québec: École Nationale d'Administration Publique, 1987.

Dorion, Henri. « Contribution à une géopolitique des Amérindiens du Canada. » In *Les Facettes de l'identité amérindienne*, ed. Marc-Adélard Tremblay. Québec: Les Presses de l'Université Laval, 1976.

_____. « Nation amérindienne et nationalisme amérindien. » *Mémoires de la Société royale du Canada/Proceedings of the Royal Society of Canada*. Fourth edition. 15, 1 (1978): 161–170.

Driedger, Leo. *Race and Ethnicity: Finding Identities and Equalities.* Second edition. New York: Oxford University Press, 2003.

Dufour, Jules. « Les Autochtones et la reconnaissance de leurs droits et de leurs valeurs culturelles. » In *Panorama du Québec.* <http://www.panorama-quebec.com>. Accessed 25 August 2004.

_____. « Les espaces septentrionaux. » *Collection : Réflexions et recherches.* Numéro spécial sur le patrimoine de demain. No 10. Montréal : Regroupement Loisir Québec, 1985.

_____. « Les Inuits du Québec auront leur gouvernement autonome. » In *Annuaire politique, social, économique et culturel du Québec 2002.* Montréal: Fides, 2001.

_____. « Les nations autochtones au Québec. Les enjeux de leur développement à l'aube du 21ième siècle. » In *Le Québec en changement. Entre l'exclusion et l'espérance,* ed. P. Bruneau. Québec: Presses de l'Université du Québec, 2000.

_____. "The Nunavik Elected UQARVIMARIK, The Nunavik Government Executive and the Nunavik Standing Committee." Projet soumis à l'attention des Parties aux négociations entourant la création d'un gouvernement autonome au Nunavik, Québec. Ottawa: Ministère des Affaires indiennes et du Nord Canada, 2003.

_____. « Le Nunavik. Vers un gouvernement autonome. » *L'Annuaire du Québec* (2005) : 625–632.

_____. *Profil régional du Nord du Québec.* Québec: Office de Planification et de développement du Québec, 1983.

_____. « Le projet Grande-Baleine et l'avenir des peuples autochtones au Québec. » *Cahiers de géographie du Québec* 40, 110 (1996): 233–252.

_____. "Report from the Commission of Self-Governance." Analyse et commentaires. Avis et commentaires rédigés à l'intention de Donat Savoie, négociateur en Chef-Nunavik. February 2003. Ottawa: Ministère des Affaires indiennes et du Nord Canada, 2004.

_____. « Les revendications territoriales des Peuples autochtones au Québec. » *Cahiers de Géographie du Québec* 37, 101 (1993): 263–290.

_____. "Towards Sustainable Development of Canada's Forests." In *Resource and Environmental Management in Canada. Addressing Conflict and Uncertainty,* ed. B. Mitchell. Third edition. Toronto: Oxford University Press Canada, 2003.

_____, and A. Binette. *Report of Consultation with the Government of Greenland, October 8–17th 2000*. Quebec: Nunavik Commission, 2000.

_____, and Marc-Adélard Tremblay. *La commission du Nunavik. Une expérience unique et extraordinaire*. Paper presented to the Ministère Canadien des Affaires Indiennes et du Nord. Chicoutimi. 2001.

_____. *Une forme de gouvernement pour le Nunavik. Propositions pour une entente finale (1ière phase) qui respecte davantage l'esprit du rapport de la commission du Nunavik*. Avis formulé à l'intention de Donat Savoie, négociateur fédéral en Chef-Nunavik. Ministère des Affaires indiennes et du Nord, 2005.

Duhaime, Gérard. « Le chasseur et le Minotaure : itinéraire de l'autonomie politique au Nunavik. » *Études/Inuit/Studies* 16, 1–2 (1992): 149–178.

_____. *De l'igloo au H.L.M. Les Inuit sédentaires et l'État providence*. Quebec : Centre d'Études Nordiques (Université Laval), 1985.

_____, Martin, Thibault, Fréchette, Pierre, and Véronique Robichaud. *A Perception Study of the Socio-economic Impacts of the Grande-Baleine Feasibility Studies on the Inuit Communities of Kuujjuarapik and Umiujaq*. Québec: GÉTIC, Université Laval, 1998.

Dupuis, Renée. *Quel Canada pour les autochtones? La fin de l'exclusion*. Montreal: Éditions du Boréal, 1999.

_____. *Le statut juridique des peuples autochtones en droit canadien*. Scarborough: Éditions Carswell, 1999.

Dysart, Myrtle. Letter to Manitoba Minister Responsible for Manitoba Hydro the Honourable Tim Sale regarding the 1992 CASIL Agreement. Nelson House, Manitoba, Canada, 2003.

Federal Ecological Monitoring Program (FEMP). *Final Report*. Volume 2. Ottawa: Environment Canada, Department of Fisheries and Oceans, 1992.

Feit, Harvey. "Hunting and the Quest for Power." In *Native Peoples: The Canadian Experience*, ed. R. Bruce Morrison and C. Roderick Wilson. Toronto: McClelland and Stewart, 1986.

Ferguson, Naill. "Sinking Globalization." *Foreign Affairs* (March/April 2005): 64–77.

Fleras, Augie, and Jean L. Elliott. *Unequal Relations: An Introduction to Race, Ethnic, and Aboriginal Dynamics in Canada*. Toronto: Prentice-Hall, 1999.

Fortin, Pierre. "Hydroelectric Power: A Renewable and Clean Source of Energy." <http://www.pollutionprobe.org/whatwedo/GPW/halifax/presentations/fortin.pdf>. Accessed 27 October 2007.

Francoeur, Louis-Gilles. « Hydro-Ilnu : les ingénieurs du gouvernement demandent une enquête. » *Le Devoir*, 24 March 2000, p. A10.

_____. « Hydro-Québec possède la moitié d'Hydro-Ilnu. L'entreprise bénéficie d'un traitement de faveur. » *Le Devoir*, 23 March 2000, p. A3.

_____. « Non à Batiscan mais oui à Hydro-Ilnu. » *Le Devoir*, 22 March 2000, pp. A1 and A 8.

_____. « Rencontre avec Thierry Vandal—La terre des grands barrages. » *Le Devoir*, June 2003, pp. 14–15.

Frideres, James S. *Aboriginal Peoples in Canada. Contemporary Conflicts*. Fifth edition. Scarborough: Prentice Hall Allyn and Bacon, 1998. Sixth edition, 2000.

Goldemberg, Jose, ed. *Energy and the Challenge of Sustainability*. New York: World Energy Assessment, United Nations Development Programme, 2000.

Gottlieb, Robert. *Forcing the Spring: The Transformation of the American Environmental Movement*. Washington, DC: Island Press, 1993.

Grand Council of the Crees. "'Reciting the Symptoms, Ignoring the Cause: The Systematic Dispossession of Aboriginal Peoples in Canada.' A Response to the Government of Canada's Third Periodic Report on the Implementation of the International Covenant on Economic, Social and Cultural Rights." Submission of the Grand Council of the Crees to the United Nations Human Rights Committee. Nemaska, James Bay, Quebec, 1998.

Granger, Billy. "Hydro Lines Threat to Caribou Herds." *Winnipeg Free Press*, 15 December 2002.

Green, Joyce A. "Exploring Identity and Citizenship: First Nations Women, Bill C-31 and the Sawridge Case." PhD dissertation, University of Alberta, 1997.

Gunn, A., Appleby, A.G., Enns, G. Whelan, O'Brien, C., Kavanagh, K., Sims, M., and G. Mann. "Northern Canadian Shield Taiga," 2001. <www.worldwildlife.org/wildworld/profiles/terrestrial/na/na0612_full.html>.

Hamelin, Louis-Edmond. « Passer près d'une perdrix sans la voir ou attitudes à l'égard des Autochtones. » *Grande Conférence Desjardins No. 5*. Montréal: Programme d'étude sur le Québec de l'Université McGill, 1999.

Hartman, G.F. "Impacts of Growth in Resource Use and Human Population on the Nechako River: A Major Tributary of the Fraser River, British Columbia, Canada." *GeoJournal* 40, 1–2 (1996): 147–164.

Hawthron, Harry B., ed. *Une étude des Indiens contemporains du Canada/A Survey of Contemporary Indians of Canada*. Ottawa: Imprimeur de la Reine, 1966.

Henry, Frances, and Carol Tator. *The Colour of Democracy*. Second edition. Toronto: Harcourt, 2000.

Hill, Roger, and Pamela Sloan. "Canada: Native Peoples and Corporations." In *Native Americas*. Ithaca: Cornell University Press, 1996.

Hirsch, Joachim. "Globalization of Capital, Nation-States and Democracy." *Studies in Political Economy* 54 (1997): 39–58.

Hoffman, Steven M. "Engineering Poverty: Colonialism and Hydro-Electric Development in Northern Manitoba." Paper presented at Old Relationships or New Partnerships: Hydro Development on Aboriginal Lands in Quebec and Manitoba, University of Winnipeg, Winnipeg, Manitoba, 23 February 2004.

_____. "Powering Injustice: Hydroelectric Development in Northern Manitoba." In *Environmental Justice: Discourses in International Political Economy*, ed. John Byrne, Leigh Glover, and Cecilia Martinez. Volume 8. Energy and Environmental Policy. New Brunswick, NJ: Transaction Publishers, 2002.

Hoxie, Frederick E., ed. *Encyclopedia of North American Indians: Native American History, Culture, and Life from Paleo-Indians to the Present*. Boston: Houghton Mifflin, 1996.

Hughes, Lotte. *The No-Nonsense Guide to Indigenous Peoples*. Toronto: New Internationalist Publications/BTI, 2003.

Hydro-Québec. *Aménagement hydroélectrique de la Péribonka. Suivi des contrats et recherche d'emplois*. <http://www.hydroquebec.com/>. Accessed 15 February 2004.

_____. *Plan stratégique 2004–2008*. Montréal: The Author, 2003.

_____. *Politique : nos partenaires, approuvée par le Conseil d'administration le 11 septembre 1998*. <http://www.hydroquebec.com/>. Accessed 15 February 1998.

_____. *Rapport annuel 2001*. Montréal: The Author, 2001.

_____. Rapport de synthèse, Centrale de l'Eastmain-1-A et dérivation Rupert, Etude d'impact sur l'environnement. December 2004.

Indian Chiefs of Alberta. "Citizen Plus." A Presentation by the Indian Chiefs of Alberta to the Right Honourable P.E. Trudeau, Prime Minister, and the Government of Canada, 1970.

Indian and Northern Affairs Canada. *Implementation of Lake Winnipeg, Churchill and Nelson Rivers Study Board Recommendations*. The 1987 Status Report of the Government of Canada. Ottawa: The Author, 1987.

_____. *Arbitration Claims, Northern Flood Agreement, Article 24.* The 1977–1987 Status Report of the Government of Canada. Ottawa: The Author, 1987.

Institute on Governance. *Understanding Governance in Strong First Nations Communities. Phase One: Principles and Best Practices from the Literature.* Ottawa: The Author, 1999.

<http://www.kairoscanada.org/e/aboriginal/Let%20Justice%20Flow%20Inq uiry%20Report.pdf.> *Justice Seekers* 3 (March 2005).

Klak, Thomas, ed. *Globalization and Neo-liberalism: The Caribbean Context.* Maryland: Rowman and Littlefield Publishers, 1998.

Knoy, Laura. "Living on Earth." Manitoba Hydro Power interview with Mary Stucky. National Public Radio Program, 6 October 2000. <www.loe.org/ shows/shows.htm?programID=00-P13-00040>.

Kobliski, Carol. *Wuskwatim: Manitoba Hydro's Deceit and Manipulation Continues. The Truth behind Manitoba Hydro's Promise of Prosperity for NCN and Other Cree First Nations.* National Aboriginal News, 2006. <http://www.firstpers-pective.ca/fp_combo_template.php?path=opinion>.

Krotz, Larry. "Dammed and Diverted." *Canadian Geographic* (February/March 1991): 36–44.

Kulchyski, Peter. "Manitoba Hydro: How to Build a Legacy of Hatred." *Canadian Dimensions* 38, 3 (2004). <http://www.canadiandimension.com/>. Accessed 25 September 2004.

_____, ed. *Unjust Relations.* Toronto: Oxford University Press, 1994.

La Forme, H.S. "Indian Sovereignty: What Does it Mean?" *The Canadian Journal of Native Studies* 11, 2 (1991): 253–266.

Lasserre, Frederic. « L'Amérique a soif. Les besoins en eau de l'Ouest des États-Unis conduiront-ils Ottawa à céder l'eau du Canada ? » *Revue Internationale d'Etudes canadiennes/International Journal of Canadian Studies* 24 (2001): 196–214.

Lawrence, M.J. *Split Lake Cree Post Project Environmental Review.* Split Lake Cree–Manitoba Hydro Joint Studies. Volumes 4 and 5. Winnipeg: North/South Consultants, Inc., 1996.

Leake, Sophie. "First Nations Land Claims Discussed at SFU Forum." *The Peak* 91, 4. <www.peak.sfu.ca/the-peak/95-3/issue4/aborig.html>. Accessed 25 September 1995.

Lepage, Pierre. *Mythes et Réalités sur les Peuples Autochtones.* Québec: Commission des droits de la personne et des droits de la jeunesse, 2002.

Lexum. *Jugement Sioui.* <http://www.lexum.umontreal.ca/cscscc/fr/pub/1990/vol1/1990rcs1025.html>. Accessed September 2005.

_____. *Jugement Sparrow.* <http://www.lexum.umontreal.ca/pub/1990rcs1075.html>. Accessed September 2005.

Loomba, Ania. *Colonialism/Postcolonialism*. New York: Routledge, 1998.

Lowe, Mick. *Premature Bonanza.* Toronto: Between the Lines, 1998.

Macdonald, Mark. "Relearning our ABC's? The New Governance of First Nations Economic Development in Canada." In *How Ottawa Spends 2000–2001*, ed. Leslie A. Pal. Don Mills: Oxford University Press, 2000.

MacPherson, Nancy, and Gladys Netro. "Community Impact Assessment for Old Crow, Yukon." In *The International Study of the Effectiveness of Environmental Assessment,* ed. Peter Boothroyd and Barry Sadler. Vancouver: Canadian Environmental Assessment Agency, International Association for Impact Assessment, and University of British Columbia, 1994.

Malouf, Albert. *La Baie James indienne. Texte intégral du jugement du juge Albert Malouf.* Montréal: Éditions du jour, 1973.

Mandlebaum, David G. *The Plains Cree: An Ethnographic, Historical, and Comparative Study.* Regina: Canadian Plains Research Center/University of Regina, 1978.

Manitoba Aboriginal Rights Coalition. *Let Justice Flow: Report of the Interchurch Inquiry into Northern Hydro Development.* Winnipeg: The Author, 2001.

Manitoba Hydro. History and Timeline. <www.hydro.mb.ca/about_us/history/history_timeline.html>. Accessed August 2004.

_____. Kettle River Generating Station. Fact Sheet. <www.hydro.mb.ca/corporate/facilities/gs_kettle.shtml>.

_____. *Manitoba Hydro-Electric Board 52ⁿᵈ Annual Report.* 2003. <http://www.hydro.mb.ca/about_us/ar_2002_environment.pdf>.

Manitoba Clean Environment Commission. *Report on Public Hearings: Report on the Wuskwatim Generation and Transmission Projects.* Winnipeg, MB: The Author, 2004. <www.cecmanitoba.ca/reports/pdf/RespectingWuskwatim Generation.pdf>.

Manitoba Department of Mines, Resources and Environmental Management. *The Social and Economic Impact Study of the Churchill-Nelson Rivers Hydro Development.* Prepared by the Social & Economic Impact Study Team, Planning Branch, for the Lake Winnipeg, Churchill and Nelson Rivers Study. Winnipeg: The Author, 1974.

Manitoba Hydro. "Background Paper #1: Overview of NFA Origins and Provisions." *Background Information from Manitoba Hydro to the Interchurch Inquiry into Northern Hydro Development.* Winnipeg: The Author, 1999.

_____. "Background Paper #2: Recent Implementation Agreements with Four First Nations." *Background Information from Manitoba Hydro to the Interchurch Inquiry into Northern Hydro Development.* Winnipeg: The Author, 1999.

_____. "Background Paper #4: Manitoba Hydro Impacts within Manitoba's Economy." *Background Information from Manitoba Hydro to the Interchurch Inquiry into Northern Hydro Development.* Winnipeg: The Author, 1999.

_____. *A History of Electric Power in Manitoba.* Winnipeg: The Author.

_____. *Manitoba Hydro-Electric Board Annual Report.* Winnipeg: The Author. <www.hydro.mb.ca/about_us/ar_2003/ar_2003_complete.pdf>.

_____. *News Release.* <www.hydro.mb.ca>. Accessed 25 September 2007.

_____. *Wuskwatim Generating Station: Project Overview.* <http://www.hydro.mb.ca/projects/wuskwatim/overview.shtml>. Accessed 23 September 2007.

Manitoba Wildlands. 2005. *Hydropower Transmission in Manitoba: Current Status and Future Planning.* 2005. <http://manitobawildlands.org/develop_hydro.htm#energy>.

Martin, Thibault. *De la banquise au congélateur. Mondialisation et culture au Nunavik.* Quebec and Paris: Les Presses de l'Université Laval and UNESCO, 2003.

_____. "The Great Whale Hydroelectric project and the Relocation of the Inuit Population of Kuujjuarapik to Umiujaq (Nunavik). Reconstructing the Community, Preliminary Perspectives." In *Sustainable Development in the North. Local Initiatives vs Megaprojects*, ed. Gérard Duhaime et al. Québec: GETIC, Université Laval, 1998.

_____. « La guerre des fourrures et ses impacts sur les communautés inuit contemporaines. » *Recherches Amérindiennes au Québec* 32, 2 (2002): 71–82.

_____. « Solidarités et intégration communautaire. Le projet Grande-Baleine et le relogement des Inuit de Kuujjuarapik à Umiujaq. » PhD dissertation, Université Laval, 2001.

Massot, Alain. *Discours des Cris et des Inuit dans la presse écrite à travers les actions judiciaires contre le projet d'aménagement hydroélectrique de la Grande-rivière-de-la-Baleine.* Montréal: Hydro-Québec, 1993.

Matthew, M. *The Cost of Quality of First Nations Education.* Victoria: First Nations Education Steering Committee, 2000.

McAllister, D., Craig, J., Davidson, N., Murray, D., and M. Seddon. *Biodiversity Impacts of Large Dams. Background Paper #1.* Prepared for United Nations Environment Programme, The World Conservation Union, and the World Commission on Dams, 2001.

McCullough, Robert F. "The Northern Flood Agreement and the Northern Flood Committee." Unpublished document. 2002.

McInnes, William. *The Basins of Nelson and Churchill Rivers, Memoir No. 30.* Ottawa: Canada Department of Mines Geological Survey, Government Printing Bureau, 1913.

McMillan, Alan D. *Native Peoples and Cultures of Canada.* Vancouver: Douglas and McIntyre, 1988.

Memmi, Albert. *Portrait du colonisé; followed by Les Canadiens français sont-ils des colonisés?* Montréal: l'Étincelle, 1972.

Memorandum of Understanding on the Study of Clean Energy Transfers from Manitoba to Ontario. Memorandum between the Government of Manitoba and the Government of Ontario, June 2003.

Miller, Jason. "A Youth Perspective on the Failure of Northern Flood Agreement Implementation in Cross Lake." Paper presented at a conference of Society for Applied Anthropology, Manitoba. 6 February 1999. Winnipeg: Rupertsland Publications Series, 1999.

Miller, J.R. *The Historical Context of the Drive for Self-Government: Continuing Poundmaker and Riel's Quest.* Regina: University of Saskatchewan, 1994.

Minnesota Court of Appeals. "In the Matter of the Petition of Northern States Power Company for Review of its 1999 All Source Request for Proposals." A03-836. 30 March 2004.

Minnesota Department of Commerce. "Minnesota's Leadership in Renewable Energy." <http://www.commissions.leg.state.mn.us/leetf/CommercePresentation.pdf>. Accessed 27 October 2007.

Minnesota Public Utilities Commission. "In the Matter of the Petition of Northern States Power Company for Review of its 1999 All Source Request for Proposals." E-002/M-99-888. 18 March 2003.

_____. "In the Matter of the Petition of Northern States Power Company for Review of its 1999 All Source Request for Proposals." E-002/M-99-888. Staff Briefing Paper, public version. 19 December 2002.

_____. "Order Rejecting Requests for Further Investigation, Approving Final Bid Selections, and Opening Docket Regarding Externality Values." E-002/M-99-888. 7 February 2001.

Minnesota Statues 2006. Section 216C.052, subdivision 8a, as added by Laws 2007, chapter 57, article 2, s.26, amended Subd. 8a.

Miswaggon, Kenny. Pimicikamak Cree Nation Statement to the Minnesota Public Utilities Commission. 19 November 1999.

Mitchell, Marybelle. *From Talking Chiefs to a Native Corporate Elite: The Birth of Class and Nationalism among Canadian Inuit*. Montreal and Kingston: McGill-Queen's University Press, 1996.

Monture-Angus, Patricia. *Journeying Forward: Dreaming First Nations' Independence*. Halifax: Fernwood, 1999.

Morin, René. "The James Bay and Northern Agreement and the Development of Aboriginal Rights." In *Reflections on the James Bay and Northern Quebec Agreement*, ed. Alain-G. Gagnon and Guy Rocher. Montréal: Québec-Amérique, 2002.

Morris, Alexander. *The Treaties of Canada*. Saskatoon: Fifth House, 1991.

Murphy, Eamon. *Memorandum Re: Review of Summary of Understandings between NCN and MB Hydro Regarding the Wuskwatim Power Limited Partnerships*. Victoria, BC, 14 January 2004.

Nadasdy, Paul. *Hunters and Bureaucrats*. Vancouver: University of British Columbia Press, 2003.

Nelson, Robert E. *Genocide in Canada*. Roseau River: Anishinabe First Nation, 1997.

Netherton, Thomas. "From Rentiership to Continental Modernization: Shifting Policy Paradigms of State Intervention in Hydro in Manitoba: 1922–1977." PhD dissertation, Carlton University, 1993.

Neville–Robitaille Commission. *Report of the Federal-Provincial Team of Officials Directed to Visit the Communities of Nouveau-Quebec*. Ottawa: The Author, 1970.

Niezen, Ronald. *Power and Dignity: The Social Consequences of Hydroelectric Development for the James Bay Cree*. Toronto: University of Toronto Press, 1993.

_____. "Treaty Violations and the Hydro-Payment Rebellion of Cross Lake, Manitoba." *Cultural Survival Quarterly* 23, 1 (1999): 18.

Nobles, James. *Energy Conservation Improvement Program.* Report from the Minnesota Office of the Legislative Auditor. Report No. 05-04, 31 January 2005.

Northern Flood Agreement. An Agreement Between the Government of Manitoba, the Government of Canada, the Manitoba Hydro-Electric Board, and the Northern Flood Committee, Inc., Representing Nelson House, Norway House, Cross Lake, Split Lake, and York Factory. 16 December 1977.

Paine, Robert, ed. *The White Arctic: Anthropological Essays in Tutelage and Ethnicity.* St. John's: Institute of Social and Economic Research, 1977.

Panitch, Leo. "The Role and Nature of the Canadian State." In *The Canadian State: Political Economy and Political Power,* ed. Leo Panitch. Toronto: University of Toronto Press, 1977.

Paraskevas, Joe, and Mia Rabson. "Referendum on Hydro Lines: Native Chiefs; Doer Says Voters Have Spoken." *Winnipeg Free Press,* 1 November 2007.

Petit, Céline. « L'éducation et la scolarisation au Nunavik et au Nunavut : Transmission et réappropriation des savoirs. » In *Les Inuit de l'Arctique canadien,* ed. Michèle Therrien. Québec: CIDEF-AFI, Inuksuk, 2003.

Petrella, Riccardo. *Le Manifeste de l'eau : Pour un contrat mondial.* Bruxelles: Editions Labor, 1998.

Picard, Raphaël. « Les autochtones et la société québécoise : l'avenir économique. » Paper presented at the conference Les autochtones et la société québécoise : l'avenir économique, Montréal, Quebec. 6 February 2004.

Primrose, Jerry. "Powering a Future: Cashing in on Wuskwatim's Billion-Dollar Generation Project." *Winnipeg Free Press* On-line. Tuesday, 23 May 2006. <http://www.ncncree.com/ncn/wuskarchive.html>.

Québec. *Les Amérindiens et les Inuits du Québec. Onze Nations contemporaines.* Québec: Secrétariat aux Affaires autochtones, 2001.

_____. *La Convention de la Baie James et du Nord québécois.* Québec: Éditeur officiel du Quebec, 1975.

_____. *James Bay and Northern Quebec Agreement and the Additional Agreements.* Quebec: Éditeur officiel du Quebec, 1991.

_____. *Québécois et Innus sur un même territoire , de voisins à partenaires: Synthèse de la proposition d'Entente de principe avec les Innus.* Québec: Secrétariat aux Affaires autochtones, 2002.

_____. *Relations du Québec avec les Autochtones. Résultats tangibles.* Québec: Secrétariat aux Affaires autochtones, 1998.

_____. "Report from the Commission Studying the Territorial Integrity of Quebec, Rapport des Commissaires sur l'intégrité térritoriale du Quebec." Chapter 4 : Le Domaine indien. Unpublished manuscript, 1971.

Québec, Assemblée Législative. Commission de l'Économie et du Travail. Les travaux parlementaires, 37ᵉ législature, 1ʳᵉ session (début le 4 juin 2003). *Journal des débats.* Wednesday, 21 January 2004, 10h00.

Québec Gouvernement et Grand Conseil des Cris du Québec. Une nouvelle relation entre le Gouvernement du Québec et les Cris du Québec : *La Paix des Braves.* Québec: Éditeur officiel du Quebec, 2001.

Québec, Secrétariat aux Affaires Autochtones (SAA). *Partenariat/Développement/Actions (Partnership/Development/Achievement).* Québec: Secrétariat aux Affaires autochtones, 1998

Rabson, Mia. "West Side Story for Manitoba Hydro." *Winnipeg Free Press.* Wednesday, 27 September 2007. <http://www.winnipegfreepress.com/local/local_picture/story/4045647p-4653377c.html>.

Radio-Canada. *Les Montagnais de Saint-Augustin poursuivent Hydro-Québec.* 14 July 2003. <http://www.radiocanada.ca>.

_____. *Hydro-Québec verse 1,5 million aux Montagnais de Saint-Augustin,* 16 Octobre 2003. <http://www.radiocanada.ca>.

Richardson, Karen, and Rebecca Smith. "Berkshire Unit to Acquire PacifiCorp for $5.1 Billion. MidAmerican Deal with Scottish Power Marks Buffett's Return to Big Acquisitions." *Wall Street Journal.* <http://www.mindfully.org/Energy/2005-Berkshire/PacifiCorp24may05.htm>. Accessed 26 October 2007.

Robichaud, Véronique, Duhaime, Gérard, and Pierre Frechette. *The 1991 Social Accounting Matrix for the Nunavik Region Economy.* Québec: GÉTIC, Université Laval, 1998.

Robinson, Eric. Ministerial Statement on the Northern Flood Agreement by the Minister of Aboriginal and Northern Affairs. 15 December 2000. <www.gov.mb.ca/ana/ministers_statement.html>.

Robson, Robert. 1993. "Modernization in the Manitoba North: The Housing Initiative." *Canadian Journal of Native Studies Annual* 13, 1 (1993): 105–138.

Rousseau, Jean-Jacques. *Du Contrat social.* Paris: Folio, 1964.

Royal Commission on Aboriginal Peoples. *Report of the Royal Commission on Aboriginal Peoples*. Two volumes. Ottawa: Communication Group Publishing, 1996.

Rozon, Gina. "Education for Self-Determination." *American Review of Canadian Studies* 31, 1 & 2 (2001): 61.

Russel, Dan. *A People's Dream: Aboriginal Self-Government in Canada*. Vancouver: University of British Columbia Press, 2000.

Saganash, Roméo D. "La Paix des Braves." Paper presented at the Conference of the American Council for Quebec Studies, Mobile, Alabama. 24–27 October 2002.

_____. "The Peace of the Braves and the Negotiation of a New Partnership in Quebec." Paper presented at the colloquium New Partnerships or Old Relationships: Hydro Developments in Quebec and Manitoba, Winnipeg. 23 February 2004.

Saku, James C., and Robert M. Bone. "Modern Treaties in Canada: The Case of Northern Quebec Agreements and the Inuvialuit Final Agreement." *The Canadian Journal of Native Studies* 20, 2 (2000): 283–308.

Salisbury, Richard F. *A Homeland for the Cree: Regional Development in James Bay 1981–1981*. Kingston: McGill-Queen's University Press, 1986.

Salter, Liora, and Rick Salter. "Displacing the Welfare State." In *Understanding Canada: Building on the New Canadian Political Economy*, ed. Wallace Clement. Montreal and Kingston: McGill-Queen's University Press, 1997.

Saul, John Ralston. "Rooted in the Power of Three." *Globe and Mail*, 8 March 2002, p. A15.

Schreyer, Ed. Letter to Cross Lake Community Residents and Cross Lake Information Bulletin. Office of the Premier, Winnipeg, MB, 31 January 1975.

Scott, Colin, ed. *Aboriginal Autonomy and Development*. Vancouver: University of British Columbia Press, 2001.

Secrétariat aux Affaires Autochtones. 1991. *Les Autochtones et le Québec : le chemin parcouru*. Québec: The Author, 1991.

Sen, Amartya. *On Economic Inequality*. Oxford: Clarendon Press, 1973.

Shoumatoff, Alex. "Who Owns This River?" *OnEarth*. National Resources Defense Council 2005. <www.nrdc.org/onearth/05spr/manitoba1.asp>.

Sierra Club. *A Review of Labrador's Recovery Strategy for Woodland Caribou*. April 2005. <http://www.sierraclub.ca>.

Simard, Jean-Jacques. *La réduction: l'autochtone inventé et les Amérindiens d'aujourd'hui*. Sillery: Septentrion, 2003.

_____, et al. *Tendances nordiques. Les changements sociaux 1970-1990 chez les Cris et les Inuit du Québec. Une enquète statistique exploratoire*. Québec: GÉTIC, Université Laval, 1996.

Simon, René. « 30 ans de développement hydroélectrique sur la Côte-Nord : que réserve l'avenir aux Montagnais. » Conference at the Colloquium Les peuples indigènes et la mise en valeur des ressources en eaux, Montréal, 1993.

Slowey, Gabrielle A. "Globalization and Self-Government: Impacts and Implications for First Nations." *American Review of Canadian Studies* 31, 1 & 2 (2001): 265–281.

_____. "The Political Economy of Self-Determination: The Case of the Mikisew Cree First Nation." PhD dissertation, University of Alberta, 2003.

Springhall, John. *Decolonialization Since 1945*. New York: Palgrave, 2001.

Steckley, John L., and Bryan D. Cummins. *Full Circle: Canada's First Nations*. Toronto: Prentice-Hall, 2001.

Stiglitz, Joseph E. *Globalization and Its Discontents*. New York: W.W. Norton, 2002.

Strausz-Hupe, Robert, and Harry W. Hazard. *The Idea of Colonialism*. New York: Frederick A. Praeger, Inc., 1958.

Suchan, Allan. 1999. "What Is the Northern Flood Agreement?" In *First Nations and Hydroelectric Development in Northern Manitoba—The Northern Flood Agreement: Issues and Implications*, ed. Jean-Luc Chodkiewicz and Jennifer Brown. Winnipeg: University of Winnipeg, 1999.

Sullivan, Don. Personal interview conducted by Steve Hoffman, April 2005.

Summary of Understandings Between Nisichawayasihk Cree Nation and Manitoba Hydro with Respect to the Wuskwatim Project. Winnipeg: Manitoba Hydro, 2003.

Treaty Number 5. "Between Her Majesty the Queen and the Saulteaux and Swampy Cree Tribes." Ottawa: Department of Indian and Northern Development, 20–24 September 1875.

Tremblay, Marc-Adélard. « L'éducation des Indiens : un modèle d'analyse des Agences blanches. » *Mémoires de la Société royale du Canada/Proceedings of the Royal Society of Canada* 16 (1978): 171–193.

_____. "Les études amérindiennes au Québec 1960-1981 : État des travaux et principales tendances." *Culture* 11, 1 (1982): 83–106.

_____. « Les enjeux ethniques dans un Canada Multiculturel : l'espace des Autochtones. » Manuscrit. 1987.

_____. "De l'éthique sociale et de l'interculturalisme : deux voies incontournables dans l'établissement d'un rapprochement harmonieux entre Autochtones et non-Autochtones." Paper presented at the Conférence de l'Université McGill sur le Rapport Erasmus-Dussault, Montréal, Québec, February 1997. Manuscrit.

_____. 1993. "Les politiques et les pratiques socio-sanitaires des Autochtones du Grand Nord québécois." Paper presented at the Commission royale sur les Peuples Autochtones, Quebec, 1993.

_____. "Le processus de création d'un gouvernement autonome au Nunavik : les Recommandations de la Commission du Nunavik." *Études canadiennes/ Canadian Studies* 52 (2002): 117–130.

_____. "La Recherche universitaire nordique dans les Sciences humaines au creux de la vague. » *Recherches Amérindiennes au Québec*, X1V, 3, (1984): 90–95.

_____. "La renaissance de l'identité amérindienne dans l'espace québécois." In *Mélanges offerts au Cardinal Vachon*. Québec: Les Presses de l'Université Laval, 1989.

_____. "Richard Salisbury et l'anthropologie du développement." *Culture* 10, 1 (1990): 5–8.

_____. « La vision du future. » In *Les facettes de l'Identité amérindienne*, ed. Marc-Adélard Tremblay. Québec: Les Presses de l'Université Laval, 1976.

_____, ed. *Les facettes de l'Identité amérindienne*. Québec: Les Presses de l'Université Laval, 1976.

_____, et Jules Dufour. « Compte rendu de l'atelier 1. » In *Regard sur la Convention de la Baie-James et du Nord québécois*, ed. Alain-G. Gagnon et Guy Rocher. Montréal: Québec-Amérique, 2002.

_____, et Carole Lévesque. *Les études québécoises en Sciences sociales sur les Peuples autochtones du Nord 1950–1989 : Conditions socio-historiques de production et profil thématique*. Québec: GÉTIC, 1992.

_____. "Quebec Social Science and Canadian Indigenous Peoples : An Overview of Research Trends." *Polaris Paper* 11, Ottawa: Canadian Polar Commission, 1997.

_____, et Josée Thivierge. « La nature et la portée de l'œuvre amérindienne de Jacques Rousseau. » *Anthropologie et Sociétés* 10, 2 (1986): 163–182.

Troniak, Eric. Personal communication to Steve Hoffman, 2004.

Tulugak, H., Adams, J., Dufour, J., Duhaime, G., Gaumont, G., et M.-A. Tremblay. *Partageons. Tracer la voie vers un gouvernement pour le Nunavik*. Rapport de la Commission du Nunavik, 2001.

Underwood, McLellan and Associates, Ltd. *Churchill River Diversion. Study of Alternative Diversions*. 20 February 1970.

United Nations Environment Programme. Declaration of the United Nations Conference on the Human Environment. Stockholm, Sweden, 5–16 June 1972.

US GAO. *Informing Our Nation: Improving How to Understand and Assess the USA's Position and Progress*. Report to the Chairman, Subcommittee on Science, Technology and Space, Committee on Commerce, Science and Transportation, U.S. Senate. Report No. GAO-05-1. November 2004.

University of Manitoba. *Characteristics of Churchill–Nelson Shorelines*. Physical Impact Study Interim Report, 1972. University of Manitoba Department of Civil Engineering. January 1973.

Van Ginkel Associates. May 1967. *Transition in the North: The Churchill River Diversion and the People of South Indian Lake*. A Study Prepared for Manitoba Development Authority. Winnipeg, May 1967.

Wabanong Nakaygum Okimawin Council of Chiefs Accord. Between the Signatory First Nations located within the East Side Planning Area of the First Part and Her Majesty the Queen in Right of the Province of Manitoba as represented by the Premier of Manitoba of the Second Part. April 2007.

Waldram, James B. *As Long as Rivers Run: Hydroelectric Development and Native Communities in Western Canada*. Winnipeg: University of Manitoba, 1988.

_____. "Falling Through the Cracks (in the Dam): South Indian Lake and the Churchill River Diversion Project." In *First Nations and Hydroelectric Development in Northern Manitoba—The Northern Flood Agreement: Issues and Implications,* ed. Jean-Luc Chodkiewicz and Jennifer Brown. Winnipeg: University of Winnipeg, 1999.

_____. "Hydro-Electric Development and the Process of Negotiation in Northern Manitoba, 1960–1977." *The Canadian Journal of Native Studies* 4, 2 (1984): 205–239.

_____. "Relocation, Consolidation, and Settlement Pattern in the Canadian Subarctic." *Human Ecology* 15, 2 (1987): 117–128.

Wall, Denis. "Aboriginal Self-Government in Canada: The Cases of Nunavut and the Alberta Métis Settlements." In *Visions of the Heart: Canadian Aboriginal Issues*, ed. David Long and Olive P. Dickason. Second edition. Toronto: Harcourt, 2000.

Warburton, Rennie. "First Nations Status and Canadian Politics." *Studies in Political Economy* 54 (Fall 1997): 119–141.

Watkins, G. Campbell. *Canada and the U.S.: A Seamless Energy Border?* The Border Papers: C.D. Howe Institute, 2003.

Weaver, Sally. "The Role of Social Science in Formulating Canadian Indian Policy: A Preliminary History of the Hawthorn–Tremblay Report." In *The History of Canadian Anthropology*, ed. Jim Freedman. London, ON: The Canadian Ethnology Society, 1976.

_____. *Making Canadian Indian Policy : The Hidden Agenda, 1968–1979*. Toronto: University Press, 1981.

Wiebe, Menno. "The Northern Flood Agreement: In Whose Interest." A paper presented at the Current Status of the Northern Flood Agreement, a conference sponsored by the Society for Applied Anthropology of Manitoba. University of Winnipeg, 1999.

Williams, Glen. "Canada in the International Political Economy." In *The New Canadian Political Economy*, ed. Wallace Clement and Glen Williams. Montreal and Kingston: McGill-Queen's University Press, 1989.

World Commission on Dams. The Report of the World Commission on Dams, 16 November 2000. <www.dams.org/report/>.

World Commission on Environment and Development. *Our Common Future*. Oxford, England: Oxford University Press, 1987.

Worster, Donald. *Rivers of Empire. Water, Aridity, and the Growth of the American West*. New York: Oxford University Press, 1985.

Wotherspoon, Terry, and Vic Satzewich. *First Nations: Race, Class and Gender Relations*. Scarborough: Nelson Canada, 1993.

Wuskwatim Generation Environmental Impact Statement. Executive Summary and Volumes 1 to 10. Manitoba Hydro and Nisichawayasihk Cree Nation, 2003.

Wuskwatim Project Development Agreement between the Nisichawayasihk Cree Nation and the Manitoba Hydro-Electric Board and Taskinigagp Power Corporation and 5022649 Manitoba Ltd. and Wuskwatim Power Limited Partnership. 26 June 2006.

Xcel Energy. 2005. *Resource Plan*. Filed with the Minnesota Public Utilities Commission as MPUC Docket E002/RP-04-1752. Minneapolis MN, 23 November 2005.

Index

A

Aboriginal

autonomy 19, 24–28, 35–36, 46, 56,
70–73, 82, 88–89, 93, 113, 244, 263, 273

languages 25–27, 30, 70, 79, 86, 89–90,
105, 122–124, 129–132, 137–139, 143,
160, 195, 198, 201

leadership 3–7, 10–12, 17, 25, 35,
47, 56, 70, 76–81, 97, 112, 116, 126,
129, 138–142, 152–156, 160–163, 227,
233–234, 238, 246–252, 261, 264, 273,
276–277, 283, 290

nations/First Nations 3–5, 7, 12,
19–37, 39, 43–54, 65–70, 73–86, 88, 90,
97, 99, 101, 107, 122, 129–139, 142–144,
151–153, 157, 162, 178–182, 199–201,
205–210, 215–216, 219–220, 224, 230–
233, 245, 259, 262, 274–275, 281–286,
290–293

political division 12, 33, 52, 122, 154,
163, 241, 261, 278

resistance 24, 31, 36, 56, 121, 128, 230,
234, 252, 273, 285, 293

rights 7, 10, 22–37, 45, 49, 56, 65–93,
118–119, 123, 127, 132–143, 167, 176–
177, 186, 191, 201, 205–212, 216–225,
242, 260–261, 266, 277, 281–294

surrender/extinguishment 10, 21–23,
33–34, 65, 68, 72, 83, 105, 119, 133–137,
174, 201, 205–209, 212, 217–221, 261,
282, 288–293

title 20–24, 27–33, 44–48, 65, 68–73,
83–84, 91, 119, 133, 174, 218, 225,
260–261, 283

unity 17, 69, 80, 284, 287–290

Aboriginal enterprises

Cree Development Corporation 211

Cree Trappers Association 211

Developement Piekuagami
Ilnuatsh 272

Hydro–Ilnu 269–270

Innu Aitun fund 271

Makivik Society 72, 90, 234, 246,
248, 251

Peshamiu Ilnuts Enterprises 271

Aboriginal organizations

Assembly of First Nations 79–81

Assembly of First Nations of Quebec
and Labrador (AFNQL) 274–275

Attikamek–Montagnais Council
(CAM) 260–261, 266

Council of Yukon Indians 90

Displaced Residents of South Indian
Lake (DRSIL) 122, 164

Grand Council of the Crees (GCC)
5–6, 119, 205, 221, 264

Innu Takuaikan band council 268–269

Kativik 72, 246

League of Indians 79

Mamit Innuat tribal council 260–261,
275–278

Mamuitun tribal council 31, 91,
260–261, 276

National Indian Brotherhood (NIB) 80

National Indian Council (NIC) 79

North American Indian Brotherhood
(NAIB) 79

Northern Flood Committee 68,
117–118, 174, 289